DEAD ENDS

DEAD ENDS

AMERICAN FOREIGN POLICY IN THE NEW COLD WAR

STANLEY HOFFMANN

BALLINGER PUBLISHING COMPANY
Cambridge, Massachusetts
A Subsidiary of Harper & Row, Publishers, Inc.

Copyright © 1983 by Ballinger Publishing Company. All rights reserved. No part
of this publication may be reproduced, stored in a retrieval system, or transmitted
in any form or by any means, electronic, mechanical, photocopy, recording or
otherwise, without the prior written consent of the publisher.

International Standard Book Number: 0-88410-003-0

Library of Congress Catalog Card Number: 82-22735

Printed in the United States of America

Library of Congress Cataloging in Publication Data

Hoffmann, Stanley.
    Dead ends.

    Includes index.
    1. United States—Foreign relations—1945-   . 2. North Atlantic Treaty
Organization. 3. United States—National security. I. Title.
E840.H583   1983   327.73   82-22735
ISBN 0-88410-003-0

To the memory of Nahum Goldman, whose wisdom, humanity, and wit are unforgettable, and to my friend Guido Goldman, whose energy, skill, and collaboration are invaluable.

CONTENTS

CHAPTER 1:   Introduction: Themes and Trends   1

PART I: *The Détente Era Revisited*   15

CHAPTER 2:   The World According to Henry
Kissinger: I, 1969-1972   17

CHAPTER 3:   The World According to Henry
Kissinger: II, 1973-1974   47

CHAPTER 4:   Requiem   67

PART II: *The Rise and Troubles of the
New Orthodoxy*   85

CHAPTER 5:   Unwelcome Complexity   89

CHAPTER 6:   Muscle and Brains   97

CHAPTER 7:   The New Orthodoxy: A Critique
and an Alternative   121

CHAPTER 8:   Reagan Abroad   153

CONTENTS

PART III:	*The Western Alliance in Turmoil*	175
CHAPTER 9:	The Crisis in the West	179
CHAPTER 10:	Drift or Harmony?	199
CHAPTER 11:	NATO and Nuclear Weapons: Reasons and Unreason	219
PART IV:	*A Strategy for the Long Term*	243
CHAPTER 12:	Security in an Age of Turbulence	245
CHAPTER 13:	Foreign Policy Priorities of the United States	273
	Index	289
	About the Author	301

ACKNOWLEDGMENTS

Chapters 2 through 13 of this volume have been previously published:

Chapter 2 in the *New York Review of Books*, December 6, 1979.

Chapter 3 in the *New York Review of Books*, April 29, 1982.

Chapter 4 in *Foreign Policy*, Spring 1981 (the version in this book is slightly abridged).

Chapter 5 in *Le Débat*, October 1980 (I have translated it from the original French).

Chapter 6 in *Foreign Policy*, Winter 1979-1980 (the present version contains passages cut from and some additions to the original).

Chapter 7 in the *New York Review of Books*, April 16 and April 30, 1981.

Chapter 8 in the *New York Review of Books*, February 4, 1982.

Chapter 9 in the *New York Review of Books*, July 17, 1980.

Chapter 10 in *International Security*, Fall 1981.

Chapter 11 in *Foreign Affairs*, Winter 1981-1982 (the present version contains passages cut from the original).

Chapter 12 in International Institute of Strategic Studies, *Adelphi Paper* no. 167, 1981.

Chapter 13 in *Alternatives for the 1980s*, no. 5: "Building the Peace-Foreign Policy for the Next Decade." Washington, D.C.: Center for National Policy, 1982.

I thank these journals and institutions for having allowed me to republish the essays.

CHAPTER 1

INTRODUCTION: THEMES AND TRENDS

I.

THE ESSAYS collected in this book were written between the fall of 1979 and the spring of 1982. They form the elements of a continuing reflection about the evolution of international relations and of American foreign policy. They also form the sequel of a book that deals with the preceding period, *Primacy or World Order*.[1] There, I tried to show that the United States had a choice between a classical policy of primacy and an innovative policy of world order, made necessary by the transformation of power in the atomic era and in the age of economic interdependence, and by the huge risks of violence and chaos present in the international system.

Primacy or World Order was finished during the first phase of the Carter administration, a phase filled with good will, illusions, and confusion. In an article written at the end of 1978, I indicated that the most serious flaw of American foreign policy at the time was the absence of any coherent strategy toward Moscow.[2] Indeed, throughout the years 1978 and 1979, the relations between the two superpowers worsened, and in the circles of officials, former officials, and other citizens concerned with international relations, a vast counteroffensive developed against Carter's apparent complacency, against his original intention of relegating relations with the Soviet Union to second place, as well as against the détente policy undertaken by Nixon and Kissinger (who later joined that reaction themselves). What made this

1

intellectual and political movement grow was a well-known series of facts that led many people to believe that the Soviet Union had entered a new phase of global imperialism, made possible by its enormous arms build-up and marked by its interventions in the Third World. The counteroffensive, supported by an increasingly large fraction of Jimmy Carter's own foreign policy team, prevailed after the humiliating seizure of American hostages in Iran and after the Soviet invasion of Afghanistan. Carter himself, in 1980, initiated the return to the Cold War. The election of Ronald Reagan in November 1980 meant the triumph of what I have called, throughout this volume, the new orthodoxy.

This book examines how the new orthodoxy and the new Cold War that it tries to wage fit an international reality that is no longer of the immediate postwar period, or the bipolar world of 1947, or the era in which the United States was the dominant world power, threatened only by a much weaker Soviet Union. The reader will soon realize that I deeply deplore the new orthodoxy, not because I believe that the Soviet Union is a benevolent or conservative state, nor because I underestimate the scope and depth of the superpowers' rivalry, but because a cold war strategy rests on an incomplete analysis of the international system and is capable of leading only to confrontations that heighten the risks for world order and international security.

II.

Much of what follows, particularly Chapter 12, describes the highly complex system in which we live: a system characterized both by a Soviet-American contest that is practically unlimited, and by an increasing number of actors who promote, often most brutally, their own interests, create their own areas of conflict, exploit to their own benefit the contest of the superpowers, and often succeed in imposing their own priorities on Moscow and Washington.

Three lasting features of the system must be mentioned. The first is the obvious rise of nationalism. There are many new and weak states that try to become nation states. The very weaknesses or leaks of sovereignty and the often illusory nature of independence lead the rulers and their peoples to react against dependence and the tyranny of the outside world. Everything contributes to nationalism: postcolonial factors (such as the elimination of the last colonial situations, as in Namibia, or the fights of old or new nations that try to liquidate in their favor the sequels of their colonial past, as in Cyprus, Kashmir, Palestine, the Horn of Africa, or in the Falkland Islands, or attempts to modify borders set by colonial powers); traditional border clashes (between Greece and Turkey, Iran and Iraq); and the rival ideologies that want to unify a divided country under their flags (Korea). Nationalism is also fed by the reaction against new forms of imperialism (in Poland, Afghanistan, and Cambodia, but also in Nicaragua), or else by the reaction against the absence or the loss of control over the tools of economic or social policy. This reaction takes the form of nationalizations, protectionist measures, and moves aimed at exploiting the resources of the sea. Often nationalism gives rulers the temptation to unify a heterogeneous country or a weak society by exploiting its neighbor's divisions. And it is exacerbated by the attempts at intervention and manipulation made by the superpowers or by other states.

The second lasting feature is the revolutionary phenomenon. (It is not necessarily a left wing phenomenon, as too many people believe; there are many revolutions of the right.) Here again there are multiple causes: social injustice and political deadlock (as in Iran, Nicaragua, El Salvador, and tomorrow perhaps in Guatemala, the Philippines, Pakistan, and Zaire), racial oppression (South Africa), the disruptions resulting from economic modernization (Mexico or the Persian Gulf countries), and tribal, ideological, or political rivalries (Chad and Ethiopia). There are also revolutions imported by foreign guns (Cambodia). Revolutions often feed nationalism and provide foreign countries with opportunities for intervention (El Salvador, Lebanon, Chad, etc.).

Finally, nothing seems more lasting than the superpowers' conflict. It is fueled by three asymmetries. The political positions of the two rivals are different. The United States is a maritime power that, like nineteenth century England, needs a fleet and foreign bases in order to make its commitments credible; but like past continental powers, it also must keep armies abroad. The Soviet Union, a continental power that occupies a world situation comparable to that of Germany in pre-1945 Europe, has, like Germany, tried to give itself the means necessary to intervene far from its borders. Thus, the competition pits a whale that is often obliged to behave like an elephant against an elephant that tries to be capable of challenging the whale. The objectives are also different. To be sure, each of the superpowers has, in many areas, an interest in preserving the status quo, but on the whole, America's mix of conservatism and reformism continues to confront Moscow's mix of revisionism and revolutionary radicalism. Finally, the strategies differ. The United States has huge military, economic, and technological assets but also great difficulties abroad because its friends often fight violently with one another, and because America itself is the favorite target of all the discontented. The United States also experiences great difficulties at home (political discontinuity, institutional flaws). The Soviet Union is capable of choosing among opportunities but remains handicapped outside of its borders by its brutality and its insufficient economic means, and at home by its rigidities.

3

Until now, despite many crises between the superpowers and many wars among the lesser powers, an international system in which each state tries to manipulate all others, in which the theoretical barriers between domestic politics and foreign policy have collapsed, and in which offensive military or economic means multiply, has nevertheless remained relatively moderate. There are three reasons for this. The first one is nuclear weaponry. Deterrence has prevented all direct nuclear confrontations and resulted in a kind of regional fragmentation of the global system. This fragile peace results also in part from the fact that the two superpowers have no direct clash of interests (the differences between their two economies contribute to this); they have, on the whole, shown mutual respect for each other's spheres of vital influence, their opposed ideologies both expect to be vindicated in the long run, and their internal stability until now has been considerable. The second favorable factor is the very heterogeneity of the system. The Cold War has not been able to absorb all other conflicts (it is often the other way around). This also contributes to fragmentation. For instance, in the horrible war that Israel launched in Lebanon in July 1982, the two superpowers have been remarkably impotent. The third factor is provided by the positive aspects of economic interdependence, which leads states either to seek economic development (or the end of economic crisis) through cooperation, or to limit their economic conflicts. This also results in a proliferation of regimes and institutions whose function is to provide a minimum of order and security.

But everything that has until now been preceded by a plus sign risks shifting to the minus. Moderation is threatened by several tendencies. In the first place, the world economy has many negative aspects. The longer the global recession lasts, the more the quest for individual advantages risks prevailing over the desire for mutual benefits; the struggle for the redistribution of power and wealth (power that is often elusive, and wealth that does not increase much anymore) risks becoming ever more fierce; the burdens that afflict developing or mismanaged states deep in debt (Mexico, Argentina, Brazil, Poland)—states that must slow down their economic growth and reduce their social expenditures—risk breeding revolt and chaos. An increasing resort to economic instruments of coercion—against Iran, Uganda, the Soviet Union, Poland, South Africa, Argentina, and already, by the Arabs, against the West in 1973—shows how limited the benefits of interdependence are.

Second, while nuclear weapons have contributed to preserving peace between the superpowers, proliferation is a serious threat, tolerable only if the conditions that have existed between Washington and Moscow (mutual invulnerability, no direct conflict, responsible leaders) could be expected to repeat themselves in all other cases, and if proliferation led automatically to the disengagement or dissociation of the superpowers. Reality is of course quite different. What would happen if the nuclear weapon became the decisive factor in inexpiable conflicts in which one party would gain a decisive advantage by striking first? And could the superpowers let an important client be annihilated or threatened?

Finally, the new Cold War threatens moderation. Military evolution is not reassuring. Nuclear technology has moved from deterrence through the threat of mutual destruction, to increased means for waging an atomic war, with counterforce weapons, as in a traditional war. Also, the balance has shifted: the Soviet Union now has the means to intimidate the intimidator—that is, the United States' ability to extend the mantle of enlarged deterrence over its allies has diminished. This could allow the Soviet Union to push its pawns ahead in peacetime, or make the Soviet Union believe that it can do so. Therefore the United States hopes to stop Soviet expansion by increasing both conventional forces in the threatened sectors, and nuclear counterforce warfighting means. Even the good aspects of the bipolar contest have a debit side. Deterrence eliminates, or delays interminably, the moment of truth—in the Middle East, for instance. Because nothing ever gets settled, conflicts reappear again and again. The obvious risks of confrontation in hot areas like Europe move violent conflicts toward the grey areas, where the threat of resorting to nuclear weapons is not very credible and where, consequently, the imperatives of prudence are less compelling.

Given those threats, two directions seem open, particularly to the two giants. One leads to the weakening of all the moderating factors that have prevailed until now, as on the eve of the First World War. The accelerated rate of nuclear proliferation, the acquisition of nuclear means by countries engaged in conflicts that threaten their survival, and the failure of economic coordination among the industrial powers and also between these and the developing countries, all could contribute to disaster by making economic vulnerability and military insecurity merge. The other direction seeks, on the contrary, to cope with the threats and to carry out the political and ethical imperatives of prudence and progress in a way that I will try to indicate in the following chapters. But success along this road requires statesmen capable of tolerating, appreciating, and exploiting complexity—not simple-minded leaders. They should be capable of recognizing and pursuing long-term interests, not momentary advantages. They should be capable of transcending the borders of their nation, and of hearing what others say.

III.

The trouble with simple-minded leaders is that, like simple-minded theorists of international relations, they tend not only to analyze all politics in terms of power, but also to equate power with the ability to coerce. Power remains the dominant concept for the study of international relations. But the flaws of a "realism" that fails to distinguish between the nature and role of power in an integrated community endowed with a central authority and the nature and role of power in the international milieu need to be pointed out more than ever. So do the flaws of a realism that does not distinguish between power as a means, or intermediate goal, that has to be tailored to specific objectives, and power as a yardstick comparable to money in economics. A traditional realism that equates power with military might, or a modern realism that analyzes the structure of the international system only in terms of the distribution of state capabilities—as if the latter were all measurable and equally significant independently of their usability and effectiveness—is an insufficient basis for a theory of international politics.[3] Today, military might is only one dimension of power among many. It is hampered by a formidable variety of domestic and external restraints on its use (restraints which apply differently to different categories of actors), and it is of limited effectiveness toward the accomplishment of a variety of goals that are increasingly important to countries whose future depends as much on the shape of the international milieu as on possessions that can be acquired by force. Power is not a fungible commodity: the world is full of cases in which military power has brought no economic advantages, and vast economic power has not lead to military might in an international system that consists of a number of different games with different structures and rules requiring very different kinds of power. Military power is often less relevant or important than the power to persuade and to entangle others in delicately balanced bargains. For such bargaining power one must have something to offer, not only something to threaten with. The changes that have almost infinitely broadened the agenda of world politics and the multiplication of arenas or chessboards introduce new complexities, and demand not only a more differentiated view of power among analysts, but also a supplement of skill among the players.[4]

As a result, the analysis of American foreign policy, its mistakes and its opportunities, presented in these essays, rests on a view of the power and (relative) impotence of the nuclear superpowers I have developed elsewhere. I am aware of the differences between Soviet and American might and behavior, both in the use of force within each side's sphere of domination (Soviet uses have been less inhibited), and in the realm of economics (Soviet involvement in the world economy remains limited). However, there have been many constraints operating on both.

In the first place, they have found it easier—largely through coercive means—to deny gains to their foes rather than to wrest gains for themselves. The United States has succeeded in preventing unwelcome victories by leftist forces in the Dominican Republic and in El Salvador. Moscow has, with the help of Cuban troops, thwarted Somali revisionism in Ethiopia; the Soviets, with the help of loyal allies in Poland, have prevented the surge of Polish liberalization from destroying the Communist regime; in Afghanistan, they have prevented an overthrow of the post-1978 regime, or a defection by the unreliable Communist leader, Amin, who became one of the first victims of Soviet "assistance." But even denial has not always been possible, especially when it would have required more military exertions by the United States than its domestic opinion was willing to tolerate (Vietnam, Angola). And the use of force to wrest gains has often been frustrating: the civil war continues, at a low level, in Angola, and the Soviets have not smashed the resistance in Afghanistan. Nor has the left wing coalition been defeated in El Salvador. Lesser powers have used force more freely on behalf of vital interests, but insofar as they are up against local nationalisms, their victories have not brought them the security they sought (as the Vietnamese have discovered in Cambodia, and, above all, the Israelis in the occupied territories and Lebanon). On the whole, against forces for national liberation, military victories have rarely led to political success—witness the South Africans in Namibia, or the Israelis, or the Soviets.

In the second place, the superpowers are often at the mercy of their allies or clients. Soviet experiences in the Arab world have been bitter: several allies, disappointed both by Soviet inability to bring them political satisfaction and by Soviet reticence in fomenting risky wars, have defected. Others, having been defeated, dragged Soviet prestige down with them. Soviet economic weaknesses have led clients of the Soviet Union, in southern Africa, to turn to Western sources of aid. The United States has found it difficult not only to coerce foes through economic sanctions (foes can either turn to alternative suppliers, or disregard and survive the sanctions) but also to use either its powers of persuasion or the threat of the stick in order to deflect allies from courses deemed contrary to American interests, because of a fear that the use of sticks on allies would undermine the credibility of America as a "big brother" (an argument often used to justify Washington's tolerance of Israeli excesses), or because the actual resort to sticks only increases the allies' determination to protect their own interests (as in the case of the pipeline which Western Europe and the Soviet Union have decided to build), or because America's involvement in the world economy could expose it to damaging reprisals.

Indeed, in the third place, the contest for influence has often led the United States to provide other states with weapons or nuclear materials that will help them pursue policies contrary to, or at least different from, American interests. In the case of the Saudis, the United States practically had to bribe them into accepting a weapons system needed for their security—and perhaps for objectives other than the anti-Soviet one which obsesses Washington. The limits on the Soviets' power to reward (besides the sale of weapons) hampers Moscow's influence. America's power to reward, in recent years, has either been self-curtailed (by the recession and domestic hostility to various forms of assistance) or else has boomeranged.

The contrast between the increase in the superpowers' available nuclear warheads and capacity to deploy conventional forces far from their borders, and the amount of actually usable or effective power, is remarkable. Power in the sense of an ability to control outcomes often tends to be limited to the home ground: the United States can shape (or misshape) its energy policy and its arsenal. Even in its sphere of domination, control cannot easily go beyond mere damage limitation. For the United States today, successful power means influencing, not controlling, others, and affecting, not determining, outcomes. This "fall from grace" does not result from American "decline," as the new orthodoxy has proclaimed in its bizarre mix of masochism and machismo. The United States could not prevent either the recovery of a devastated Soviet Union, or the Soviet determination to avoid humiliations comparable to the Cuban missile crisis Moscow had provoked. The United States deemed it in its own interest to promote the recovery of the powers it had defeated in World War II, and that of its allies. Its interests and values dictated support to decolonization and to the establishment of various international regimes to assure a modicum of order and security in the open international economy that was one of America's main objectives. But in a crowded world there is less elbow room for the mighty, and regimes by definition require the cooperation of many and compromises by all. Chapters 12 and 13 specifically suggest a strategy that takes these new realities into account.

Three directions deserve mention here. One is an effort to devise, with the Soviet Union and its allies (such as Cuba), ad hoc "rules of the game" to limit the intensity and risks of the inevitable contest, and to allow domestic developments in troubled countries to take their own course without massive and uncontrolled outside interference. (With respect to Cuba, several opportunities appear to have been missed.)[5] The second direction is the necessary liquidation of colonial situations, whether they persist in the Middle East, South Africa, or Eastern Europe—the means for achieving decolonization being, of course, different in each case (in Eastern Europe, the long-term aim ought to be Finlandization). The third direction is a drastic reconsideration of the role of nuclear weapons in the superpowers' strategies: away from the warfighting scenarios that result largely from the American attempt to give nuclear weapons a major function in extending deterrence to allies. This function can be made credible only by developing counterforce capabilities that would be difficult or impossible to control once employed.

Since one does not want to make the world safe for major conventional wars (and since the Soviet Union enjoys several advantages in this respect on all its borders), and because conventional disarmament is far away, the residual threat of escalation to nuclear war must continue to play a deterrent role in preventing conventional aggression. The tension will persist between efforts at ensuring strategic and crisis stability[6] (which tend to relegate nuclear weapons to the deterrence of *nuclear* attacks) and the fear that a disappearance of the residual risk of escalation could favor traditional wars and Soviet advances. But the alternatives are either an intolerable drift toward nuclear conflict, through an increasingly destabilizing arms race, or a ruling out of "war itself, as a means of settling differences at least between the great industrial powers."[7] The latter is an important objective for the long-range future. In the meantime, restoring a modicum of stability and moderation to the nuclear contest, and limiting the risks of conventional clashes by a combination of military measures, informal understandings, and preventive diplomacy, are the order of the day.

IV.

The responsibility of the United States is obviously huge. Will it prove to be a good navigator? Another purpose of this book is to examine the postulates, main elements, and results of American foreign policy in the last few years. When I tried to make a balance sheet of the first Cold War and of the détente era in *Gulliver's Troubles*[8] and in *Primacy or World Order*, I was generally critical and emphasized the errors of analysis and the failures of American diplomacy. However, there had been many successes and sometimes, as in the late 1940s and again under Kissinger, coherent conceptions. But the essays gathered in this volume deal with a much more considerable fiasco. They examine why the ambitious theories of Henry Kissinger led neither to a lasting détente nor to a better "structure of peace," and why the good ideas and welcome initiatives of Carter drowned in a total shipwreck. They also criticize the basic assumptions of the new orthodoxy that brought Ronald Reagan to power and give a predominantly negative idea of the first years of Reagan's diplomacy. In other words, they explore a variety of dead ends. They also try repeatedly to suggest a better way.

They overlap somewhat, because of some recurrent themes. The first concerns the intellectual crisis of American foreign policy. What is striking today is a kind of complacent resignation to emptiness. The election campaign of 1980 was marked by the triumph of the new orthodoxy: Reagan expressed it most vigorously, Carter provided a softer version of it, but everything happened as if a return to the Cold War would save politicians and even many intellectuals from having to think about the relevance of reflexes that had, on the whole, contributed to America's power in the simple world created by the victory over Germany and Japan but were quite inadequate in the complex world of the 1980s. The bankruptcy of what I call, in Chapter 8, Reagan's decalogue, has not yet led to an "agonizing reappraisal" of the postulates behind the new American diplomacy. The team in power, whose composition has changed, vacillates between the new orthodoxy and a kind of low level pragmatism, between symbolic poundings of the table or rhetorical thrusts, and the dismay one senses under the ideological veneer whenever its members are obliged to recognize that others do what they like and do not yield to the new American voluntarism.

The debate over the economic and social role of the federal government, over the respective virtues and flaws of Keynesian economics and of supply-side economics, over the future of American industry, or over the struggle for minority rights has not yet been accompanied by any serious debate on the future of foreign policy. The champions of the new orthodoxy warn Reagan against all departures that could dilute it. Henry Kissinger tries not to harm his own future by being too critical, while presenting in his memoirs his past policy as a model. The Democrats criticize case by case. The impulse that private institutions of research and analysis could or should give has not come yet. It is as if the Vietnam syndrome (which has not disappeared), the internal and external failure of Kissinger's strategy, and Carter's fiasco had left no other alternative than the temporary and rather pitiful return, not of the repressed, but of the obsolete. As usual, but even more than usual, public opinion wants both peace and power, and fears both Soviet expansion and the threat of nuclear war. This means that it supports the new orthodoxy only conditionally. It also means that a coherent policy can only be provided from the top.

A second theme concerns the relations between the superpowers and the necessity of an American diplomacy quite different from everything that has been tried with Moscow. As in Kissinger's conception, one would have to conduct simultaneously resistance and cooperation. One must know both how to contain and how to collaborate. This appeal to common action, or to the acknowledgement of common interests (for instance, in economic affairs), results neither from the delusion that one might thereby change the nature of the Soviet regime, nor from the illusion that one could somehow divert Moscow from tempting unilateral political gains. Good effects could only appear in the long run. Nor is this an appeal for a duopoly or a division of the world into spheres of influence, since I am convinced not only that it would be bad for most nations, but also that the superpowers are simply incapable of imposing their will on all others. Nor is the Soviet regime one with which to share world control, even if it were possible. But I have tried to argue that the new détente I would like us to reach would have to be different from that of the 1970s. It would have to be much more modest: we cannot make Moscow underwrite America's conception of stability. I also have tried to explain that the legitimate rejection of any duopoly should not entail the exclusion of the Soviet Union from bargains and areas where it has important interests, because such an exclusion can only make it seek gains at its rival's expense more brutally and unilaterally.

The third theme is that of "the troubled partnership" and the interallied crisis that has worsened during the past three years—the vast difference in the evaluation of the world scene between Western Europe and the United States. They now differ both about relations with Moscow and about the nature of the international system. We find a desire for a mixed relationship and a multipolar analysis on the one side of the Atlantic, and renewed hostility and a bipolar conception on the other. Irritation is also caused among the allies by Washington's monetary and economic divagations and unilateral moves. Part 3 of this volume deals specifically with this theme. The United States has the ability to alienate its allies, either when it ignores the interest they have in preserving links with Moscow, or when it pursues (in the Middle East) a policy that is dangerous for the Europeans, or—indeed, principally—when it subjects the economies of allied countries to the bad effects of decisions taken exclusively on the basis of American domestic concerns or calculations. It is not clear whether America's ability to provoke, or to be clumsy, is matched by a European ability to act. But what the French Foreign Minister Claude Cheysson has called "a progressive divorce" between Western Europe and the United States can be explained not only by disagreements in foreign policy and a clash of economic interests, but also by differences over the domestic role of the state. Even Mrs. Thatcher's Britain has not dismantled the welfare state that has been built up for more than forty years, whereas the United States is passing through a phase of deep reaction in economic and social affairs.

This reaction only worsens the lack of understanding shown by American diplomacy, and by many Americans, toward revolutions or rebellions aimed at repressive regimes in the Third World. This is the fourth theme of this volume: the fear of communism—anxiety about any left wing movement (especially when it speaks with Marxist jargon) opening the door to Moscow or to an ally of Moscow and carrying subversion abroad—has more than ever nailed America to the mast of the status quo. This is a blind policy, for it is not by providing weapons to the local army, police, or state terrorists that Washington will be able to preserve its influence in the long run. This can be done only if in exchange for its aid, Washington demands and obtains the end of repression and the enforcement of reform, or else withdraws its support if the regime that calls for help persists in error or terror. It is true that revolutions often end up as sinister as the governments against which they had rebelled, and it is indeed inconceivable that capitalist America would encourage or help these revolutions. But encouragement and aid to reactionary and murderous regimes (as in El Salvador, the Philippines, or Argentina) are both morally lamentable and politically counterproductive. Unfortunately, the triumph of the new orthodoxy has not only pushed America further down this road, but has also given this policy a new ideological cloak: praise for authoritarian regimes, or at least rationalizations for tolerating and helping such regimes.

This brings me to the last theme: the link between America's domestic problems and foreign policy. The economic policies of the dominant power in the world capitalist economy have an impact on other countries that is often badly calculated or ignored in Washington. Moreover, the turmoil of domestic politics, the economic somersaults of recent years, and the weaknesses of American institutions deprive American diplomacy of a great deal of its potential effectiveness. It is clear that the power of interest groups or single-issue lobbies (such as the pro-Israeli lobby, the grain producers lobby, or the Committee on the Present Danger) often succeeds in shaping or in misshaping national strategy. It is certain that the Watergate affair—by which I mean the follies committed by Mr. Nixon and his bizarre entourage (not the brave efforts of the press or of Congress for preserving American institutions)—has not served the prestige or authority of the President. It is obvious that the choice of Jimmy Carter, followed by the choice of Ronald Reagan, as candidates of their respective parties—the first one being an unknown without any experience other than local, and the second one a passionate champion of strongly felt but extreme and sketchy ideas—has not helped either. It is evident that the astonishing machinery for foreign policymaking under both Carter and Reagan has often given American diplomacy the appearance of a ship out of control.

Intellectual laziness or fatigue, the absence of any long-run strategy toward Moscow, increasing recriminations against the Allies, and a frequent incompatibility between domestic priorities or imperatives and the requirements of a coherent diplomacy: all these factors explain both the determination (symbolized by Mr. Reagan) to reverse the trend in order to put an end to the decline of America's power and prestige and to return if possible to the days when America was number one, and the visible inability to control others and to dominate events. Of course, America is strong enough militarily, the dollar is powerful enough, America's technological resources are still vast enough for Washington's influence abroad (for instance in the Arab world or in Southeast Asia) to remain considerable, or for America to be able to contain, in Central America, revolutions it deems disastrous to its interests. Many countries continue to ask for America's weapons or America's money; this interest by so many clients and suppliers saves Washington from much possible retaliation. But none of this gives the United States the ability to lead the world where its leaders would like. And the less they succeed, the more the nostalgia for control through will and power persists; the less they seem to ask themselves if, in any case, today's world is still capable of being dominated even by superpowers. The greatest obstacles to the mere possibility of the alternative strategy recommended in this volume (the reasons why, under the pressure of unchangeable realities, no more than some bits and pieces of this alternative are likely to become official policy) lie within the United States—in the national psyche and style, in the political and economic systems, and in the organization of the government. One of the most lamentable aspects of the (rather one-sided) recent discussion of America's role in the world is that it is so much easier for some to blame other Americans for America's "decline," for lack of will or for lack of morality, than it is either to examine coolly the transformations and trends in the world, or the reflexes, myths, patterns, and inhibitions that America owes to its history, to its own "exceptionalism," to its very success story in the past, to the combination of insecurity and hubris engendered by its emergence as the dominant power in 1945, and to the domestic turbulence and deterioration of the past decade and a half.

NOTES

1. Stanley Hoffmann, *Primacy or World Order* (New York: McGraw-Hill, 1978).
2. Stanley Hoffmann, "The Perils of Incoherence," *Foreign Affairs: America and the World in 1978* (special issue, 1978):463-491.
3. Stanley Hoffmann, "Notes on the Limits of 'Realism'," *Social Research* 48 (Winter 1981):653-659.
4. Cf. Robert Keohane and Joseph Nye, *Power and Interdependence* (Boston: Little Brown, 1977).
5. Wayne S. Smith, "Myopic Diplomacy," *Foreign Policy* (Fall 1982):157-174.
6. Leon S. Sigal, "Warming to the Freeze," *Foreign Policy* (Fall 1982): 54-65.
7. George Kennan, *The Nuclear Delusion* (New York: Pantheon, 1982), p. xxvi.
8. Stanley Hoffmann, *Gulliver's Troubles* (New York: McGraw-Hill, 1968).

PART I

THE DÉTENTE ERA REVISITED

THE THREE essays in this section deal with the two parts of the détente era (1969-1979). The first two examine American foreign policy from 1969 to 1974 as it has been described and justified at length by Henry Kissinger in the two volumes of his memoirs published so far. The third essay deals with Jimmy Carter's diplomacy.

All three try to present a fairly complete balance sheet. However, the central issue is the Soviet-American conflict and the degree to which international relations could be reduced to or separated from this conflict. This was one of the major differences between Mr. Kissinger and Mr. Nixon on the one hand, and Jimmy Carter and a sizeable part of his team on the other. Another difference was that between the highly ambitious and complex but coherent concepts of Kissinger, and the contradictions of the Carter era that resulted both from divisions within the team and from the frequent inability of the President to translate his aspirations into policies.

Concerning Henry Kissinger, it is important to distinguish his strategy from the conception of containment developed by George Kennan after the end of the Second World War. In a brilliant recent book, John Lewis Gaddis has referred to many similarities between Kissinger and Kennan.[1] It is true that Kissinger has often *written* about the need to recognize limits, the advent of multipolarity, the imperative of defining lasting American interests in geopolitical terms (rather than letting them be determined by real or assumed outside threats), and the importance of distinguishing vital from secondary interests, and foreign policy behavior from domestic behavior— notions that are all close to George Kennan's. But Kissinger's actions, as I

15

have tried to show in Chapter 2, really resulted from an extraordinarily extensive notion of American interests, which could not let even minor or marginal challenges go unopposed. There is no doubt that both the containment element of his strategy and the complex network of incentives and threats aimed at inducing Soviet self-restraint resulted from a worldview in which the United States, while enlisting the support of others whose resources had to be marshalled now that American power was no longer quite as overwhelming as in 1947, was the nation that had to define the nature of world order and, so to speak, to assign roles to all the others—not at all George Kennan's view. Kissinger's view was a bold attempt to combine universal containment, à la Eisenhower and Dulles (with whom he shared both the idea of avoiding getting dragged into costly conventional conflicts by the Soviets or their allies, and a Manichean view of the world), *and* the Rooseveltian concept (or conceit) of enticing and ensnaring the Soviets into cooperation on America's terms. Both policies are decidedly unlike Kennan's.[2]

As for Jimmy Carter, while Robert W. Tucker asserts that he *had* a strategy, with which Tucker disagrees violently because he considers it to have been fatal for American power, I continue to believe that this was not the case, and that his administration can best be described as a constant collision of incompatible would-be strategies, some explicit, some implicit, and never carefully worked out.[3]

NOTES

1. John Lewis Gaddis, *Strategies of Containment* (New York: Oxford University Press, 1982).

2. For further elaboration, see my chapter in the forthcoming book edited by Joseph S. Nye, *Managing the U.S.-Soviet Relationship.*

3. Robert W. Tucker, *The Purposes of American Power* (Baltimore: Praeger Publications, 1981).

CHAPTER 2

THE WORLD ACCORDING TO HENRY KISSINGER: I, 1969-1972

I.

IN *WHITE House Years*[1], Henry Kissinger has given us an overwhelming account and a formidable defense of American foreign policy, as devised and carried out by Henry Kissinger, from the first Nixon inauguration to the signing of the Vietnam peace agreement four years later. Kissinger's earlier works were remarkable for the intellectual self-assurance and the penetrating analytical intelligence they displayed. They were not easy to read. The marshaling of arguments and the array of maxims brought to mind the heavy, purposeful march of Roman legions. In his enormous memoirs, Kissinger shows the same gifts, and adds light touches reflecting a sardonic humor that had not been much in evidence in his academic years, but flourished as his success in action began to match his self-confidence.

He also, far more than in his previous books, lets his emotions show—the warmth of his gratitude to Nelson Rockefeller, or his affection for Chou En-lai, the depth of his exasperation and "impotent rage" when either the North or the South Vietnamese blocked his designs, and most frequently his anger or contempt for domestic opponents. The book is often brilliant, the flow of arguments and the author's mental concentration are prodigious, but the mass of detail is likely to discourage readers who are not professionally interested in foreign policy. The tone moves from the masterful to the garrulous; and despite many admirable sections, and chapters in which he communicates his own exhilaration, there is something airless and oppressive about the book.

This too has to be explained, for it is not caused only by the many passages in which he celebrates his diplomacy's achievements, or by the tendency to repeat points almost verbatim from chapter to chapter (which better editing could have cured). It is as if the reader were entering a mighty fortress, with many glittering rooms but several dark galleries and dungeons, innumerable closets, and narrow openings filled with weapons for resisting attacks—guns or boiling oil.

About every political memoir, a first question is: for whom is the author writing? In the case of statesmen who wrote after they reached, or thought they had reached, the end of their careers, the audience is posterity. De Gaulle, for instance, wanted his memoirs to be both a celebration and an inspiration (or a reproach). Posterity is much on Kissinger's mind, either when he draws pictures of his leading contemporaries or when he outlines his goals, explains his tactics, and defends his most controversial decisions. But Kissinger is not at the end of his career, and his book is a weighty force thrown into the battle for a second chance, or at least for continuing public service. This accounts for the vigor with which he conducts his defense, his occasional digs at his successors, his often brutal dismissal of foes he knows he would have to fight again, or (on the contrary) are now out of the way, and in either case deserve no quarter, and his prudence in dealing with figures with whom he tangled mightily but whom he cannot afford to offend. His treatment of Melvin Laird is one example, and an enthusiasm for John Connally that was far less evident in 1971 is another. Although he mentions his "intention to reconcile" (p. xxi), he is at his most aggressive wherever he feels most on the defensive: in his chapters on Chile, Bangladesh, Iran, and Cambodia where his enemies are denounced for having done "their utmost to forestall any effective assistance to the beleaguered country, as if to punish the free Cambodians for not living up to the role of victim to which they had been consigned," (p. 1384). This is not a serene work.

A second question raised by political memoirs is: how truthful are they? A detailed answer will have to wait until we have more of the record: the memoirs of other actors, unpublished documents (especially intelligence reports), and the famous tapes of the president and his assistant. Two kinds of problems arise. First, when Kissinger reconstructs his "design" (for instance, for the Middle East), to what extent does he tell us what he really thought and planned at the time, to what extent does he tell us now that what he obtained later is what he had wanted all along? Yitzhak Rabin, in his *Memoirs*,[2] reports that in October 1971 Kissinger, referring to United States peace efforts in the Middle East, confided to him that he would never handle any "matter that he deemed hopeless." Was Kissinger's opposition to the State Department's initiatives due to a simple conviction that they were doomed, or to his preference for a complex plan aimed at producing a deadlock that would force the radical Arabs to turn to Washington? Was this plan, for which he claims authorship and credit repeatedly, any different from Israel's policy under Golda Meir, which consisted of refusing concessions (except very minor ones) and of increasing Israel's strength in the conviction that its enemies, incapable of a new round of war, would come to Canossa?

Secondly, is Kissinger's account of the facts that led to a decision, or of the proposals and counterproposals in a negotiation, entirely candid? I will discuss later the evidence he gives on Cambodia—and what he leaves out. In his account of SALT I, he is very discreet on points that have later led to criticisms: his lack of interest in controlling MIRVs and his formula for limiting increases in silo dimensions for land-based missiles, which did not foresee that the Soviets would put powerful new missiles into existing silos and gain a (theoretical) advantage through a combination of superior throw-weight and multiple warheads of their own. In his account of the Vietnam negotiations he tends to interpret America's successive proposals in such a way as to put maximum emphasis on continuity, and to present the North Vietnamese as the ones who made the decisive concessions (in giving up their objective of a coalition government and their insistence that we overthrow Thieu).

But it is not at all clear that we had really given up asking for mutual withdrawals from South Vietnam (unacceptable to the North Vietnamese) as early as October 1970: Nixon's proposal of October 1970, Kissinger recognizes, was "fuzzy" on this point; and the United States' offer of 1971 still mentioned the withdrawal of all outside forces. This goes a long way toward explaining Thieu's rage, in October 1972, at an agreement that legalized the presence of Hanoi's troops in the South (a point acknowledged by Kissinger, but which contradicts his assertion that this agreement contained no more than what Thieu had endorsed before). Kissinger's account of discussions on Vietnam with the Soviets in April and May 1972 minimizes their importance and implicitly contradicts Tad Szulc's story in his *Illusion of Peace*.[3] Obviously, generations of scholars and graduate students will test Kissinger's story issue by issue in order to get closer to the truth.

A third question raised by political memoirs is: what does the author reveal about himself—not his acts or concepts, but his personality? Kissinger, on the surface, is reticent. He is gracious in acknowledging his own intellectual arrogance, occasional pettiness (toward Secretary of State Rogers), vanity (as in his interview with Oriana Fallaci), one or two tactical mistakes, and some deviousness. While he spares us little in describing his tactics abroad, he does not tell us much about the ways in which he consolidated and expanded his power at home over the bureaucracy and his influence over the press. He can be generous: several of his portraits show compassion and empathy, even for men such as Gromyko, who must have maddened him countless times.

But he displays also two less attractive features. One is a compulsion to be right. He is never so lavish in his praise of Nixon as when the president agreed with Kissinger's preferred course. Whatever goes well was his initiative. To be sure, Nixon also had thought of the opening to China, but, says Kissinger, the president's perspective was more tactical—he was seeking "short-term help on Vietnam." Kissinger's was strategic—"the policy's impact on the structure of international relations" (p. 164). Whenever something goes wrong, it is someone else's fault—or else history later comes to the rescue and vindicates the original design.

Thus Kissinger's plan for a "reversal of alliances in the Middle East" finally worked, "but it took a long time, further crises, and an anguishing war to complete it" (p. 379). He does not ask whether these crises and this war weren't partly the result of his policy. India and the Soviets are copiously blamed for the Bangladesh crisis of 1971—far more so than massacres carried out by Yahya Khan's forces. In the failed Laos operation of 1971 the fault, he writes, lies with the military; in the failed attempts by the United States at preventing Allende from becoming Chile's president in 1970, the bureaucracy was too slow, too timid, and too clumsy. Watergate is the devil *ex machina* that ruined Kissinger's post-January 1973 policy for Vietnam and, along with "the erosion of the leadership structure even in the Congress, the isolationism born of the frustrations of Vietnam, and an emerging pattern of geopolitical abdication" (p. 1143), it destroyed his policy toward Moscow, a careful "balance of incentives and penalties."

This need to be right merges with his other unattractive bias: vindictiveness. He has three targets (two of them overlap). Academics get blamed for their "lack of compassion" and "over-weening self-righteousness" (p. 515), the "abasement of the middle-aged before the young," and "the dismissal of rational discourse by those with the greatest stake in reason" (p. 1199). When his former colleagues urged him to accept Nixon's offer of the job of National Security Assistant, he suggests that their advice was "tinged by the desire to know someone of influence in Washington who could provide . . . vicarious access to power" (p. 15)—not the most charitable explanation.[4] Liberals, throughout the book, are described as "sentimental," unreliable, soft-headed, and wracked by guilt. (Already in *A World Restored* he had expressed a preference for conservatives and revolutionaries—both having predictable purposes and methods—over liberals. Mao, much to his delight, expressed the same feeling. It was precisely because, in Kissinger's eyes, Allende was a true revolutionary that he took him seriously enough to want him kept from power.) Liberals are not only shallow but irresponsible and—as in the case of the antiwar leaders—"merciless": "the doves have proved to be a specially vicious kind of bird" (p. 295).

The third target is none other than Richard Nixon. True, Kissinger celebrates repeatedly Nixon's ability to make tough, unpopular, and bold decisions; "much intelligence and much knowledge lay behind his accomplishments" (p. 1468). The book's last long paragraph, which is his most penetrating look at his boss ("What extraordinary vehicles destiny selects to accomplish its design," p. 1475), is quite moving. And yet Nixon, "strong in his decisions," was "inconclusive in his leadership" (p. 482). Whether he is aware of it or not, Kissinger, in dozens of brush strokes, gives a portrait of Nixon that is just as deadly, and far more informed, than the cartoons sketched over the years by the hated members of the Eastern "Establishment"—capitalized throughout the book and referred to with apparent confidence in its existence. Nixon, who felt (correctly) despised by it, and Kissinger, who had been adopted by it, who respected some of its members (such as Acheson or McCloy), but who despised much of it for its mix of condescending arrogance and superficiality, had been brought together not only by common ideas but by their sense of being (relative) outsiders. But *White House Years* is not only the history of a partnership. It is also the story of a divorce.

Kissinger's portrait of Nixon is devastating in two ways. One is the accumulation of anecdotes that reveal the growing resentments, the psychological insecurity, the craving for reassurance and the thirst for publicity, the preference for indirection, the fear of rejection, the dislike of face-to-face confrontations, the need for isolation and "cocoons," the secretiveness and suspiciousness, the lack of grace and style, the inability to elicit respect and obedience, and the love of pomp and splash of a man who had been humiliated and battered so long that success in the 1972 elections, far from bringing satisfaction or relief, incited him only to "a premonition of ephemerality" (p. 1471), and to what Kissinger calls the "appalling performance" and "political butchery" (p. 1407) of November 8, 1972, when he asked for the resignation of the White House staff just after his victory.

The anecdotes about Nixon are often funny—Nixon eager to go to Maxim's between the memorial ceremony at Notre Dame that followed de Gaulle's death and an afternoon reception by Pompidou; or Nixon's departure from the Vatican in a military helicopter after having harangued the Pope about left wing priests in Latin America; or Nixon ordering the blockade of Haiphong and the bombing of Hanoi while gesticulating with a pipe and "playing MacArthur"; Nixon toasting the Shah and telling him that all successful leaders have "the ability to marry above themselves" (p. 1263); Nixon's enthusiasm for Connally whose "swaggering self-assurance was Nixon's Walter Mitty image of himself'' (p. 951); Nixon suggesting Thomas Dewey as a possible emissary to China months after Dewey's death, and so forth. But the effect is to give a picture of a man incapable of the greatness to which he aspired, craving for crises that would lift him above the daily routine, but gnawed by a "strange sense of his inadequacy" (p. 944) that was "the psychological essence of the Watergate debacle" (p. 1095), and consumed by a desire for revenge over his enemies.

The other way in which Kissinger gets at Nixon is not by stressing his foibles and instability but by telling the story of their own relationship. All was well in 1969-1970, when Kissinger helped Nixon to prevail over the bureaucracy they both distrusted—Nixon, because he deemed it filled with enemies, Kissinger because he had always feared it as a quagmire that absorbs creativity and dooms policy to routine. And they overcame together the crises in Cambodia, Cuba (the Cienfuegos affair), and Jordan. But things started going sour in 1971. Nixon sent Kissinger to China, but was afraid "of being upstaged by his own Assistant," who, after achieving a real breakthrough with Chou En-lai, found his plane had been ordered to land "at a distant corner of Andrews Air Force Base, inaccessible to newsmen and photographers" (p. 786). Kissinger carried out Nixon's orders during the Bangladesh crisis, but since the policy was unpopular, Nixon wanted "to get out of the line of fire" and to push Kissinger into it: "Nixon could not resist the temptation of letting me twist slowly, slowly in the wind, to use the literary contribution of a later period" (p. 918). Kissinger says he resented that "stern lesson in the dependence of Presidential Assistants on their chief."

The following year, he resented even more a sharp tactical disagreement with Nixon over his secret trip to Moscow in April, an episode on which he spends several bitter pages—far more space than Nixon, who in his own memoirs rather fairly concludes that Kissinger may have been right.[5] And the split deepened during the tense last phases of the Vietnam negotiations, when Kissinger tried to reach an agreement with (and in) Hanoi before the presidential election, while Nixon was willing to try one more military escalation just after his reelection. When Thieu rejected the agreement, Kissinger "began to be nagged by the unworthy notion that I was being set up as the fall guy in case anything went wrong" (p. 1377).[6]

The "peace is at hand" press conference of November 1972 and the Fallaci interview provoked a crisis of "emerging competitiveness' with Nixon (p. 1409). It led to new tactical differences, first when the negotiations resumed after the election, and later when both Nixon and Kissinger decided to break them off. Nixon—for once—wanted a low-key suspension of the talks, followed by a heavy U.S. bombing of North Vietnam that would not be announced by a presidential speech. Kissinger wanted Nixon to announce this plan and to try to rally the public behind it.[7] Nixon prevailed and ordered Kissinger to give a press conference in which he would "stress the President's consistency, unflappability, firmness, patience, and far-sightedness" (p. 1450). This, according to Kissinger, explains why, during the Christmas bombing Kissinger had endorsed, he "did little to dampen the speculation" that he had opposed it, "one of the episodes of my public life in which I take no great pride" (p. 1456). Nixon, infuriated, had Kissinger's phone tapped; Kissinger decided he would resign during 1973.[8]

This story helps to explain why Kissinger so relentlessly splashes his ambivalence about Nixon all over the book. There are similarities between the two men: neither forgave wounds to his self-esteem; both craved approval and flattery. Kissinger treats Nixon, on balance, less generously than Nixon treated Kissinger in his own book, and there are two good reasons for this. One is personal. Since Nixon's administration was, until 1973, Kissinger's only base of power, Kissinger had had to accept the humiliations which the White House minions inflicted on him. In his book he could no more, it seems, keep himself from settling this account than he could refrain from a very unflattering portrait of McGeorge Bundy—a man who plays no part in his story—thus getting even for having been treated, by Bundy, at Harvard, "with the combination of politeness and subconscious condescension that upper-class Bostonians reserve for people of, by New England standards, exotic backgrounds and excessively intense personal style" (pp. 13-14).

The other reason is, of course, Kissinger's resentment over Watergate: a president more eager to heed Chou's remark on the danger of coverups (p. 1081), and less unable "to leave the inhospitable and hostile world he inherited" (p. 1471), would not have undermined all the foreign policy triumphs that he and Kissinger had, in their eyes, achieved, by provoking the collapse of executive authority. For Kissinger, having had to serve Richard Nixon, rather than Nelson Rockefeller, is a stain that won't go away.

II.

Some people owe their psychological or sociological insight exclusively to their resentments and their fears. This is not Kissinger's case. These may sharpen his wits and dip his brush in acid. But he has three great gifts that serve him equally well in his writings and his statecraft.

One is an almost devilish psychological intuition, an instinct for grasping the hidden springs of character, of knowing what drives or what dooms another person. He was at his best as a face-to-face negotiator precisely because of this rare talent. Had he been less tempted by action and more capable of that "fantasy life" of "romantic imaginings" in which, he says, Nixon indulged (p. 1475), he might have been a good novelist. The gallery of portraits is the best part of the book. Readers will have their own favorites (and everyone will notice that some statesmen with whom Kissinger had many dealings harldy appear—Willy Brandt being the most conspicuous). My favorites are the vivid portraits of Chou, Heath, Brezhnev, and Mao—who is described with a power and subtlety that seem worthy of him (pp. 1057-1066). As in his account of Nixon, for example, Kissinger backs up his incisive analysis of character with incisive anecdotes. We see Chou, late at night, taking Kissinger on a walk where they cross two bridges, without a word referring to a conversation months before when Kissinge had told Chou that he felt like a character in Kafka's *Castle*—the plumber who is summoned and denied entrance—because of the presence of soldiers guarding the bridges connecting the various guest cottages (p. 745), and Brezhnev trying to make a toy cannon work during a conference and strutting "like a prizefighter who has knocked out his opponent" when the cannon finally went off (p. 1140).

All of the portraits convey the relation between a personality and the culture that has shaped it. And Kissinger's second gift is that of a man particularly attuned to the nuances of cultural difference (the word "nuance" is one of his favorites, along with "intangible," "comparison," "exalted," "insecure," "petty," and "unsentimental"). People who have been transplanted from one country to another, who have a certain distance both from the history and mores of the society from which they were uprooted and from the memories and rituals of their adopted country, often develop this sense. They lose it only if they are too eager to assimilate into the mainstream of their new culture—something that was never Kissinger's case.

Kissinger is very good at evoking atmospheres and their relation to the business of power: Washington dinner parties and receptions, where "the relationships are created without which the machinery of government would soon stalemate itself" (p. 20), the president's lonely hideaway room, the villa filled with Fernand Léger paintings where Kissinger met the North Vietnamese, the peculiarities of protocol in each country he visited. One of the most fascinating sides of this book is the analysis of different political styles, molded by distinctive historical experiences and geographical imperatives. Kissinger thus compares brilliantly the Chinese and the Soviet styles of negotiation (not to mention cuisines). "The Soviets insist on their prerogatives as a great power. The Chinese establish a claim on the basis of universal principles and a demonstration of self-confidence that attempts to make the issue of power irrelevant" (p. 1056). Mao and Chou represented a nation that "had absorbed conquerors and had proved its inward strength by imposing its social and intellectual style on them. Its leaders were aloof, self-assured, composed. Brezhnev represented a nation that had survived not by civilizing its conquerors but by outlasting them . . . he sought to obscure his lack of assurance by boisterousness" (p. 1138).

The Vietnamese, he notes, have outlasted their conquerors by driving them insane. A Japanese leader "does not announce a decision, he evokes it" (p. 324). Japanese decisionmaking by consensus is endless, but execution is disciplined; in the United States, it is the other way around. In the Middle East, "formal positions are like the shadows in Plato's cave—reflections of a transcendent reality almost impossible to encompass in the dry legalisms of a negotiating process" (p. 342).

Nobody has analyzed more pithily Western European ambivalence toward the United States—the fear of American rigidity compounded by the fear either of American retreat or of superpower condominium. French foreign polity under the Fifth Republic was prickly but "serious and consistent," at times "steadier and more perceptive than our own," whereas British statesmen "were content to act as honored consultants to our deliberations" (pp. 420-421). And "one sometimes could not avoid the impression that to discuss international affairs with [Italy's] foreign minister was to risk boring him" (p. 102). One could cull a bestiary of negotiating styles from this book.

One could also draw from it a vast monograph on the workings of American bureaucracy in foreign affairs, and a short Little Red (or rather White) Book, an appendix to *The Prince,* on the art of diplomatic bargaining. For Kissinger's third gift is one that puts into practice his insights into personalities and cultures: it is the gift for the manipulation of power—exploiting the weaknesses and strengths of character of his counterparts, either by neutralizing them (if they were adversaries) or turning them into allies or accomplices by addressing their needs and playing on their fears of other countries. This did not always work: his attempt at negotiating a textile agreement with the Japanese began as "an intricate Kabuki play" that "turned out to be more like a Kafka story" (p. 337).

Kissinger's prerequisite for the exercise of this gift, as he suggests throughout the book, is a firm control of the U.S. bureaucracy—which is precisely what Nixon also wanted. The president "was determined to run foreign policy from the White House" (p. 11), and Kissinger devised the machinery that was supposed to make it possible. But it never worked well enough, and those who believe that confusion and cacophony began with the Carter administration are in for a surprise.

If there is one constant theme that runs through every chapter of this complex book, it is that of the battle for control between on the one hand, Nixon and Kissinger and, on the other, the bureaucracy—the State Department, Defense, the CIA, and the Treasury during Connally's "frontal assault on the White House staff system" (p. 951). It was a vicious circle: Nixon and Kissinger, exasperated by the bureaucrats' lack of imagination, frequent resistance, and propensity to leaks, reserved more and more control over the key issues to themselves, but this only compounded the problem, since the execution of policies had to be largely entrusted to departments that had not been consulted or even informed. More and more Kissinger carried on the real business of foreign policy through secretive "back channels"—with Dobrynin over SALT and all other U.S.-Soviet relations, with Chou, with Ambassador Rabin and Golda Meir (at the expense of Foreign Minister Abba Eban), and later with Sadat. But the same issues were being treated simultaneously by the State Department, or in the formal SALT negotiation at Helsinki.

This created frequent confusion when America's negotiators did not know the agreements in the making through the back channels; it also gave the Soviets opportunities to try to play one team against the other. It created deep resentments among American diplomats ignored or undercut by the White House. It even created suspicion in Moscow and Peking, for Soviet and Chinese diplomats wondered why the Americans wanted so much secrecy. It meant that vital decisions (for instance, those concerning Cambodia in April 1970) were taken behind the backs or against the opposition of Secretaries Rogers and Laird. It meant that at the summits in Peking and Moscow, set up without Rogers's participation, Kissinger had to enlist the cooperation of Chou and of Gromyko in handling our own resentful State Department. (In China, this did not work: when the State Department, which had been kept in the dark, was informed of the text of what became the Shanghai communiqué, it demanded a host of changes—and obtained some, behaving exactly as Thieu was going to do a few months later, when he was finally informed of the text of the peace agreement Kissinger had negotiated along with Le Duc Tho.)

When Kissinger was charged with executing a policy, the sluggishness and opposition of the bureaucracy could complicate and delay, but no more. When responsibilities were shared, or supposedly belonged to the State Department but were subject to White House review, policy could become incoherent: for instance, in the Middle East in 1969-1970, when Rogers launched peace plans which Nixon and Kissinger did not endorse, or during the Bangladesh crisis when Rogers opposed the "tilt" toward Pakistan. The bureaucracy, in what it deemed "its" domain, often failed to consult the White House! Nixon's startling announcement of August 15, 1971—the monetary and economic measures that provoked a crisis with Western Europe and Japan—was made without either Rogers or Kissinger being consulted.

> The Nixon method of government worked well when the military problem was relatively straightforward and could be carried out in one daring move. It was effective also for purposeful solitary diplomacy conducted by a trusted associate working with a small staff. . . . Difficulties arose when a sustained military effort was needed, or when the diplomacy was too complex to be handled by the security adviser's office. . . . Then the absence of consensus or even understanding inhibited coherence and commitment. [p. 997]

Nixon's reluctance to impose his will perpetuated the lack of discipline, and drove him increasingly into secrecy and distrust. Thus his methods made possible some remarkable initiatives, but also led straight to the crisis that destroyed him in 1974, and weakened the presidency.

Kissinger was more than willing to overlook those risks, both when in office and in writing most of his memoir. For the brand of diplomacy he wanted to perform cannot tolerate pluralism in the various institutions concerned with foreign policy, or the long delays that building a consensus among them would entail. He concentrated on the games to be played with foreign interlocutors, not domestic bureaucrats. For him the job of the U.S. bureaucracies was to give him the data for the decisions he and Nixon would make, and to carry out these decisions.

Bureaucratic maneuver annoys him. What fascinates him is diplomatic maneuver, as he makes clear in countless maxims and comments on the art of relating force to goals, and on the advantages and perils of crises. These confer "an unusual capacity for creative action" (p. 597), but they must be "overpowered early" (p. 890). "One's actions must be sustained; they must appear relentless, inexorable" (p. 604). In the final phase one must resist "the natural temptation to relax and perhaps to ease the process by a gesture of goodwill . . . The time for conciliation is after the crisis is surmounted" (p. 629).

He tells us the requirements of secret diplomacy, the way of linking issues in a bargain so as to extract advantages, and the way of delaying agreement on the issues which one's opponent is in a hurry to settle until he has given in on the others. One must never appear too eager, yet one should not (as the Soviets tend to do) compromise one's gains by being too greedy or by asking for something unattainable; one should not make any unilateral concessions, yet one ought to avoid excessive haggling.

Kissinger also instructs us on triangular diplomacy (which "must rely on the natural incentives and propensities of the players" and "avoid the impression that one is 'using' either of the contenders against the other," p. 712), on giving an opponent "a formal reassurance intended to unnerve as much as to calm; and which would defeat its purpose if it were actually believed" (p. 712), on the error of raising too soon an issue on which "readiness to compromise does not exist" (p. 349), on the occasional need to substitute boldness if one lacks power, and on the uses of insolence, "the armor of the weak" (p. 1327).

If there seems considerable self-satisfaction in such advice, it is true that during the period covered by this book he was rarely caught at his own game: pathetically, his only personal diplomatic defeat was inflicted by Thieu, in October 1972, when the South Vietnamese leader turned the deadline agreed upon by Kissinger and the North Vietnamese into a weapon against the whole agreement as brilliantly as Kissinger had used the deadline of the U.S. election in order to extract a "cascade" of concessions from Hanoi. (Both Thieu and Le Duc Tho used insolence to "stonewall" when in positions of weakness. Kissinger in this book does the same in reply to criticism from the left and from liberals.) Like an athlete reminiscing about a game he won because he was in top form. Kissinger relives his tactical calculations and manipulations with relish, and thus reveals what sustains a master politician in the daily drudgery of dealing with "the contingent." But what was the design that all the ingenuity he so fondly recalls was supposed to serve? What strategy required these tactics?

III.

Kissinger's tactical maxims leave no doubt: the professed disciple of Kant,[9] he is a follower of Hobbes in his assessment of human nature and of the behavior of states in the international state of nature. (Twice he mentions, with some awe, that Pompidou, who helped him conduct his secret negotiations with the North Vietnamese, "never used these kindnesses to extract anything in return" [p. 420 and again p. 440].) As he sees them, nations are driven by diffidence, greed, and glory; they are often propelled by the murderous certainties of ideology, compelled to use their power for their preservation or their expansion. What order can nations achieve in this "state of war" which Hobbes deemed bearable in his day, but which has become a threat to the common survival in the age (foreseen by Kant) when total destruction is possible and nations are so intimately interdependent?

Americans, Kissinger tells us, have had three traditions: "an idealistic tradition that sees foreign policy as a contest between evil and good," a pragmatic tradition of problem solving, and a legalistic tradition (p. 915). They had all failed. "Emotional slogans" (p. 1088) had kept America oscillating from overinvolvement to isolationism. The time had come when "moral exuberance" could no longer be condoned: "we were becoming like other nations in the need to recognize that our power, while vast, had limits" (p. 57). "It was my conviction that a concept of our fundamental national interests would provide a ballast of restraint and an assurance of continuity'' (p. 65). What America needed, and Kissinger wanted to establish, was a geopolitical tradition. ("By 'geopolitical' I mean an approach that pays attention to the requirements of equilibrium," p. 914.)

Kissinger the realist sounds here like Hans Morgenthau writing on the balance of power. But Morgenthau has often been severely critical of Kissinger. The drama of this doctrine of realism is that, while it conceives of world order as the product of a careful balancing of power, as a set of restraints on excessive ambitions, and as a compromise between conflicting interests, it allows for many different versions of nirvana, and different evaluations of threats and opportunities. Containment too—as described by George Kennan, and as executed (not to Kennan's satisfaction) by Acheson and (not to Acheson's satisfaction) by Dulles—had been an attempt to teach realism to Americans. But Kissinger is critical of containment: it "treated power and diplomacy as distinct elements or phases of policy" (p. 62); by concentrating on building "situations of strength" at a time when we were strong and the Soviets weak, we allowed them to catch up, and thus to be in a much more favorable position on the distant day of negotiation. "Treating force and diplomacy as discrete phenomena caused our power to lack purpose and our negotiations to lack force" (p. 64). We had to learn a better integration of power and policy in an age of nuclear weapons, competing ideologies, and diffusion of political power.

The question remains: for what purpose? What was the "geopolitical design"? It is here that surprises begin. In the first place, Kissinger's repeated assertions about the need for a policy purged of emotional excesses and reconciled "to imperfect choices, partial fulfillment, the unsatisfying tasks of balance and maneuver" (p. 1089) are nowhere accompanied by a description of the kind of world Kissinger was trying to bring about. If there was a vision beyond the geopolitical game, if the complex manipulation of rewards and punishments needed to create equilibrium and to restrain the troublemakers was aimed at a certain ideal of world order, we are left free to guess what it might have been. Maybe it is Kissinger's horror of grand designs mass produced by "the wayward representatives of American liberalism" (p. 1089) that explains this reticence. At any rate, he is much more mysterious about his purposes than about his method, and about his destination than about his approach.

Second, the approach itself reminds one that geopolitics was a German school of thought based on the notion of constant and inevitable struggle. And Kissinger now reminds one of Karl Schmitt's fundamental distinction—in which he saw the key to politics—between friends and foes. Kissinger recognizes that the nuclear stalemate between the superpowers results in a kind of fragmentation of world politics: there is both a global balance of nuclear power, and a series of regional balances (or imbalances). But at the heart of his conception there are two propositions.

The first is that the decisive and dominant issue is the conflict between the United States and the Soviet Union. This extends to every part of the world and, given the nature of Soviet ideology, includes "the internal policies and social structures of countries" (p. 117) as well. Soviet policy, whatever its "ultimate aims" or the Soviet leaders' "real intentions" (wrong questions, says Kissinger), wants "to promote the attrition of adversaries by gradual increments." Soviet strategy is "one of ruthless opportunism" (p. 119). There is no "terminal point to international tension" (p. 123) that could be achieved by "sentimental conciliation" or "liturgical belligerence," for we are "dealing with a system too ideologically hostile for instant conciliation and militarily too powerful to destroy" (p. 123).

The second fundamental proposition is that "to foreclose Soviet opportunities is thus the essence of the West's responsibility" (p. 119). It is a permanent task, not (as containment was thought to be) "an exertion that has a foreseeable end." The nature of that task is the management of the balance of power, which requires "perseverance, subtlety, not a little courage, and above all understanding of its requirements" (p. 115).

What are these requirements? Above all, we must create in our adversary a perception of "an equality of power": if it is perceived, "it will not be tested." "Calculation must include potential as well as actual power, not only the possession of power but the will to bring it to bear" (p. 115). We must understand that our performance in any part of the world has an effect on this balance of real and perceived power; therefore, the way in which we respond to any local crisis ought to be related to, and determined by its relation to, the central contest.

Kissinger rigorously applied this maxim in cases such as Chile, where he saw in Allende's election "a challenge to our national interest" not only because of Allende's revolutionary and anti-American program but because it happened "against the backdrop of the Syrian invasion of Jordan" (Syria being a Soviet ally) "and our effort to force the Soviet Union to dismantle its installation for servicing nuclear submarines in the Caribbean" (p. 654). He acted in the same way in the Middle East, where in 1969 "delay was on the whole in our interest because it enabled us to demonstrate even to radical Arabs that we were indispensable to *any* progress and that it cannot be extorted from us by Soviet pressure" (p. 354). The division of the world into radicals and moderates is as important to Kissinger as the division between Moscow and Washington; Moscow being seen as the ally of the radicals, and Washington the protector of the moderates.

Vietnam was, of course, part of the same chain: he tells us many times that his "initiatives with Peking and Moscow would have been impossible had we simply collapsed in Vietnam" (p. 1046). He supported Pakistan against India because Pakistan was our ally and China's friend, whereas India had signed a treaty with Moscow, and India's war threatened "our geopolitical design" (p. 879). Our friends must be supported whatever they may do within their own countries: hence Kissinger's determination to stick by Yahya Khan, Thieu, Lon Nol, the shah, and so on. Still, when their acts could adversely affect the central conflict, we must check their course: thus as Nixon "frostily" reminded Willy Brandt, we did not support his *Ostpolitik,* we merely "did not object" (p. 966); but we gave "the inevitable a constructive direction" (p. 530) by linking it to America's own policy toward the Soviet Union, and thus we "became responsible for the ultimate success of Brandt's policy" (p. 824). Our enemies, defined as whoever aligns himself with the Soviets, must be resisted and frustrated; our friends must be guided.

Kissinger's notion of linkage applies not only to power relations among nations and entire regions but also to political issues arising with the Soviets. Not only are "the actions of a major power inevitably related," and not only do they have "consequences beyond the issue or region immediately concerned," but we must try to link "deliberately" separate objectives in a negotiation, "using one as a leverage on the other" (p. 129). Hence the efforts of the Nixon administration to make "progress in settling the Vietnam war something of a condition for advance in areas of interest to the Soviets, such as the Middle East, trade or arms limitation" (p. 129); and we linked SALT to the Berlin negotiation, on whose success, in turn, the Soviet-West German treaty depended. "We saw linkage, in short, as synonymous with an overall strategic and geopolitical view. To ignore the interconnection of events was to undermine the coherence of all policy" (p. 129).

Linkage was part of the attempt to restrain the Soviets with a careful mixture of penalties and incentives. Trade, for instance, was treated as "a political instrument," to be favored "in measured doses" when the Soviets behaved cooperatively, and withheld otherwise (p. 840). "Penalties for adventurism" include "military assistance to friends resisting Soviet or Cuban or radical pressures" (p. 1254). They also include the use of force.

On this point, Kissinger is prolix: on the one hand, the "basic choice is to act or not to act"; "there are no rewards for exhibiting one's doubts in vacillation: statesmen get no praise for failing with restraint. Once committed they must prevail" (p. 498). "Gradual escalation tempts the opponent to match every move"; a leader, once committed, has the "obligation to end the confrontation rapidly. For this he must convey implacability" (p. 622).

On the other hand, the purpose of force is to restore a balance of power, without which negotiations are bound to be counterproductive for one's own side. And it is best to resort to force quickly, when a major crisis can still be avoided and the adversary is not yet fully committed. The objective of this strategy is "an end of the constant Soviet pressure against the global balance of power," to which "in our minds efforts to reduce the danger of nuclear war by the control of arms had to be linked" (p. 1250). Reacting strongly, violently if necessary, in the early stages of Soviet expansion would save us from having to choose between either "the collapse of the balance of power or a colossal confrontation" (p. 1158).

It must be clear that Kissinger's geopolitical design is not at all adequately described by the word détente. It was a scheme for universal, permanent, and successful containment, marshaling all our instruments of power more effectively than before, and aiming at "an end to the constant probing for openings and the testing of every equilibrium" (p. 1143). Kissinger, indeed, appears as the Compleat Cold Warrior. To be sure, he would allow for some cooperation with Moscow, but as a reward for good behavior, as an incentive to moderation, and because of the risks in the nuclear age.

Détente was a name for the forced Soviet acceptance of the status quo, obtained by "a firm application of psychological and physical restraints and determined resistance to challenge" (p. 1143). It was also "a device to maximize Soviet dilemmas" (p. 1255), a tactic aimed at demonstrating "to our public and to our allies that we were not the cause of conflict" (p. 1076). "We could not permit the Soviets to monopolize the world's yearning for peace" (p. 1203). SALT I made us give up one weapon—the ABM—Congress was going to destroy anyhow, but it froze the Soviet offensive build-up (a debatable point) while allowing us to catch up (pp. 1244-1245). Triangular diplomacy has to serve the aim of containing the Soviets without provoking them into greater aggressiveness, and

> it was a three-dimensional game, but any simplification had the makings of catastrophe. If we appeared irresolute or leaning toward Moscow, Peking would be driven to accommodation with the Soviet Union. If we adopted the Chinese attitude, however, we might not even help Peking: we might, in fact, tempt a Soviet preemptive attack on China and thus be faced with decisions of enormous danger. [p. 1076]

Kissinger asks whether the Soviet's shift to détente was a tactical maneuver—a question that could be put to him.

This was, as I have written elsewhere, a design of Bismarckian proportions.[10] "Our relations to possible opponents should be such, I considered, that our options toward both of them were always greater than their options toward each other" (p. 165). The United States was to be the supreme manipulator of the triangle, and of course the supreme beneficiary of détente: the Soviets would be contained all over the world, and rewarded with measured deliveries of grain. Their proxies would be either punished, or induced to turn to us, as in the Middle East, from where, Kissinger announced in 1969, we wanted to expell the Soviets. "Three years later," he now claims, "we made this prediction come true" (p. 580)—another debatable point. Balance of power and American hegemony become synonymous. Just as "it is up to *us* to define the limits of Soviet aims" (p. 119), it is up to us to teach everyone else the boundaries of the permissible, to trace the borders of their diplomatic and social experiments.

The problems with this ambitious strategy were legion, and Kissinger is singularly unwilling to confront them. In the first place, it assumed a far greater ability to force the Soviets to play "our" game than it was wise to expect. During the period in question Soviet military might and their capacity to project it grew, in no small part because the United States was bogged down in Vietnam. Not only the weaknesses but the strengths of our own friends and allies created openings for Soviet influence—in the Middle East and in Southern Africa, for example. Were we really in a position to deny them "all opportunities for expansion"? Since we wanted to keep them out of our *chasses gardées*, and since they wanted to preserve the autonomy of their political and economic system, how many chances "for genuine cooperation" could we dangle before their eyes so as to "inculcate habits of moderation and bring about a more constructive future" (p. 1204)?

Kissinger had criticized the containment doctrine for its suggestion that creating situations of strength would ultimately lead to harmony. But his own strategy left room for only two options: a constant manning of barricades, permanent crisis management, an endless vista of confrontations and tests, or else Soviet acceptance of the inevitable U.S. dominance. The latter was unlikely, for it presumed total success by the United States, for which the conditions existed neither at home nor in the world. The former was bleak.

Let us assume that the design made sense. Was it compatible with the American system of government? First, it required an extraordinary capacity for acting swiftly and flexibly all over the globe. Centralization of command allows for speed and suppleness. But it also entails concentration on few fronts: a small staff can't cope with everything. The beast in Kafka's fable can't run to all the corners of the burrow at once. Kissinger tells us that his plan for the Middle East, in 1969-1972, was, through intransigence—that is, by our refusing to put pressure on Israel to make any accommodation whatever with Moscow and its allies—to get to the point where "some Arab state showed a willingness to separate from the Soviets, or the Soviets were prepared to dissociate from the maximum Arab program" (p. 1291). By the early spring of 1972, *both* of these developments had occurred: the Soviets were hinting strongly at their desire to deviate from that program (although they could not initiate this deviation themselves). At the summit they agreed on a weak statement of principles (Kissinger says he "never understood" why they did so [p. 1294]) which Sadat indeed interpreted as a Soviet breach of solidarity with the Arabs. And Sadat himself, disillusioned with the Soviets, had opened a secret channel to Kissinger and suggested an American initiative.

Even after Sadat's expulsion of the Soviets in July 1972, however, the United States took no such initiative. Kissinger—in the only chapter that sounds faintly embarrassed—pleads unconvincingly that Soviet proposals were unacceptable because they assumed a permanent Soviet presence in the Middle East. And yet—knowing what was happening to their position in Egypt—the Soviets had offered to withdraw in the event of a comprehensive settlement. As for Sadat, Kissinger recognizes that he thought for too long that Nasser's successor was still playing Nasser's game: "great men are so rare that they take some getting used to" (p. 1299)! In other words, opportunities were missed (and the October war made more likely), partly by Kissinger's fixation on the Soviet angle of the Middle Eastern problem, partly by the simple fact that the summits and Vietnam left him little time, partly by the fact that 1972 was an election year: "I was too immersed in Vietnam and Nixon in the campaign to do any serious negotiating" (p. 1300). This is far from the only case where Kissinger's conception and manipulation of grand strategy are shown as defective by his own evidence.

In the second place, Kissinger's strategy required that domestic politics allow American leaders to pursue their delicate game abroad without constraints or pressures. He denounces, from chapter to chapter, those who wanted to cut the military budget at a time when the Soviets were building large missiles, or who sympathized with India over Bangladesh, or who tried to limit the Executive's freedom of military action in Cambodia, Laos, and Vietnam. But there can be no guarantee that a policy whose success depends largely on secrecy and speed will be automatically supported by a public and a Congress that are simply told to wait for the results. Surely the secrecy of the 1969 bombing of the sanctuaries in Cambodia was due at least as much to the desire not to sharpen domestic opposition as to the desire to protect Sihanouk. The tools of Kissinger's strategy—linkage, the unrestrained use of force for specific objectives—could be effective only in the hands of one person. Yet their very nature tempted others, in Congress or in the public, to try to impose different ways (more crude or more moderate) of using them.

The style of Kissinger's strategy was itself an invitation to damaging leaks, which in turn would provoke more or less legal retaliation, such as the wiretaps or the onslaught on Daniel Ellsberg; and these measures in turn would make Congress and the public more restive. In this sense, Kissinger cannot escape all responsibility for Watergate, if we mean by Watergate a pattern of Executive abuses. Watergate became a personal tragedy for Kissinger not only because it was the price of having served Nixon but also because it symbolized the revolt of the very democracy on whose behalf the geopolitical battle was being waged.

We have assumed so far that the design at least made sense abroad. But this too is open to challenge. The problem is not *whether* Soviet designs ought to be thwarted; the debate is over *how* to do it, and about the conception of the world that underlies Kissinger's strategy. To Kissinger, the struggle between Moscow and Washington is not just global in scope, it absorbs, so to speak, every other conflict or issue. Peace, or containment, is therefore indivisible. Every crisis anywhere tests our ability to stand up to the Soviets. And the credibility of the United States depends on our capacity to meet every test. Thus, in case after case, Kissinger's policy was to make the Soviets squarely responsible for what was happening, and to act in such a way that they would either put pressure on their clients to cease and desist, or dissociate themselves from their clients.

Is this the real world? Or does it not substitute for the real world an artificially simple and tidy one, in which friends and foes, radicals and moderates are neatly lined up, and in which nationalism—surely as important a force as communism—gets thoroughly discounted? If one sees the world as more complex and fluid than in Kissinger's scheme, if one realizes that most states are not simply the superpowers' proxies—India and Syria are described as waging "proxy wars" for the Soviets (p. 1255)—but pursue their own interests, the notion of indivisible credibility and of a strategy geared exclusively to the Soviet Union becomes eminently questionable. A Soviet presence or privileged position is not necessarily permanent. We may have a good reason for being occasionally on the same side as the Soviets in order to prevent them from capturing a cause or movement. And we may have many incentives to deal with Soviet clients while they still are beholden to the Soviets, precisely because they may not want to mortgage their independence, or because their radicalism is rhetorical, or compatible with our concerns. Looking to Moscow for a key (as Kissinger did in early 1969, when he wanted to send Cyrus Vance there with a peace plan for Vietnam) can be a mistake. On the other hand, as we discovered in Vietnam, some "proxies" are of such a hostile will of their own that neither Soviet pressure nor Soviet political disengagement helps us much.

Kissinger's conception can thus be criticized in the first place because—strange as it seems—it limits America's flexibility and may turn into a set of self-fulfilling prophecies. It obliges us to treat practically all unfavorable events as confrontations, and yet it may be very wise to avoid confrontations one can't win—and some situations (as in the Horn of Africa)

DEAD ENDS

offer little or no scope for American success. Kissinger wanted us to establish priorities. Yet in his design every incident must be treated seriously, since even if it has no great intrinsic significance, losing the test would encourage our adversary to test us again. But if the Soviets are indeed intent on seizing every good opportunity, why would they fail to exploit one just because we blocked them elsewhere earlier?

To treat countries allied to Moscow (for their own national reasons) merely as Soviet proxies risks tightening their bonds to Moscow (it was Chou En-lai who wisely advised Kissinger to end the Vietnam war rapidly so as to reduce Soviet influence in Indochina), or putting oneself on the losing side (as in the Bangladesh crisis), or missing opportunities (as with Sadat). Indeed, to treat one's own allies as proxies may bring rude awakenings: Thieu, in the last part of 1972, derailed our negotiations by asserting his own interests. And Kissinger has some trouble defending, in a footnote, our friend the shah's decision to press for high oil prices through OPEC.

Kissinger's conception is one that, in its obsession with Moscow, discounts the internal problems of other countries, and dismisses local circumstances. This is a recipe for disaster. Thus he reduces the Chilean domestic situation of 1969 to a simple choice between revolutionary communism and democracy, either ignoring or misreading the complexities of the Allende coalition and the opposition to it. In 1972, Kissinger refused to support Brandt—who was having trouble getting his *Ostpolitik* treaties through the Bundestag—because the Soviets weren't helpful in Vietnam: had Brandt lost, there would have been a major crisis in U.S.-West German relations (Schmidt has been more generous in trying to help Carter with SALT II).

In the case of Bangladesh, Kissinger blames "the majority of informed opinion" for having "sought to judge the confrontation on the subcontinent on the merits of the issue that had produced the crisis" (p. 914). We had to stay associated with Pakistan because dissociation would have been tantamount "to the U.S.-Soviet condominium so dreaded by Peking." There would therefore have been no Peking summit, and without it there could be no Moscow summit (p. 886). But the one thing, it seems, we could not do was to ask Yahya Khan to release Mujib, without whom Kissinger's dream of a "peaceful" solution of the Bangladesh problem (after so much bloodshed) was bound to remain a mirage, at Indira Gandhi's mercy. "The merits of the issue" not only produce a crisis: they are also the key to a solution.

The signing by Sadat of a treaty with Moscow was wrongly seen by Kissinger as evidence of Soviet domination and confirmation of the conviction he expressed to Rabin that no settlement could be concluded without a Soviet-American understanding—on our terms.[11]

36

The geopolitical vision Kissinger advocates looks above all at military balance. Yet in the Middle East, where the United States provided huge military assistance to Israel, William Quandt rightly notes that "the military balance proved not to be the key to regional stability and the prevention of war."[12]

Kissinger's conception can be criticized for another reason as well. Like Metternich, he is caught in a contradiction. He seeks an order of restraint, yet his global view obliges him to universal intervention. He wants the Soviets to separate their domestic ideology and practices from their external conduct, yet his very recognition of the fact that "a domestic upheaval in any country can cause a major shift in international alignments" (p. 68) leads him to justify as blatant an intervention in another nation's affairs as the attempt to prevent Allende from becoming president. Indeed, he regrets that the United States did not use arms and economic assistance as political weapons earlier and better in Chile. Our failure to do so "transformed us by 1970 from the dominant element of 1964 into a sort of mother hen clucking nervous irrelevancies from the sidelines" (p. 664). Kissinger wants to "shape events in the light of our own purposes" (p. 683)—those events may be another nation's own political life. But of course, in Kissinger's view, nobody's affairs are exclusively his own.

The third criticism arises from the human cost of such a strategy—admittedly a "sentimental" concern. Kissinger's conception turns people into pawns, countries into tools. Kissinger and the CIA encouraged the Kurds to agitate in Iraq so as to divert Iraqi forces from the Arab-Israeli conflict. When, in 1975, the shah decided to "settle the Kurdish problem with Iraq" (a nice unsentimental euphemism), we approved. Chile's General Schneider was killed as a result of a half-comic, half-serious confusion produced by the famous Forty Committee's orders (Frei, the former Chilean president, whom we had financed in the past, refused to play the part Kissinger had assigned to him). And the classic case of a people sacrificed is, of course, Cambodia. Had we not intervened, Kissinger writes, "Vietnamization and American withdrawal would then come unstuck" (p. 475). "Cambodia was not a moral issue . . . What we faced was essentially a tactical choice" (p. 515). "Strategically, Cambodia could not be considered a country separate from Vietnam" (p. 486).

This does not mean that Kissinger presents his strategy as amoral: morality is defined as the defense of our values and the resistance to totalitarianism. But this is an ethics of intentions, or purposes, that neglects consequences, and makes "credibility," in effect, the highest value. Whether a nation ensures its credibility by fighting unwinnable wars, by intervening blatantly in the affairs of others, by turning secondary issues into tests of strength, or by sacrificing others to its design is, at least, an open question. De Gaulle asked Kissinger in 1969 why the United States did not leave Vietnam; he answered that "a sudden withdrawal might give us a credibility problem." De Gaulle asked where; Kissinger mentioned the Middle East. "How very odd," de Gaulle replied. "It is precisely in the Middle East that I thought your enemies had the credibility problem" (p. 110).

Indivisible credibility is a recipe for political hubris, military overextension, and moral callousness. "Those without strong values cannot withstand the ambiguities, pressures, and anguish that are inseparable from great responsibility" (p. 1033). But "strong values" can apparently carry you anywhere. In Kissinger's conception, the ends justify the means, and the end (in both meanings of the word)—the stable, balanced world where the radicals and the Soviets will have been tamed—is attractive enough to vindicate a great deal of misery on the way. Kissinger wanted to put an end to America's oscillations from one form of idealism—isolation—to another—crusades. But he fails to see both how his division of the world into friends and foes resembles the crusaders' itch to divide it into good and evil, and how the way in which he proposed "to teach our people to face their permanent responsibility" (p. 125) was bound to produce a new swing toward the sentimental liberalism he despises.

If Kissinger's book is, at times, oppressive, it is because the "historian's perspective" (p. 54) he says he brought with him to power is both so grim and so thin. This is a world in which power is all: equilibrium is not just the prerequisite to order, the precondition for justice, it *is* order, it amounts to justice. Inspiration is provided not by an ideal, not by the attractiveness of the outcome—unless one makes a fetish out of a condition (balance)—but by the magnitude of the stakes. Ultimately, it is not surprising if no substantial conception of world order emerges. Religions are poor at describing paradise: it is with this world that they deal. And Geopolitics is Kissinger's religion—its god is the balance of power, its dogma is linkage, faith is credibility, and the high priest is a United States acting on Henry Kissinger's maxims.

IV.

All the flaws in Kissinger's conception come together in his discussion of Vietnam and Cambodia. It fills one-third of the volume. Just as Kissinger's ultimate vision of world order is elusive, he does not begin by telling us what his and Nixon's policy in Vietnam was trying to achieve. He tells us what was to be avoided—we had "the duty" to prove that the North Vietnamese ambition of imposing communist rule (or a fake coalition government) in Saigon was wrong (p. 311)—and what was at stake: "the future of other people depended on their confidence in America" (p. 311). Thus we had to fight on "until Hanoi's perceptions of its possibilities changed" (p. 311). What did this mean?

There were never more than two possible outcomes when Kissinger was in office. One was a victory of Hanoi—either on the battlefield or at the conference table. The other was a defeat of Hanoi—the North Vietnamese accepting in effect the survival of the regime of Saigon, under American protection, just as South Korea has survived since 1953. The fundamental ambiguity in Kissinger's account is revealed when he talks of the agreement negotiated in 1972 as a compromise—which is why, he says, up to the "breakthrough" of October 1972, both sides had rejected his strategy: each one "still yearned for a decisive victory" (p. 1328). But a compromise was ultimately impossible, because it was not acceptable in the long run to either side and it could be no more than a lull. Ultimately either Saigon or Hanoi had to be in control.

Consider what Kissinger calls a satisfactory compromise, one with which he was so happy in October 1972 that he pleaded with Nixon to let him sign it almost at once, and did not communicate the text to Thieu until the last moment in the belief that Thieu would be impressed by the magnitude of Hanoi's concessions (p. 1357). What he saw as a compromise provided Saigon not merely with a "decent interval" but with "a decent settlement" (p. 1359): Saigon, "generously armed and supported by the United States," could cope with "moderate violations," the United States "would stand by to enforce the agreement and punish major violations," Hanoi would be deterred by the prospect of such punishment and the incentives of economic aid (p. 1359). In other words, this was victory—not complete, since Hanoi did not have to withdraw its forces in the South, but it could not reinforce them and they occupied little ground.

The reason for Thieu's fury was not just that "the South Vietnamese, after eight years of American participation, simply did not feel ready to confront Hanoi without our direct involvement" (p. 1375)—although the reluctance of much of the South Vietnamese population to fight on behalf of the ruling regime had long been a fundamental problem for the United States. It is also that Thieu doubted that indirect American involvement would be forthcoming. Kissinger hoped that "joint exertions" between the United States and South Vietnam would preserve the peace (p. 1356); he writes that "if doubts as to compliance were to be allowed to block a satisfactory agreement, then the war would never come to a negotiated end" (p. 1354). But doubts were justified, both about compliance (by either Saigon or Hanoi), and about America's willingness permanently to act as policeman to exact compliance from Hanoi. Here again Watergate—and the decline in support for Nixon's Vietnam policy that accompanied it—serves Kissinger as a convenient excuse for failure.

But even without Watergate, there was no justification for believing that an agreement that "depended on the vigor with which it was enforced" (p. 1361) could rely on the only effective deterrent: the certainty of U.S. forces reintervening. Nixon promised this to Thieu, but it was not credible even before Watergate. For years Congress had been trying to accelerate America's withdrawal; the two escalations of 1972, which involved no ground forces, provoked storms at home; Vietnamization had been an attempt to meet such criticisms (in vain).

Kissinger condemns those domestic upheavals throughout his book. Either he knew that the internal balance of forces in U.S. politics would not allow the United States to restore the external one in South Vietnam if there were a violation by Hanoi, in which case Thieu's suspicions would be justified, and the agreement was no more than a time- and face-saving charade. Or else (and this is undoubtedly the case) he once again underestimated domestic battle fatigue, misjudged his ability to make Americans believe that their standing in the world depended on their persistence in a hopeless undertaking, and absurdly overestimated Nixon's capacity to repeat in the future the temporary rescue of Saigon in 1972.

When after Thieu's request for sixty-three changes in the agreement, Hanoi in turn reopened many issues (with the rather obvious aim of forcing the United States to return to the October text), Kissinger concluded that "they have not in any way abandoned their objectives or ambitions with respect to South Vietnam" (report to Nixon, p. 1435). How could he have believed they had, and if they hadn't, could he believe that "reestablishing a better balance of risks" (p. 1445—another euphemism for bombing) would be available forever? The Christmas bombing may not have been the horror some critics denounced at the time; nevertheless it killed at least hundreds of people simply because Thieu needed time and a psychological lift that would enable him to sign at last. Returning to the October text after Thieu had so violently rejected it would have been "tantamount to wrecking the South Vietnamese government." Kissinger writes that "though I considered the agreement a good one" in October, "intervening events would turn acceptance of it into a debacle" (p. 1429). This was a bloody charade—we got Hanoi to accept trivial changes that made no difference at all in the end.

Is one more "credible" for recognizing the inevitable early, and cutting one's losses, or for pursuing a futile course, escalating not only the means but the stakes, and adding to the sufferings that the winner was going to impose at the end, those inflicted by the attempt to delay his inevitable victory? When Kissinger finally obtained the separation of Peking and Moscow from Hanoi, what the China initiative had started was completed: he had "reduced Indo-China to its proper scale—a small peninsula on a major continent" (p. 1049). Yet even then he acted as if American credibility demanded the vindication of the policies we had pursued from Eisenhower to LBJ, just as his geopolitical design was meant to be an apotheosis of containment.

There are bad places for a fight. In Vietnam, we (and the hapless South Vietnamese) never had a good alternative. We could "bug out," either unilaterally or by negotiating a "coalition" formula to save some face. Or we could dig in and stick to our protégé in order to reassure our other allies—but our enemy would still be there, unless we destroyed him completely, something our values, as well as our calculation of risks, prevented us from doing. And in the meantime the futility of the effort would ensure that we'd look for a way out. At the end, the "honor" we had saved in 1973 was "lost" in 1975. Although Kissinger proclaims that "the security of free peoples everywhere would (have been) jeopardized by an essentially narcissistic act of abdication" (p. 1016), our allies were less than delighted to see what we were doing for them. They doubted its worth, and they feared that our exertions in this dubious cause might drain us of energy for better ones. In Vietnam, geopolitics were against us, and neither linkage nor dissociation could help.

Having, however, declared our policy moral, and all alternatives immoral as well as geopolitically dangerous, Kissinger can indeed affirm that he had little choice when the Cambodian crisis of 1970 broke out. There is a mad logic at work here. The new Nixon-Kissinger strategy, aimed at the same old objective of saving Saigon, entailed a greater willingness to use force outside South Vietnam (remember Kissinger's strictures against gradualism). And it also entailed Vietnamization: the combination of American withdrawals and South Vietnamese build-up. Cambodia, whose neutrality had been dented by Hanoi (as had that of Laos)—no one denies it—was the natural victim of these changes. As early as January 8, Nixon ordered a report on "what, if anything, we are doing to destroy the buildup there" (p. 241): the secret bombing was at least as much caused by this desire to loosen old constraints as by the North Vietnamese offensive at the end of February 1969.

The bombing did, as William Shawcross has shown, begin to undermine Sihanouk.[13] Kissinger denies what General Abrams has acknowledged to a Senate Committee: the bombing and other operations started pushing the North Vietnamese deeper into Cambodia.[14] When Lon Nol's coup occurred, the North Vietnamese and Peking tried to get an agreement from Lon Nol about the sanctuaries. Even though no direct aid was provided to him for several weeks, according to Kissinger, Lon Nol's ultimate intransigence must have had something to do with an expectation of American support.

On the other hand, Nixon authorized (contrary to Kissinger's wishes, he tells us) South Vietnamese attacks across the border; and several Khmer units trained in Vietnam were "launched on a grand scale into Cambodia."[15] The North Vietnamese started moving westward. They must have known that the American command in Saigon was preparing an attack against one of the sanctuaries. Kissinger minimizes the importance of the South Vietnamese raids. When he says that "there had been no considera- tion of attacking the sanctuaries before April 21" (p. 487), he surely does not mean in Saigon, as is shown in the memo to Nixon which he quoted in an earlier version of his book and then removed.[16] He claims that the North Vietnamese were threatening Phnom Penh, and that Sihanouk, by "effec- tively declaring war on the new government," had ceased to be a possible alternative: his "return would have meant not a restoration of neutrality but the victory of his new communist patrons, whom he had lost all capacity to control" (p. 467). But it was not to the North Vietnamese advantage to take charge of a vast and unfriendly country (in which Lon Nol was fostering massacres of Vietnamese); it was in their interest to have in power someone who would let them maintain their line of communication and their sanc- tuaries.

What made it impossible for us to deal with Sihanouk was neither Le Duc Tho's rhetoric (which supported Sihanouk) nor Sihanouk's alliance with his communist ex-foes but our "geopolitical" notion that whoever sides with the communists must be opposed, and above all the requirements of Vietnamization. The North Vietnamese in Cambodia were threatening a vital part of South Vietnam; we had to withdraw without endangering Saigon's survival; Nixon had expressed anger at the existence of the sanc- tuaries from the beginning. The fall of Sihanouk and the westward moves of the North Vietnamese provided the opportunity to embroil them in Cam- bodia—by our helping Lon Nol as Nixon wanted to do almost at once—as well as the opportunity to hit them from South Vietnam.

For America's strategy, a restoration of Sihanouk under North Viet- namese "protection" would have been a major setback. But for the Cam- bodian people, it would have provided a far better alternative than the war that ravaged the country and allowed, at the end, the Khmer Rouge—not the North Vietnamese—to take over. In 1970, the Khmer Rouge were a handful, with no prospects of power. Kissinger several times attributes the devastation of Cambodia to the U.S. opponents of the war, who crippled the scope of U.S. military assistance legally available for Lon Nol, and thus obliged the Cambodian forces "to rely on our planes as their only strategic reserve" (p. 519).

But he does not include in his account what Shawcross stressed: that it was Kissinger who chose the most ambitious strategic option for the war in

Cambodia, and got it approved by the National Security Council in October 1970 (Shawcross, p. 179 ff.). This strategy, designed to help Vietnamization, became a liability, both because of Lon Nol's incompetence and because the South Vietnamese, to whom the departing Americans were entrusting every bigger missions, had to overstretch their resources to keep the North Vietnamese from taking over Cambodia. Our way of helping "free Cambodia" by relentlessly destructive bombing for several years prolonged the agony and did much to prepare for Pol Pot's rule. Kissinger may be right in saying that the Nixon administration had inherited the war in Vietnam. But not only did it accept the legacy, it extended the war to Cambodia.

The same geopolitical needs, global and local, kept Kissinger from trying to deal with Sihanouk before the peace agreement in Vietnam (and, as Shawcross shows, not much more actively later): "negotiations with him could not succeed so long as he was titular head of the communist force, insisting on total victory" (p. 1414). He "could not resume his pre-1970 balancing role unless there were two parties left to balance" (p. 1415). But by 1973, Sihanouk could not have returned except as head of the anti-Lon Nol forces (which would have been far better for the Cambodians than Pol Pot). We remained inhibited both by the belief that the North Vietnamese could somehow "deliver" the Khmer Rouge—it took Kissinger a long time to recognize that their relation to Hanoi was rather like that of Hanoi to Peking—and by the fear that a negotiation with Sihanouk while the war in Cambodia persisted could undermine the shaky regime in Phnom Penh, and perhaps by the belief that a continuing war in Cambodia might provide relief for our ally in Saigon. Thus, as in Saigon, we stuck to our client, and encouraged him to persist; but in Cambodia we could not even obtain a ceasefire.

V.

External triumphs destroyed by domestic tragedy: a president's weird character, an irresponsible Congress. This is one of the main themes of this volume, and it will undoubtedly be the thread of its successor. But the questions Kissinger's relentless and impressive work leaves in the reader's mind are quite different. To what extent were the successes proof of the validity of Kissinger's "geopolitical" design? Was the détente of 1972 a vindication of his approach, or a passing episode? Was it only an attempt by Brezhnev "to calm the threat from Russia's Western past so that he could deal with its Chinese future" (p. 1142), rather than an assent to Kissinger's theory of linkages, networks, rewards, and penalties?

DEAD ENDS

Was the China summit a triumph of triangular diplomacy, or a delicate marriage of convenience, in which one of the partners wants a far closer embrace than the other deems in his interest, although he may have to submit to it lest the more ardent partner should feel jilted and resume a flirtation with their mutual enemy? How wise was American policy in the Middle East and in Iran during those years? Was the colossal effort to find an "honorable" way out of Vietnam proportional to the results? Also, was the pursuit of so single-minded and intense a policy compatible with America's institutions, and if not what were the alternatives open to us? Kissinger, immersed in tactics, recounting the bureaucratic battles, and imperturbable in his reading of history, does not raise these questions. But those who are tempted by nostalgia for the Kissinger era, ought to think seriously about them.

NOTES

1. Henry Kissinger, *White House Years* (Boston: Little Brown, 1979).
2. Yitzhak Rabin, *Memoirs* (Boston: Little Brown, 1979), p. 201.
3. Tad Szulc, *The Illusion of Peace: A Diplomatic History of the Nixon Years* (New York: Viking, 1978).
4. Kissinger, describing the "breakthrough" session with the North Vietnamese on October 11, 1972, refers to some banter between them and him: "I blamed all deadlocks on Xuan Thuy, whom I proposed to banish from the room. Tho threatened to take my chair at Harvard away from me if I were not more reasonable (his threat turned out to be more meaningful than mine)" (pp. 1352-1353). Harvard's Government Department kept Kissinger's chair available to him for two years beyond his formal resignation from Harvard, and offered it back to him when he left public service in 1977.
5. Richard M. Nixon, *The Memoirs of Richard Nixon* (New York: Grosset and Dunlap, 1978), p. 592.
6. There are interesting discrepancies between Kissinger's account on p. 1388 and Nixon's on p. 698 of his *Memoirs.*
7. On this point also, Kissinger's *Memoirs,* p. 1429 ff, and Nixon's, pp. 727-729, are not in accord.
8. There are several oblique hints of Kissinger's increasing displeasure with his aide, General Haig, during this last phase of the Vietnam negotiations: Haig, serving as liaison between Kissinger and Nixon (and soon promoted to Army Vice Chief of Staff), seemed to side increasingly with the president. But Kissinger is far less explicit about Haig than about Nixon.
9. See Peter Dickson, *Kissinger and the Meaning of History* (Cambridge: Cambridge University Press, 1978), and Kissinger's undergraduate thesis, "The Meaning of History," which Dickson analyzes.

10. Stanley Hoffmann, *Primacy or World Order* (New York: McGraw-Hill, 1978), Chapter 2.

11. Rabin, *Memoirs,* p. 201.

12. William Quandt, *Decade of Decisions* (Berkeley: University of California Press, 1977), p. 163.

13. William Shawcross, *Sideshow* (New York: Simon and Schuster, 1979); and my review, "The Crime of Cambodia," *The New York Review of Books* (June 28, 1979), pp. 3-4.

14. By 1972, says Kissinger (p. 1111), Abrams "increasingly took refuge in routine."

15. Shawcross, *Sideshow,* p. 131.

16. See *The New York Times,* October 31, 1979.

THE WORLD ACCORDING TO HENRY KISSINGER: II, 1973-1974

I.

L ESS THAN two and a half years after the publication of his first volume of memoirs, Henry Kissinger has given us an equally dense and hefty sequel. *White House Years* covered the first term of Richard Nixon and ended with the Paris peace agreement on Vietnam in January 1973; *Years of Upheaval*[1] is his account of the stormy period that began in February 1973 with his first visit to Hanoi, and ended in August 1974 with Nixon's resignation. The first book dealt with fifty months in 1,500 pages; the second volume tells about eighteen months in nearly 1,300 pages—almost three pages per day. If the third volume, which will describe the Ford years, is as long, Kissinger will have set something of a record. Since, in the two and a half years during which he wrote *Years of Upheaval*, he also did a lot of public speaking, traveling, advising, and political maneuvering, the reader can only be impressed, once more, by the powers of concentration, the mental energy, the argumentative skills, and the apparent fierce desire for total recall evident in his book.

The events covered are momentous indeed: the unraveling of the Paris agreement, the continuation of triangular diplomacy with Peking and Moscow (entailing two meetings with Mao, two visits to Brezhnev in the Soviet Union, and two Soviet-American summits), the black comedy of the "Year of Europe," 1973, the overthrow of Salvador Allende, the surprise and the shock waves of the October 1973 war in the Middle East, the first oil

DEAD ENDS

crisis, Kissinger's shuttle diplomacy, the beginning of the antidétente campaign in the United States, Richard Nixon's "last hurrah"—his Middle East journey—and, of course, throughout, the Watergate melodrama, without which, as Kissinger explains, he would not have been appointed secretary of state in August 1973 (indeed, he repeatedly asserts that he would have resigned some time in 1973). And yet a careful reader of the first volume is likely to be less stimulated or aroused this time: not because the events are less stirring, but because, apart from the story Kissinger has to tell, so little else is new.

On the one hand, Kissinger's overall philosophy of international affairs, the concepts of which he speaks so proudly, were already laid out in the first volume; there are, inevitably, neither surprises nor innovations here. On the other hand, there are enough repetitions to exasperate even admirers of Kissinger's analytic gifts and epigrammatic style. Not only does he tell us, all over again, what his basic beliefs are—his strategy and his operational code—but within Volume Two we find several overlapping accounts of the same subject, for example, the Nixon administration's "challenge . . . to educate the American people in the requirements of the balance of power" (p. 50).

Kissinger's role in the wiretapping of aides comes up in several places. (Thesis: he did the minimum that was required, appropriate, and legal. Antithesis: he expresses his "regret at the anguish that may have been caused to any individual." Synthesis: he is dismayed at having been harassed "in lawsuits and in print . . . by some who knew very well that I was torn between doing my duty . . . and sparing them personally," pp. 121-122.) Of the Year of Europe he remarks twice that "it was right to try" (p. 194 and p. 734). Without saying anything new he reiterates his points about the convergence of conservatives and liberals against détente; his judgment of Senator Jackson; his evaluation of the new nuclear situation created by superpower parity, and of the bureaucracy's position on SALT negotiations; his distinction between great men and ordinary leaders or mere experts.

On the rivalry between him and Secretary Rogers, on the proper relations between the National Security Counctil (NSC) staff and the State Department, on the shah of Iran, on Chile, and on détente, whole passages seem to repeat Volume One almost verbatim. A statesman, says Kissinger, must be a visionary and a teacher. For lack of a good (or brave) editor, and because of Kissinger's tendency to deal with each subject in several chapters, and to recapitulate in the later ones what he told us earlier, pedagogy tends to degenerate into pedantry.

What Kissinger tells us about the machinery of government in foreign policy can also be called "more of same." The indiscretions that made

Volume One so fascinating for outsiders (and often shocking to insiders concerned with the emperor's clothes) are fewer here—partly because, as of September 1973, Kissinger was both secretary of state and national security adviser, and the punishment inflicted on the Department by the NSC had stopped.

Still, in the preceding six months, many of the bizarre practices described in the previous volume persisted. In Middle East policy, "three parallel diplomatic tracks were developing" (p. 206): Kissinger's "back channel" with Ambassador Dobrynin, his secret channel with Hafiz Ismail (Sadat's national security adviser), and the State Department's attempt at obtaining an interim disengagement of forces along the Suez Canal. Only Kissinger knew about all three at first (but American diplomats in the Middle East soon found out, in embarrassing circumstances).

Moreover, Kissinger, partly in order to explain delays he deplored, or to dissociate himself from proposals he says he disliked, refers to bureaucratic deadlocks over both the plan to retaliate with force against North Vietnamese violations of the Paris agreement ("a great lost opportunity," p. 326) and over the American negotiating position for SALT II ("for the first time since I had come to government I was bureaucratically isolated—and confronted with palpable absurdities," p. 265). If his rather bitter account of the American side of SALT II in 1973-1974 is correct, even his double position as head of the State Department and head of the National Security staff did not ensure his predominance over the Pentagon in this case. As for the divergences—about which so much has been written—between the Pentagon and himself during the October war, he manages at the same time to acknowledge them, to minimize their effects, and to present himself as the American official most solicitous of Israel's needs and most eager to fit the supply of arms to Israel into an overall diplomatic strategy.

II.

To say that there is little new, conceptually or in the analysis of foreign policy-making, does not mean that what is familiar to readers of the first volume is necessarily without interest. Indeed, the strengths of this book are the same as those of its predecessor.

First, there is much merit to Kissinger's decision to go into almost exhausting detail in his account of important diplomatic negotiations. True, this allows him to display his own skills as a mediator or as a manipulator of people and events; but writers of memoirs do not go through their past in order to minimize their achievements. Also, as he explains in his foreword, what he gives us is his side of the story; other participants may have a very different view and (as we shall see), he is often far from convincing. But the very length of his account is likely to provoke other players to offer their rebuttals and amendments, as happened with Volume One.

And even though readers who are not professional diplomats or students of foreign policy may find that Kissinger's description of, say, the Syrian "shuttle"—thirty-four days in April-May 1974—is almost as draining as the events were for the actors, there is much to be learned about an art that will have to become much better analyzed and understood if one wants to be able, gradually, to replace violent change with peaceful settlements: the art of mediation, the uses (and the perils) of ambiguity, the skillful resort either to delay or to deadlines, to deadlock or to showdown in order to prevent failure or to make progress, and the little tricks that can make the difference between fiasco and success (such as having a proposal that originates from an adversary presented to the other by the mediator as his own, or refusing to present a proposal one knows to be unacceptable, etc.). Just as his account of the China "breakthrough" and of the negotiations with Hanoi in Volume One provided many glimpses into—respectively—the diplomacy of convergence and the diplomacy of inexpiable conflict, the more than 500 pages devoted here to the diplomacy of the Middle East war are a most important contribution to the record.

Second, once again, Kissinger is at his best as a portraitist. He adds new touches to his accounts of Mao, Brezhnev, and Edward Heath—Mao's ambivalence about modernization, Brezhnev's "split personality—alternatively boastful and insecure, belligerent and mellow" (p. 233), Heath trying to make "a citadel of personal excellence" (p. 140) in order to rise to leadership in an upper-class party despite his lower-class background. His portrait of Dayan captures the charm, egotism, moodiness, and intuition of a man unique among his colleagues in "the sweep of his imagination, the nimbleness of his intellect, the ability to place Israel in a world context" (p. 563).

There are shrewd evaluations of such opponents of Kissinger as Michel Jobert, Henry Jackson, and James Schlesinger. For the first time, there is a portrait of Brandt, and along with testimony to his historical importance, Kissinger makes devastating remarks about him: not only had he "made himself irrelevant (and in some respects dangerous)" in changing the course of history, but "he possessed neither the stamina nor the intellectual apparatus to manage the forces he had unleashed. He in fact became their prisoner, wallowing in their applause . . ." (pp. 144-145). The most moving portrait is that of Sadat, of his growing passion for peace, of his mix of generosity and shrewdness, of his "almost carnal relationship with authority" (p. 648), his need for solitary reflection, his "pervasive humanity."

(What makes the portrait convincing is Kissinger's awareness of his friend's flaws—"the defects of his virtues.")

Since so much of the book deals with the effects of Watergate, the reader may expect descriptions of the main actors in that drama. The sketches of Ehrlichman and Haldeman are a bit perfunctory. But the portrait of Haig—Kissinger's aide who became Nixon's final chief of staff—is a characteristic blend of compliments and barbs, showing admiration for his "will-power, dedication, and self-discipline" (p. 1197), as well as for the way in which he learned some of Kissinger's own tricks, first in order to eliminate possible rivals on Kissinger's staff, later in order to ensure his own preeminence even over Kissinger. Haig's "rough methods" and "insistence on formal status" (p. 1197) are not recent.

The portrait of Nixon, begun in Volume One, is considerably deepened here, especially in the final chapter. I had thought that some of the comments about Nixon in *White House Years* were rather mean. Here, a kind of lucid, unsentimental compassion prevails in the description of a man "awake during his own nightmare" (p. 1181), "the first victim of his own unharmonious nature" (p. 1183), never at peace with himself because he had no central core, because "the various personalities within him" were always at war, because of inner doubts resulting in deviousness, because of his overwhelming fear of being rejected and his insecurity—the belief that his whole career had been accidental (p. 1186). "Few men so needed to be loved and were so shy about the grammar of love" (p. 1184). He "sought to move the world but he lacked a firm foothold," and therefore "always turned out to be slightly out of focus" (p. 1186). He "accomplished much but he never was certain that he had earned it" (p. 1186).

Before this final judgment, Kissinger gives dozens of examples of Nixon's increasingly more desperate attempts to claim credit for the foreign policy achievements of his aide, and of the growing gap of silence and estrangement between them (especially after Kissinger's deliberate and spectacular threat to resign, at the famous Salzburg press conference in June 1974).

As good as the portraits are the short essays on what could be called national styles. Kissinger describes the Chinese communists as consummate Machiavellians, "scientists of equilibrium, artists of relativity" (p. 50), and he points out the contrast between Mao, "attempting to inflict upon his country the tour de force of a permanent revolution," and his people, who "have survived not by exaltation but by perserverance" (p. 64).

He is at his best in his account of the Saudi style, "oblique and persistent, reticent and assertive," marked by "a caution that has elevated indirectness into a special art form" so as to avoid being subjected to "entreaties, threats, and blandishments" (p. 659), and in his short treatise on

Japan, where "consensus became a method to explore the most effective way of dealing with the future rather than . . . a system of ratifying the status quo" (p. 736). "What could be more effective," he revealingly asks, "than a society voracious in its collection of information, impervious to pressure, and implacable in execution?" (p. 738). He is also very perceptive about the remarkably similar, and harrowing, negotiating styles of Israel and Syria, both convinced that all their "troubles come from abroad" (p. 779), both bogged down in short-term calculations, partly because of domestic difficulties.

Finally, Kissinger is superb at analyzing foreign policy predicaments—the contradictions a state experiences over a given issue: the Europeans' ambivalences toward America, or the Soviet Union in the Middle East oscillating "between the malign and the confused" (p. 200). (Kissinger describes Soviet diplomacy as a clumsy, heavy-handed, unimaginative opportunism: "they were willing enough to fish in troubled waters but . . . loath to run major risks," [p. 1051] "their strength was not a master plan but the exploitation of the confusion of their adversary" [p. 1051].) "The Israelis could not grasp the Syrians' primeval sense of honor; the Syrians did not understand that Israeli assertiveness was an amalgam of fear and insecurity" (p. 1083). His account of the differences between the United States and China over the management of Soviet power, his analysis of the position of each participant at the Geneva conference that followed the October war, and his description of the role of a mediator ("to find why an agreed goal can be in the *common* interest for *different* purposes," p. 1056) are remarkably acute.

III.

Such are the rewards, and they are many. But, as in the first volume, there is here an enormous amount of pleading, sometimes concealed behind the smooth, entertaining, or long-winded narrative, sometimes eloquently presented as if by a lawyer in a trial court. What must be stressed are, first of all, some of the fundamental biases or defects that have marred Kissinger's performance; and second, how these flaws have affected policy toward the main questions covered by the book.

One flaw has more to do with character than with concepts, with personality and pride (or vanity) than with vision. Whenever something goes wrong, it is someone else's fault. Yet the book shows that a number of mistakes were made by Kissinger himself. For instance, he launched the Year of Europe without having ascertained in advance what the response to his initiative would be (the very thing he blames the State Department for having done in the Middle East, p. 207). He failed to understand Sadat's policy before the October war and remained convinced that Egypt would not initiate a war that it had no chance of winning. He deplores the "personal feud" (p. 17) between Prince Sihanouk and Lon Nol, who had overthrown him, which is about as wise as it would be to lament about the failure of Pétain and DeGaulle to join and subordinate "their egos to the necessities of their nation" (p. 17). He misinterpreted Senator Jackson, believing he would accept a compromise on Jewish emigration from the Soviet Union as long as Kissinger was willing to give him full credit for it to improve his standing with the American Jews!

The colossal failure to grasp Sadat's design of making war on Israel and then offering peace, and Sadat's success in "paralyz[ing] his opponents with their own preconceptions" (p. 460) are blamed abstractly on "our definition of rationality." The proposal for a $2.2 billion package of aid to Israel, on October 19, 1973, which triggered the Arab oil embargo, Kissinger calls *Nixon's* request (p. 873). It is the Establishment's collapse that explains the domestic stalemate over Vietnam (p. 84). Haldeman's "lack of direction . . . aggravated by an even more rudderless group of associates" (p. 97) accounts for Watergate. The deadlock over SALT is explained by the Pentagon's and the State Department's absurd and opposite views.

Above all, Watergate becomes *the* cause of everything that went wrong: the continuation of the war in Cambodia, the undermining of the fragile peace in Vietnam, the Middle East war (p. 125), the fiasco of the Year of Europe, the failure of détente (p. 300 ff.), the sluggishness of the SALT-II negotiations (p. 1160), and the Cyprus debacle (pp. 1190-1192). No doubt Watergate weakened the authority of the president. But Kissinger himself shows how much—in the Middle East—he was able to compensate for that decline. In almost every instance, as we shall see, the reasons for deadlock or disarray went much deeper. Had Watergate never occurred, and had many of the failures proven unavoidable, Kissinger would have been deprived of a most convenient, Procrustean, excuse.

The resort to Watergate brings out a second flaw—a conceptual one this time. It concerns the place of domestic politics in Kissinger's view of and strategy for international affairs. There is a strange contradiction here—or rather a web of contradictions. On the one hand, insofar as the United States and its allies are concerned, Kissinger almost consistently underestimates the extent to which a state's external performance and strength depend on domestic cohesion and consensus. Internal weaknesses are seen as nuisances that have to be deplored but should not be allowed to affect foreign policy, as if one were dealing with separate compartments. Kissinger mentions Chou En-lai's request to the United States to take special care of Turkey, Pakistan, and Iran; at no point does he examine adequately the internal factors that made Iran and Pakistan rather weak links in America's chain of allies.

In the United States, domestic opposition to the war in Vietnam and to the bombing in Cambodia is treated not as an *element* that had to figure in foreign policy calculations, but only as an *impediment* to that policy. And Watergate is treated as a disastrous impediment, but never discussed as something far more serious than a series of silly moves and bad judgments by presidential aides, compounded by Nixon's wrong tactics and failure to "lance the boil" (as Kissinger did in Salzburg). If one does not understand that "Watergate" meant the destruction, by the president, of the bond of trust that links the presidency to the people, and of the position of defender and enforcer of legality entrusted to him by the Constitution, one ends up seeing it in only, or almost only, a kind of destructive rebellion against authority by willful leaders, partisans, and the press.

Kissinger has learned—the hard way—to understand the neoconservatives, whom he treats with some awe. Liberals he tends to reduce to caricature (p. 239), and protest movements that are not of the right he rarely tries to understand at all. The only exception to this flawed consideration of internal affairs, interestingly enough, occurs in Kissinger's treatment of Israel: he shows far more tolerance for domestic factors of paralysis there than he does in the case of the United States.

On the other hand, when Kissinger deals with "progressive" or "radical" regimes, he is fierce. He may, on occasion, deplore some excesses of the rightwing regimes (Pinochet, the shah), but when it comes to the left, he lumps together "left tyrannies of the Third World" and communist totalitarian regimes, and, with the significant exception of China, he shows implacable hostility to them for two reasons. One is their domestic crimes, deemed necessarily more extensive than the exactions of mere authoritarian regimes because the latter are "a vestige of traditional personal rule," that has "inherent limits," whereas totalitarianism is "a caricature . . . of democracy" (p. 313).

This very debatable political theory leads, of course, to grimly conservative conclusions. One is that the liberalization of authoritarian regimes is likely to lead to disaster: accelerating reform and sharing power are mistakes. There must be no concessions; either the causes of civil war should be preempted long in advance, or else conciliation can be shown *after* victory (p. 313). As the chapter on Allende shows, Kissinger views left wing revolutions as demonic.

The second reason for Kissinger's hostility is that such revolutions and regimes tend to spread their malfeasance beyond their borders. This is why the fall of Allende, in which Kissinger denies any American participation

day international politics risks becoming a recipe for resignation or paralysis. But it is only if one begins by acknowledging complexity and diversity that there is any chance of designing an intelligent strategy. The troubles of the Reagan administration, which result from the contrast between its initial world view and a highly resistant world, are most instructive in this connection (see Chapter 8). Today, many of the original supporters of the administration feel that they have been betrayed, whereas the only thing that has happened is a gradual and grudging acknowledgment of complexity in all its forms—regional realities, economic issues, the need for a mixed policy toward the Soviet Union—by those in power.

NOTES

1. See for instance Robert E. Osgood, "Containment, Soviet Behavior and Grand Strategy," *Policy Papers in Internal Affairs, 16* (1981):1-18.

2. Alexander Dallin and Gail Lapidus, "Ronald Reagan and the Russians," in Kenneth A. Oye et al., *Eagle Defiant* (New York: Longmans, 1983).

3. See the remarks of Jeremy Hough in Osgood, *op. cit.*, pp. 48-54.

4. George Kennan, *The Nuclear Delusion* (New York: Pantheon, 1982), p. XXVI.

CHAPTER 5

UNWELCOME COMPLEXITY

IN EUROPE as in the United States, enlightened thinkers got into the habit of considering Jimmy Carter with a mixture of condescension and contempt. Judgments went from sarcasm to exasperation. By 1980, many regretted Kissinger and Nixon without worrying too much about the incompatibility between America's constitutional dogmas and the secret and unwholesome practices of these two statesmen. To be sure, these two champions of Machiavellian realism, balance of power politics, and "unsentimental" diplomacy had shown themselves more skillful than the novice from Georgia. But it hasn't sufficiently been noticed that the latter's foreign policy and the Kissinger-Nixon strategy, despite all their differences, ran into the same obstacles.

In the first place, the world view on which they all rested turned out to be inaccurate. I have discussed this elsewhere. Let it merely be said here that the conception that Nixon and Kissinger shared owed too much to the 19th century (Mr. Nixon's book, *The Real War*, is filled with a touching nostalgia for the British Empire). The conception Carter and his advisers shared was based on a premature and certainly overoptimistic model of a world in which the interdependence of states succeeds in eroding fundamental and traditional differences between domestic and foreign policy; between the search for the common good and the just order, on the one hand, and the obsession of survival and security in an anarchic disorder manageable only by the use of force on the other hand.

In the second place, and this is what will be examined here, both doctrines met a domestic obstacle. They were undermined by the inability of the public, the media, and the political class to accept the idea of a complex policy. Forty years after the appearance of the United States as a major power on the world scene, nothing is more striking than the nostalgia for simplicity—the difficulty to recognize that the time of grand and sharply edged designs is over, and that there is no single or decisive remedy for the evils that plague the world in general and American policy in particular.

Let us take the case of Nixon's and Kissinger's diplomacy. Nothing could have been simpler than the strategy of containment that had lasted from 1947 to 1968. This is precisely what Kissinger finds wrong with it in his memoirs. The policy assumes that if one builds barriers against the Soviet Union long enough, sooner or later Moscow will get tired and accept the American conception of international stability and moderate behavior. There is no need for diplomacy in the relations with the adversary; foreign policy consists above all in the collecting of allies and in the transfer of military and economic resources needed to turn them into bastions. In the 1960s, the flaws of this kind of simplicity had become obvious. The arms race and the danger of confrontations such as the missile crisis in Cuba made negotiations with the rival necessary. And the protection of the victims of "communist aggression" by the United States had turned into a major disaster in Vietnam.

The foreign policy of Nixon and Kissinger tried to reintroduce complexity in two important ways. First, one had to move from a game with two players—a game that was a little bit more military than diplomatic—to a game with three, which would be more diplomatic than military; hence, the rapprochement with China and the determination to maintain a delicate balance between Moscow and Peking so as to force each of the two big communist states to have good relations with Washington. Second, it was also necessary in relations with Moscow (partly thanks to this triangular game) to achieve a mix of containment and cooperation, and to apply to the Soviet Union a careful mix of carrots and sticks—or at least incentives and threats of sanctions—to provide Moscow with good reasons to behave well. The purpose was to replace containment, through dams and barriers, with self-containment.

This entailed patience and the ability to pursue apparently contradictory moves. However, this diplomacy turned sour as early as 1973. This was partly due to the fact that neither Peking nor Moscow played the role that American diplomacy had tried to foist upon them. But it was also due to the refusal of a sizable part of the American public to accept it. For some Americans, any détente with a major communist power—any cooperation with Moscow, any flirt with Peking at Taiwan's expense—means embracing evil. For others, since the Soviet Union is absolute evil, what was needed was not a balancing game between Moscow and Peking, but as close an entente with China as possible. For many Americans, the military and economic agreements signed with the Soviet Union could only be examples of American foolishness; triumphs of Soviet cunning aimed at weakening American vigilance and at squeezing out of the United States resources needed by the Soviet war machine. The very idea of transforming hostile relations into mixed ones was being challenged. The notion of a diplomacy without any other lodestar than reason of state, capable of being idealistic wherever idealism was useful and profitable, and of displaying cynical realism wherever it was necessary, also provoked the most violent opposition from those who believed that the American reason of state cannot be anything but the triumph of the rule of law, justice, and progress. Simplistic pseudorealists and indignant idealists formed a coalition against Kissinger and his complexities.

Whatever might have been said or written, the diplomatic intentions of Carter in 1977 were not simplistic; the pendulum had, it is true, swung back toward the idealistic pole. There was much less talk about balancing policies and much more talk about human rights. But another kind of complexity appeared in the statements of the new leaders. They wanted to wage their own kind of triangular policy with Moscow and Peking (a policy which presupposed the preservation of American military might and main alliances), as well as a very ambitious "global policy" aimed at solving the world's economic problems, slowing down the spread of nuclear weapons, and promoting human rights. In all these areas, American initiatives could not fail to antagonize many of America's allies and clients. In other words, the idea of mixed relations, semihostile and semifriendly, was now extended to our allies. An additional element of complexity was provided by the State Department's determination to deal with regional conflicts—in the Middle East, in East and southern Africa—or even with civil wars—as in Central America—on their own terms and on their own merits: by taking into account local and regional realities and no longer, as in Kissinger's days, by applying to it the yardstick of the Soviet-American contest, and by projecting on these conflicts the anxiety derived from the real or imaginary links that might exist between the ratio of forces in conflict in the area and the ratio of the two superpowers' forces.

The incoherence and clumsiness of Jimmy Carter's policy explains to a very large extent the fiasco of this new quest for complexity. But once more, domestic storms accompanied turbulence outside. Idealists grumbled about Carter's contradiction: he proclaimed his determination to fight for human rights in the Soviet Union, but not in South Korea or the shah's Iran. Simplistic pseudorealists who had already attacked Nixon's and Kissinger's détente attacked Carter even more ferociously. Kissinger at least had held that the U.S.-Soviet relationship was the keystone of international relations, although he had wanted to spread a bit too much honey on that relationship. Carter was trying both to persist in such an error (by negotiating SALT II) and to give to all kinds of half-baked issues priority over the contest with the Soviet Union (at the risk of turning reliable allies into adversaries through his crusades against nuclear energy or for human rights, or because of his mistakes in economic and monetary policy).

The most important event in 1979 in the United States—long before the hostage seizure in Iran and the invasion of Afghanistan—was the formation of a huge simplistic consensus that brought together the bulk of the Republicans, the right wing (Jackson and Moynihan) of the Democrats, and the new intellectual right (*Commentary*, the people and the journals of the Center for Strategic and International Studies at Georgetown, the American Enterprise Institute, and the Hoover Institution), as well as a sizeable fraction of the media. The most astonishing aspect was Kissinger's decision to join this consensus and to come closer to those who had attacked him between 1973 and 1976, in order to erase those old divergencies, to concentrate fire on the current common enemy, Carter, and perhaps to become the leader of the movement (which he failed to do: Ronald Reagan and his entourage have accepted a truce, but not full reconciliation, and certainly not subordination). Less astonishing, perhaps, was the effort made by Nixon to find a place in this operation: all he had to do for this was return to the elementary anticommunism and anti-Soviet mood of his youth, which is exactly what he did in his *Real War*.[1]

Kissinger, on the contrary, had to make people forget that he had been both the theorist and the diplomat of détente. In his memoirs, while he justifies his triangular diplomacy, he presents his policy toward the Soviet Union as a diabolically more clever version of containment, as a means of forcing the Soviet Union to accept out of necessity and self-interest the American rules of the game, and of ensnaring the Soviet Union in a net of ties manipulated by Washington. The whole book emphasizes geopolitics: he conceals the initial complexity of his détente strategy (a word he rarely mentions in the first volume, but which he uses a great deal in the second, published at a time when disillusionment with Reagan's simplistic foreign policy was beginning), whereas the simple-minded view that consists of seeing everywhere only the effects or the reflection of the two superpowers' rivalry is given preeminence. Kissinger thus inflicted on his own diplomacy a kind of face-lifting surgery, to reshape it according to the mood of the day. When Ronald Reagan asserts that all difficulties, always, everywhere, result from the Soviet Union; when journalists, intellectuals, and politicians proclaim that everything that is going badly for America can be attributed to the decline of its military power and that a huge increase in defense spending could solve the problems, they can turn to Kissinger's first volume for comfort.

UNWELCOME COMPLEXITY

In a speech he gave at Harvard on June 5, 1980, Cyrus Vance denounced the new nostalgia and the dangerous illusion of military solutions to problems that are not military. There exists indeed a nostalgia for the 1950s; for the period when America had a huge military and economic superiority. But one has to look deeper. Two images seem to divide people's minds, two archetypes that serve as their shelters when the weather in the world becomes stormy, despite all contrary lessons inflicted by history.

First, there is the fascination of force and muscle: this is politics as derived from western movies or from Popeye cartoons—the sheriff who preserves or restores public order against thieves and reassures honest citizens, or the gallant sailor who, when confronted with big bullies, eats spinach, flexes his arm, uses his fist and triumphs in front of Olive who is, of course, delighted. In this conception, foreign policy is a struggle in which force dominates and where a gaggle of weak countries or shady politicians need a powerful, vigilant, and pugnacious America to prevent aggression and subversion by the enemy. There are, of course, nuances, between those who stress the moral virtues and the salutary mission of the sheriff, and those (like Nixon) who proclaim in Machiavellian terms the uses of cunning: the need to make deals with the bad guys who are on the good side in order to oppose the only bad guy who matters, and the importance of not being too choosey about means. But whether it is preachy or cynical, the celebration of American power and will, with all its echoes of social Darwinism or Protestant theology, is a kind of talisman.

The other vision is that of pure virtue. It is that of a radiant America careful about means, and champion of democracy, economic development, and social progress (without revolution) abroad. Here, what matters is the conversion of pagans, the help provided to the needy, and the spread of enlightenment. While there exists a highly idealistic version of the stereotype of force (remember "High Noon"), there is no cynical and Machiavellian version of the missionary image. This perhaps explains why politicians who live in a world where force matters often try a synthesis of the two kinds of idealism: that of the sheriff and that of the good American. This is what American diplomacy attempted in the 1950s and 1960s, since it offered both peace through America's power and progress through economic and political development—that is, the spread of those methods that have made the United States what it is.

But it so happens that the outside world corresponds neither to the first archetype nor to the second. In different but convergent ways, the tragedies of Vietnam and Iran ought to have demonstrated both the limits of power—when military bases rest on rotten foundations—and those of the American type of nation-building. However, the debates of the last thirteen or fourteen years have not really dealt with the complex realities of the outside world.

When the champions of force are obliged to realize that this world resists sheriffs, they start hunting witches and scapegoats: the United States would have prevailed if it had been more powerful, or if it had used force or encouraged others to use it without hesitations or limits. When the champions of purity look at America's failures, they beat their own breasts: the United States is guilty for having exported more swords than plowshares, for having tolerated too many evil regimes and too many egoistic elites, for having too often compromised its own ideals and dipped its principles in too many impurities. Between the attack on weakness or softness and self-flagellation, between "let us find the guilty ones among us" and "we are all guilty," it is the analysis of outside realities that is missing. For both groups, ultimately, the remedy is within: let us get stronger or let us get cleaner. It is our condition to examine our own pulse, physically or morally. The great debate on SALT and the smaller debate on the shah's fall have had almost nothing to do with the treaties' provisions or the situation in Iran. The question was whether the United States was still strong enough and sufficiently aware of its power, and whether the strategic agreement was an expression of self-confidence and reason or a kind of capitulation or abdication. The question was also whether the United States had been right to support an allied king in his ambition to become the Persian Gulf's protector, or wrong in encouraging a tyrant. And if, throughout 1979, there appeared to be a great national debate about the Soviet Union (its ambitions, intentions, and expansion), it was in reality an American self-examination: Had we done all we could to impose our will on events; had we recovered from Vietnam; had we gotten back our old self-confidence? While the apostles said that in these inflation- and unemployment-ridden times America had to begin by solving its own problems and by being more concerned with poverty in the world, the champions of the will to power shouted that one had to expel from power those who had accepted defeat in Vietnam.

For a while the great majority of those who deal with foreign policy returned to the original holy simplicity: the world as a duel between "us" and "them." A very small minority laments the now fashionable dismissal of the liberal recipes for painless economic development of the Third World. The problem that may dominate the agenda of diplomats in years to come is the problem of revolutions. The economic, political, and social conditions of developing countries seem to rule out solutions imposed by external force, to make socialist or liberal recipes look ridiculous, and to provide the U.S.-Soviet contest with its most likely battlefields. But the problem of revolutions remains barely understood, badly studied, and not taken seriously enough. The reason is that all these things are highly complicated: South Korea is not Iran, Salvador is not Nicaragua, and South Africa is not Rhodesia. And one prefers to deal with problems that seem capable of being resolved through calculations and equations: How many nuclear warheads does it take to hit an enemy's land-based missiles, how many holes in the ground to prevent the enemy's warheads from destroying the mobile missiles America wants to bury underground? Kissinger, in his memoirs, writes that the U.S. army replaced strategy with logistics. All too often diplomacy is replaced by the calculation of military forces, the precondition is mistaken for the whole and, in the relations with the Soviet Union, a debate on strategic doctrines drives out the necessary debate on political strategy. In the universities, in research centers, and in the civil service, there are not enough specialists on foreign countries, but military experts are in abundance. Nobody knows what an atomic war would be like, but there have already been many revolutions.

Foreign policy, said Tocqueville, requires the use of almost none of the qualities characteristic of democracy. But is it democracy that explains the need for simple grids and elementary conceptions? Surely unfitness for secrecy, impatience, mediocre coordination, and impassioned shifts of opinion (noticed by Tocqueville) are democratic features. But the rejection of complexity comes from somewhere else: from that "national vanity of Americans" that he wrongly attributed to the democratic spirit (many aristocracies had displayed, not the national pride, "reserved, careless and haughty," that he had noticed in Britain, but a much more aggressive and turbulent vanity than America's). However much one proclaims the end of America's exceptionalism, faith in the unique character and mission of the United States has survived all shocks.

Even after Vietnam, Watergate, the humiliations of inflation, and dependency on Middle Eastern oil, the United States remains wedded to its conviction that it is not like any other country, that it is a model or a beacon (the rush of refugees from Southeast Asia or Cuba, not to mention immigrant workers from Mexico, hasn't done anything to shake that faith). Of course, each country is sure of its distinctiveness. But in the case of the United States, distinctiveness remains inseparable from moral and material primacy. Excessively complex designs tend to seem like machinations drowning America in a collective quagmire, and depriving it of its originality and superiority. The simplistic designs I have evoked here have the merit not only of transforming a complicated tangle into a crystal-clear drama where the good fight against the bad (or where those who are advanced raise to their level those who are unenlightened), but also of giving the leading role to the United States, whether it is the role of sheriff or teacher. And if national vanity easily turns into narcissism, it is because the idea of a world in which one is merely an actor among many others remains deeply repugnant. But clinging to simplistic and heroic schemes risks accelerating decline and worsening a lack of adaptation (whose existence is acknowledged but whose deeper causes one refuses to study).

DEAD ENDS

The hold of the two atavistic stereotypes explains in part the increasingly obvious divorce between the United States and Western Europe: it is the story of Pygmalion. The United States has seen itself (indeed it still sees itself) as the military protector and the initiator of the prodigious economic recovery of Western Europe. It is American federalism that served as a model and inspiration to the founders of the European community. DeGaulle, when he went to battle against both U.S. primacy in the world and integration in Europe, created in the United States not only deep resentment, but also the conviction that he represented nobody but himself. (Britain, West Germany, Italy, and the smaller Western European countries kept reassuring Washington of their support.) Today, however, the truth breaks through. The Europeans, while remaining America's clients in security matters, are beginning to define their own diplomacy and develop conceptions that are entirely opposed to America's simplistic formulae: détente is deemed divisible, whereas Washington thinks it is indivisible, therefore dead; the Europeans resist the elementary geopolitics of Kissinger, and refuse to divide the countries of the Third World and, in particular, the Middle East, into moderate and radical camps. Moreover, the model of federalism seems to have been abandoned. The European Economic Community is a hybrid in which the chiefs of state and government are more important than the European Parliament or the supranational commission. Neither political life nor social policy in Europe has become Americanized. Hence, a certain amount of disenchantment in the United States.

Instead of asking whether the responsibility for this turn of events lies with the inadequate models and the somewhat mindless experts of the postwar period, and while deploring European ingratitude, many Americans believe that if only the United States recovers the taste for and tone of leadership, everything will be all right again. Once more, it is the problems of common defense that receive the greatest amount of attention, instead of an analysis of the new conditions of European politics and social and economic life in Western Europe. Between an America that clings to its primacy and a Europe that opposes it (but does not have the means to replace American leadership) there are few chances for a fertile dialogue.

NOTE

1. Richard M. Nixon, *The Real War* (New York: Warner Books, 1980).

CHAPTER 6

MUSCLE AND BRAINS

I.

MUCH OF the incoherence of President Carter's foreign policy—its awkwardness, fragmentation, its frequent changes of direction, the poor timing of decisions, the occasional loss of initiative—derives from one central fact. From the beginning there has been a hole in the doughnut: the administration has never had a clear policy toward the Soviet Union. On the nature of the Soviet challenge, on the direction in which Washington should try to move US-Soviet relations, there has never been an administration consensus.

American policy has thus been condemned to oscillate and stagger. This absence of a clear vision and strategy has affected U.S. policy in other parts of the world: in Africa, in the Far East, to some extent in the Middle East, and even in Latin America. The Carter administration originally wanted to diminish the Soviet-American dimension in foreign policy and to concentrate on all the other issues. After thirty years of obsession with that rivalry—first in the form of the Cold War, then through a détente strategy that saw in the relationship among Washington, Moscow, and Peking the key to world affairs—this seemed a reasonable stance. But both the nature of Soviet strategy and power, and the administration's own determination to be tougher on Moscow than was Secretary of State Henry Kissinger in his détente days—a desire to treat the Soviet Union as an equal superpower only in the military realm—were bound to frustrate the early hopes. What to do next has never been defined.

In mid-1978 the president imposed an armistice on the two camps within his administration—the tough globalists and the more discriminating moderates—so as to give priority to SALT II. But this neither resolved the conflict nor guaranteed ratification of the treaty. For in the quasi-vacuum left by the absence of a strategy, the opponents of SALT were able to mount with relative impunity a powerful assault that could count on some sympathies, or at least benign indulgence, within parts of the administration. The treaty was left at the mercy of silly incidents like the "discovery" of a Soviet combat brigade in Cuba.

Once the passage of a single treaty becomes the only clear goal of American policy toward the Soviet Union, other problems are mishandled. Each issue reawakens the division between those who wish to turn every incident into a test (in this case, by raising the general topic of Cuban activism or Soviet support for it) and those who counsel prudence. And, not so paradoxically, with each issue considered for itself, the damage it can do to the SALT process gets overlooked. As long as there is no strategy, there will be no way of putting each phase of the rivalry in perspective; there will be conflicting perspectives, and the administration will be at the mercy of congressional reactions. It will be the victim either of Pavlovian reflexes or of parochial concerns.

It is time to reexamine the nature of Soviet-American relations and to suggest directions for the next administration, so as to avoid repeating past mistakes.

II.

There is no doubt that the United States finds itself in a predicament, but there is no agreement on its nature. To be sure, there is a new orthodoxy that identifies the present American plight as the result of a retreat before an ascending Soviet steamroller. It has been asserted that the Soviet Union has launched a geopolitical offensive, precisely because military might is the only dimension in which it is a superpower. It has also been stated that the combination of current internal Soviet tensions (due to economic inefficiency, the claims of non-Soviet nationalities, and succession troubles) and strategic advantages in the early 1980s might lead Moscow to take greater risks and behave more aggressively than in the past.

This view imposes far more coherence and design on Soviet policy than is warranted by reality. As Robert Legvold has noted, military power has never been quite the central and blunt instrument of Soviet foreign policy that so many say it is.[1] Surely, without such power the Soviet Union would neither have won World War II nor have obtained territorial gains and superpower status after the war. Nor would the Soviet empire in Eastern Europe survive without the Red Army.

But is Soviet policy a deliberate, planned, and masterly march toward world domination? More plausibly, it is a relentless attempt at achieving equality with the United States—at breaking the American monopoly of control of the high seas or of means to intervene all over the world—and at imposing Soviet participation in the settlement of all major disputes. It is also the skillful exploitation of opportunities, many of which arise spontaneously or through the independent efforts of a Soviet client or ally. The Soviet Union has moved, but with considerable caution. The litany of Angola, the Horn of Africa, South Yemen, Afghanistan, and Vietnam throws together disparate events, tied by two threads: low risks, and opportunities provided by previous Western mistakes, defeats, or (as in Afghanistan) indifference.

If it is military might that bolsters the Soviet claim to world power, then the appropriate American strategy is to constrain that might through SALT and other arms control bargains; to match it, and to help others match or deter it, where it is already deployed; to see to it that third party conflicts do not provide the Soviet Union with opportunities to project and inject its power in a manner detrimental to U.S. interests.

The new orthodoxy pretends to react against an alleged depreciation of military power among the American public and the foreign policy establishment after Vietnam. It distorts the nature of the military competition with the Soviets, analyzing it as if it were still necessary to exorcise the ghosts of the 1930s, or as if Pearl Harbor had traumatized some minds forever.

The new orthodoxy says that the United States has put all its eggs in the basket of deterrence, more specifically the doctrine of mutal assured destruction (MAD), whereas the Soviets are following a war-winning strategy. This is a distortion of reality. It is true that in the 60s we proclaimed the virtues of MAD. However, the more the Soviets succeeded in reducing our erstwhile huge superiority, the less credible a strategy of massive retaliation for all occasions became; the more warheads we had, the more opportunities appeared for selective and accurate targeting. As a result, the idea of bolstering deterrence by a limited counterforce strategy—not a first-strike force aimed at disarming our enemy, but the targeting of military objectives—reappeared in the Nixon administration and was confirmed by Harold Brown. It may not be a war-winning strategy (nobody has yet explained how nuclear war can be won), but it is certainly a war-fighting strategy. A general counterforce strategy was announced in 1980.

Conversely, Soviet strategy is not a simple war-winning strategy that treats nuclear weapons like ordinary ones. Soviet leaders have repeatedly acknowledged the folly of nuclear war or nuclear superiority. However, Soviet conceptions differ from ours. In Moscow, deterrence is seen not as the opposite of war, nor as sharply distinct from defense, and not because the Soviets' objective is victory in the classical sense, but because they assume that war is still possible, and must, if it comes, aim above all at the destruction of the enemy's forces. To them, therefore, deterrence means being capable of deterring us from striking first; and this is best done by having the ability not only to devastate cities, but also to destroy a sizable fraction of our nuclear forces—preemptively if necessary (not out of the blue, but at the height of a crisis). This difference in the conception of deterrence results partly from an old Soviet sense of technological inferiority, partly from a traditional Russian emphasis on defense, and partly from the prominent role of the Soviet military in strategic decision-making.

The problem with this difference is that it allows for wide divergences in the assessment of Soviet strategic purposes: Does this design aim at *winning* a nuclear war, or only at deterring us from resorting to nuclear weapons and limiting damage to Soviet society if such deterrence fails? A "war-fighting" strategy can aim at either or both of these goals. My own assessment is that it actually aims at the latter: the Soviets are fully aware of the enormity of our capabilities (hence their determination to be able to reduce them), and the limitations they have accepted in SALT II are far more compatible with the second interpretation than with the first.

However, even the second interpretation presents serious problems for us. For there is still another alternative. Is the Soviet conception of deterrence essentially defensive (that is "intimidate the intimidator so he can't pressure you"), or is it primarily offensive, aimed at winning *without* resort to nuclear weapons ("intimidate him so as to pressure him and to expand")? Indeed, the Soviet goal may be to pressure and expand, not through the use of conventional weapons, but through blackmail, by exploiting politically Soviet advantages in regional balances and in the composition of nuclear forces. This is where the issue of Minuteman vulnerability comes in. For a long time we have been almost obsessed by a nightmarish scenario: at the height of a political crisis, we would let ourselves be intimidated by the Soviet ability to destroy our ICBM force, leaving us with no alternative to capitulation other than mutual destruction. This scenario strikes me as perverse, and as an extraordinary instance of self-intimidation.

First, in purely military terms, it is hard to believe that the Soviets could ever be sure that an attack on all our land-based forces—which would cause considerable civilian casualties—would *not* trigger our remaining retaliatory force (about 75 percent of our arsenal!) into devastating the Soviet Union. For the Soviets, it would be a cosmic roll of the dice, gambling on perfect success on their side and cool, rational control on ours. As for selective Soviet strikes against our land-based missiles, they would leave us with enough ICBMs to retaliate against their land-based forces. The scenario of a nuclear war of attrition is highly dubious. The gradual destruction of the enemy's first-strike forces, and even military installations, is not sufficient to ensure "victory" as long as his second strike force is intact: one would win only if the "loser" spared the "winner's" own cities. The ultimate threat, in the nuclear age, remains the menace of city destruction, and counterforce nuclear war can "succeed" only if it deters the loser from carrying out the supreme threat. This is independent of the momentary military balance, since the ability to hit the enemy's cities instead of (or in addition to) its forces exists whether one is superior or inferior in first-strike forces.

Second, if after a Soviet first strike aimed at our whole ICBM force, we chose not to retaliate against their cities, we would have another alternative to capitulation. Given our advantages in bombers and air-launched cruise missiles, we would have residual capabilities of hitting military targets, including the remaining Soviet land-based missiles (assuming they wait for our counterblows; but if they don't wait, and aim at our ports, factories, and airfields, the civilian casualties might be enough to provoke radical escalation). Moreover, we would still have enough warheads left to be able to hit Soviet cities later. In short, there is no decisive Soviet advantage in striking first.

Third, the vulnerability of land-based forces is not an American problem only. Indeed, it is not clear that any of the mobile basing systems discussed until now (other than those that would, in effect, turn land- into sea-based missiles) would guarantee invulnerability, given the vast numbers of warheads available to each side. Even with the planned MX, we could probably not destroy the whole Soviet ICBM arsenal in a first strike, nor be sure to escape Soviet massive retaliation if we did; the balance of terror is much less delicate than Albert Wohlstetter had suggested almost twenty-five years ago.

Fourth, in political terms, the scenario suggests that during a crisis there are likely to be few rungs on the ladder of escalation, and that we would soon be faced with choosing between calamity and capitulation. This has not been the experience of the past thirty years. The biggest danger of armed confrontation between the superpowers exists in areas and over issues where the prospect of a resort to strategic nuclear weapons is too distant to concentrate the mind on the imperative of prudence.

Fifth, and most importantly, it is impossible to prove that the outcome of political conflicts has been determined by the exact ratio of strategic military forces. In the Middle East, it was not American nuclear superiority but Israeli conventional superiority that won the Six-Day War in 1967 and thwarted the assault mounted by Anwar El-Sadat and Hafez Al Assad in 1973. Both sides—not just the Soviet Union—refrained from the use of force during the Berlin crises of 1948 and 1958-1961, despite American nuclear superiority; if the United States prevailed, this was because it had shown resolve and demonstrated the importance of the issues at stake.

While superior, the United States never challenged the Soviet exercises of force in Eastern Europe or the erection of the Berlin Wall. In the Cuban missile crisis, it was America's local advantage, plus the same demonstration of resolve and an ability to put on the Soviets the risk of initiating the use of force, that led to victory, rather than the imbalance of strategic forces. Admittedly, the United States may try to fortify its resolve and to make the importance of the stakes at issue more manifest by having "essential equivalence" in nuclear forces, as defined by Defense Secretary Harold Brown. But nuclear equivalence—or superiority—did not help in Vietnam, and there are other ways to bolster resolve and demonstrate commitment.

The primary U.S. military effort ought to be aimed at shoring up regional balances because of the very autonomy of these balances, not because the United States can no longer count on offsetting a conventional imbalance with nuclear superiority. (In any event, the real deterrent is the risk of nuclear war, not American nuclear superiority.) None of the scenarios that entail the use of strategic nuclear weapons really make sense—not massive retaliation and not counterforce. The function of these weapons is likely to remain deterrence. This means that the real danger lies in problems of regional instability in a world strategically fragmented under a stable superpower nuclear umbrella.

In the specific case of Western Europe, what is needed is both modernization of conventional forces and an effort at restoring the theater nuclear balance. The balance must deprive the Soviets of any reason to believe that their advantage in mobile and precise weapons capable of hitting Western Europe could allow them to exploit their conventional superiority and keep a conventional war from escalating to the nuclear level; it must also provide an incentive for mutual limitations and reductions in theater nuclear forces.

However, regional balances depend decisively on underlying political and economic factors. To the lessons of Vietnam we must now add the lessons of Iran. A well-defended Western Europe, but one that would drift away from the United States because of American economic mismanagement, or one that would be internally weakened by economic crises or by partisan disputes over rearmament, would be worse for the United States than the status quo.

Those who speak of the retreat of American power lump together very different factors. One is an inevitable comparative decline. The preponderance of military and economic power enjoyed by the United States in 1945 could not last; it was clear that the Soviet Union would want to close the gap. (The massive American program of 1961 and the humiliation inflicted on the Soviets during the Cuban missile crisis gave them powerful jolts and incentives.) The economic recovery of the Western allies and the economic integration of Western Europe were, after all, American objectives. The rise of the Organization of Petroleum Exporting Countries (OPEC) is another element in the comparative decline; ironically, what has given OPEC its power is the spectacular economic growth of the advanced capitalist states, based on cheap energy.

A second factor is quite different. It consists of recent events perceived as American defeats, including the shah's downfall in Iran and the weakening of the U.S. position in Turkey and Pakistan. In practically every instance, the American failure was due not to a lack of material power but to a deficiency in political analysis and skill. The United States was unable to use its power and to control the outcomes. It failed to anticipate events, to exploit opportunities, to get out of situations before they became hopeless, and to align itself with the forces that were destined to prevail (not in order to capitulate to them but in order to influence them). This has to do not with muscle but with brains.

On the other hand, the world as seen from Moscow is no rosier than the world as seen from Washington. China's drive for development, its rapprochement with Japan (largely because of Soviet bungling), the U.S.-sponsored partial peace in the Middle East, continuing negotiations over Zimbabwe and Namibia, the consolidation and enlargement of the European Economic Community, the cooling of Soviet relations with India, and continuing discontent in Eastern Europe, not to mention quagmires in Eritrea and Afghanistan—all of this shows that growing might is not a perfect answer on the other side either. And while Americans seem obsessed with the services Cuba provides for Moscow, they overlook the advantages the United States has derived in Africa from the Egyptians (in the Sudan), the Saudis (in Somalia), the French (in Zaire), and the British (in Zimbabwe).

A third factor in the alleged U.S. retreat is lack of will or resolve. But will, resolve, and taking a stand can all too easily be code words for grandstanding, show without substance, and empty rhetoric—or, as in Vietnam, recipes for disaster. The key problem is that the old instruments of control, the application of military force or assistance, and the provision of economic aid are simply inappropriate or insufficient in three kinds of issues that dominate today's agenda: economic problems such as the energy crisis, inflation, and recession; disputes between states, both of which happen to be friends or allies; and internal disorder in friendly countries whose troubles are too deep to be resolved by covert action.

Thus, the real drama lies in the contrast between an expectation of control and the difficulties of influence. It lies not in the absence of power but in a kind of impotence of power, in a world where the successful use of one's power is at the mercy of chances provided by others (as well as of often crippling domestic processes and priorities)—a world in which America's own preponderance, its position as guardian of the status quo and maker of many rules and regimes, assures that it will be the invevitable target of all the discontented.

The American crisis cannot be found where the new orthodoxy professes to find it. This does not make it any less real. Indeed, it is much deeper than the idiosyncracies and flaws of the Carter administration, and it is likely to outlive them. It has external and internal components. To the external ones already listed, one must add the fundamental asymmetry between the Soviet and U.S. positions in the world. The United States has, of course, certain advantages: the comparative effectiveness of its economic system and its key role in the open international economy.

But there are also handicaps. Geopolitically, as the main status quo power in a world of change, the United States is on a kind of universal defensive, while its rival can pick and choose the points for attack from among the many ferments of trouble. Because of American values and domestic inhibitions (or institutions). Washington is less free to use abroad its instruments of power than a system devoid of such checks and balances. And the economics of interdependence creates a host of constraints: the United States finds itself buffeted between inflation and recession, trade expansion and protection. It has narrow margins of maneuver. The costs of retaliating against clients or friends who exploit it are too high.

Although there are more than enough reasons to worry about the future of America's role in the world, if one looks at trends in the world economy, or at world population figures, or at political and social conditions in developing countries, or at racial issues and festering conflicts in most areas, one should be more disturbed by some institutional, conceptual, and perceptual deficiencies that mark the way in which Americans look at the world. These are the internal elements of the crisis. First, the legacy of the Kissinger era has been troublesome. In a sense, despite Kissinger's attempts, American foreign policy has not yet recovered from the bankruptcy of the cold war strategy (a bankruptcy due partly to the policy's shortcomings, partly to its very successes).

Second, we suffer from a major institutional problem. It is partly the Carter administration's fault. Its two chief mistakes were the creation—in fact—of two State Departments (with a strong Secretary of State and a National Security Adviser endowed with operational responsibilities), and the bad management of relations with Congress. Since it lacked an overall strategy, it was never able to do the indispensable job of rallying Congress around its policy (even, if necessary, by extending the role of key members in Congress beyond mere consultation). As a result, it has either let itself be surprised by unexpected resistance, or jostled by unwelcome pressures, or else it has yielded unwisely the initiative to unreliable allies (like Senator Church, in the case of the Soviets in Cuba). Partly, however, the constitutional problem is far more serious: for the first time since the end of Wilson's presidency, the system of checks and balances is fully operating in the foreign policy of a country that plays a leading role in the world—as had not been the case either when it was only an insulated (or self-insulated) power, or when the urgency of the world struggle in fact suspended the checks and balances in favor of an "imperial presidency." This is happening at a time when, in Congress, party discipline and the old leadership are crumbling; when votes on foreign issues are therefore discrete, fragmented manifestations of constituency concerns, or else the products of the single-issue groups' efforts (such as the Committee on the Present Danger), but not the expression of a coherent vision; when the collapse of the old distinction between domestic and foreign affairs leads men and women elected on domestic issues to treat foreign affairs as an extension of internal ones; and when, in Congress and the media, the post-Vietnam and post-Watergate suspicion of the presidency puts the burden of proof on a president who remains under a cloud of suspicion, contrary to the very tradition of trust that used to distinguish most vividly the United States from much of democratic Europe. George Kennan's redoubtable question—are American institutions compatible with a world role (a question that seemed absurd in the days of the Cold War)—has become unavoidable and haunting, since Kennan's solution, a drastic cut in this role, is not practicable for either external or internal reasons: such a retreat *would* serve our rival's cause and exacerbate the national dread of weakness.

Two aspects of what used to be called national psychology are perhaps the most alarming elements of the crisis. The first is the tough-guy approach to international affairs. The number of problems that are likely to be resolved or even just improved by displays of force and dramatic acts of commitment is limited. And yet there is in the United States a belief that every event is a test of American will and virility. There is an addiction to a kind of "High Noon" style of international diplomacy, a nostalgia for big sticks and heroic strikes, for a world policed by America's sheriffs or marshalls, for the simple moral division between good and evil that such a world entails.

The Carter administration has been good at resisting these pressures, but one does not win plaudits by pointing out mistakes not made—especially not when the official voice is as hesitant and cacophonous as in its first three years, and when (as in the recent Cuban crisis) the ditch out of which one occasionally crawls is of one's own making.

The second manifestation of a flight from the imperatives of political analysis and skill is the obsession with calculations of strategic nuclear equivalence, and in particular with the alleged vulnerability of the Minuteman ICBM force. It is as if numbers of warheads or launchers and figures of throw-weight and potential destruction provided one with a gruesome but firm and measurable handle over the messy uncertainties of international relations. The overemphasis of politically improbable doomsday military scenarios is, like the recurrent belief in dominoes, proof of a never-abandoned quest for precision and predictability. Such a quest is dangerous, because it takes attention away from the indispensable understanding of the ways in which the United States contributes to its estrangement from others. It distracts from the essential study of the myriad of complex economic, social, and political forces that intersect in more than 150 countries. Americans desperately need to understand those forces if they want to be able, not to control them (for this is beyond any single nation's reach), but to affect them and to prevent them from pushing the United States into the decline we seem to fear so much.

There are many ways in which great powers fall into decadence. Military ineptitude is only one of them. Getting out of touch with what is happening outside and being institutionally incapable of coping with the world are others. It is not military weakness that threatens the United States most today, precisely because it has paid attention to it and at times overreacted. (Remember the missile gap?) The more serious threats are institutional paralysis, which is reflected in the furor over SALT II, and economic mismanagement, which is evidenced by the inability to curb inflation, without a recession, and to stabilize the value of the dollar. All of these and the failure to adopt an energy policy are more destructive of American influence abroad than all the military problems put together.

III.

It certainly could be argued that the next administration ought to observe the primacy of domestic politics—trying, insofar as it can, to improve relations between the White House and Capitol Hill and handling far more imaginatively and vigorously the problems of growth and energy. But as far as external issues are concerned, nothing is more important than a new Soviet-American relationship.

I will suggest certain assumptions and propose directions for the formation of such a policy. The assumptions may be dismissed as obvious. And yet we have not always acted according to them. Three concern us, three concern the Soviets, and two concern the two rivals.

1. U.S.-Soviet policy *is* global policy, not just one corner of the tapestry. Dealing with Moscow is a problem that affects almost every international issue, and both Soviet growing might and its growing needs will inject Moscow increasingly into world affairs.

2. Soviet perceptions and actions are shaped by American moves. As noted above, our own rearmament of the early 1960s triggered the Soviet effort that is bearing results now. Our failure to curb MIRVs has created the Minuteman vulnerability problem. Our decision to exclude the Soviets from Middle Eastern diplomacy after October 1973 has probably increased Soviet activism in Africa and in the Persian Gulf area. Our embrace of China against the Soviet "polar bear," in the spring of 1978, may have tightened the ties between Hanoi and Moscow.

3. There is no American interest in a return to an unmitigated Cold War. There are many reasons why this would be bad for us: the danger for peace, the cost of an uncontrolled arms race, the disadvantage of moving the competition to the one arena—the military one—that happens to be the strongest asset (almost the only strong asset) of the Soviet Union, the tensions such a duel would create between the United States and its major allies, and the risk of being (as so often in the past) pushed into making the wrong decisions in regional conflicts and in economic relationships simply because of a desire to "stop Soviet meddling," that is, the tendency to treat issues not for themselves but for their effects on the Moscow-Washington contest.

4. The Soviets, like us, encounter constraints and contradictions in their external and internal environment. Not everything they seek is achievable at once. Increasing energy needs will conflict with the need to maintain the Soviet grip over Eastern Europe. Controlling external clients is costly; not controlling them enough exposes Moscow to the risk of being manipulated by them. And there is, inside the Soviet Union, a bureaucratic and institutional pluralism that complicates decision-making.

5. As I have indicated above, there is no Soviet master plan. There is a determination to weaken Western positions, whenever possible, and to spread Soviet influence, but the link between military power and political ambition is neither simple nor direct: the growth of the latter has often preceded that of the former, and might has often failed to yield influence (as in relations with Western Europe, Japan, or China).

DEAD ENDS

6. The Soviet Union still has an overriding fear of encirclement, and is determined to preempt any attempt at enclosure.
7. Both superpowers face, in the immediate future, difficulties resulting from severe problems of succession.
8. Competition between Washington and Moscow is unavoidable. There is no convergence of social systems and no way to oblige the Soviets to subscribe to the American view of international relations. The American notion of stability—the preservation of the status quo or, at worst, of an orderly process of change—is unacceptable to the Soviets. This does not mean that they have a stake in universal turmoil and are incapable of grasping a mixed strategy, as opposed to zero-sum games. But they have not given up their ideological reading of present trends and future prospects. Thus, to pose the U.S.-Soviet problem in terms of a choice between rivalry and friendship, or between cooperation and competition, is misleading. The choice is between modes of competition. Yet it exists. Some say that Moscow, like Imperial Germany, may provoke the encirclement it fears. But is 1914 more attractive than 1938? Self-fulfilling prophecies, alas, can be realized by both sides. What America does will affect Soviet behavior.

The directions future U.S.-Soviet relations should take are defined by certain principles. The most fundamental one is that within the competition there are common interests. In economic relations, for example, each side can gain from trading with the other. And there is a domain that might be called "convergent differences." Even though stability is not a common concern, there is an opportunity for statecraft here: The pursuit of each side's competitive goals can actually take place best in an international milieu of moderation.

Both sides need to avoid taking excessive risks and pushing confrontations to the point where there are no choices other than humiliating retreat or playing with fire. Both sides have at least a partial stake in the status quo. The Soviets are a status quo power with respect to their gains from World War II and because of their border with China. In several areas, while they might ideally want a shift in a pro-Soviet direction, their fear of an American reaction makes them prefer the status quo to the kind of turmoil that could provoke such a reaction (thus, Soviet prudence in Iran). Their limited engagement in the world economy, as well as that of their satellites, was enough during the post-1973 world recession to keep them from gloating too much over the "crisis of the capitalist system"; today they too have a stake in the curbing of worldwide inflation.

In other words, while the Soviet search for expansion of power and influence may well be relentless, prudence—dictated by a common concern

108

for survival and for development and economic well-being—suggests there is also an interest in a modicum of predictability, which sharply distinguishes Soviet behavior from that of Nazi Germany. The Soviet Union, as a great power and as a stultifying bureaucracy, shows very little enthusiasm for sudden crises. Many crises in which Moscow was suspected to be pushing pawns were actually moments when the Kremlin quieted things down (for instance, the Jordanian crisis of 1970). Indeed, it is this very prudence that cost the Soviet Union the support of Egypt in 1972.

Another reason for the joint interest in moderation is the desire of both superpowers to limit the capacity of third powers to manipulate them, or to act altogether without them. The U.S. goal ought not to be to try to get the Soviets to deliver their clients in regional conflicts, for neither superpower is always able to do so. Clients have their own wills, and the effort itself would risk undermining the credibility of a superpower's commitment to its clientele; this was one of the mistakes in the Kissinger version of détente. The effort should be to get the Soviet Union to dissociate from its clients when they go too far and behave too rashly.

A second principle is that the United States should seek a definition not of common rules of *the* game, but of common rules for the different games that will continue to be played. This is not a verbal trick. The expectation of a common game—another mark of the Kissingerian détente policy—leads to inevitable frustration, and therefore to a permanent threat of unraveling whatever network of ties may have been woven, since every new sign of recurring Soviet "misbehavior" breeds demands for sanctions. They must be expected to pursue their game. The United States should try to get them to play it in more acceptable ways. To reply that Moscow's game is itself unacceptable is a moral stance, not a political proposition, since there is no way to force them to stop.

The distinction can be illuminated by the 1979 Cuban fracas: Washington declared the status quo unacceptable, but could clearly not oblige Moscow to withdraw its troops; and so it had to fall back on National Security Adviser Zbigniew Brzezinski's remarkable statement that the Berlin Wall is also unacceptable, and the perfectly sensible objective of getting Soviet assurances about the mission of the force. Ultimately, the Soviets had to be taken at their word, and the "unacceptable" had to be redefined as the feared combat nature of the force, not the presence of 2,000-3,000 troops that earlier understandings never ruled out.

The objective, then, is to find whatever common ground exists between the two sides' divergent strategic doctrines, political assumptions, and policy objectives in such a way as to organize the coexistence of competitive strategies. (Does this mean that the United States should allow the Soviets to play in the Caribbean, and that they should allow the United States to play in Eastern Europe? Yes, although the legitimate security concerns of each side must oblige the other to be careful on each other's turf.)

There are several obvious implications. One is the need to maintain the global and regional balances of power in order to prevent each rival from excluding the other and its game from any area, whether by force or through the political blackmail made possible by overwhelming force. But the level of violence of the contest must be reduced. The two sides must gradually define what means are permissible where. (This is precisely what the 1962 U.S.-Soviet understanding over Cuba tried to do and what the Cienfuegos affair of 1970 made more precise.) The contest must also be moved as much as possible away from the pole of confrontation toward the pole of cooperation. Competition can take many forms—from outright confrontation to cooperative contests. In the long run, it is in the American interest to move more toward the latter end of the spectrum, because there are many vital issues that cannot be handled without some participation by the Soviet Union. Only if there is some density of cooperative relations in which the Soviets have a stake, may considerations of linkage be effective (for instance, between economic help from the West and Soviet external behavior; explicit linkage to domestic behavior is not likely to work). Strategic arms control agreements should not be explicitly linked to anything. But their own progress will depend on the superpowers' ability to manage their contest less antagonistically. As long as cooperation is represented essentially by nuclear talks alone, this puts excessive weight on a fragile bond and makes it hostage to frustrations and confrontations.

It is precisely because the Soviets are the chief U.S. rivals and troublemakers that such a policy is essential. If they shared American strategic doctrine, so heavy an arsenal of regulations as SALT II would be unnecessary; informal understandings and parallel force decisions would suffice.

How should these principles be applied?

A first realm is that of arms control. Insofar as the conventional arms race is concerned, objectives must remain modest: confidence-building measures in Mutual and Balanced Force Reductions talks, and exchanges of information as a first step toward later restraints in Africa, the Middle East, and the Indian Ocean areas where the goal is political solutions. As for nuclear weapons, Leslie Gelb is probably right in suggesting that long and complex deals such as SALT II are not the best method: the political costs (indeed, even the military ones, such as the MX) outweigh the benefits.[2] But SALT II would have made it easier for both sides to concentrate on discrete and shorter negotiations later.

Prompt attention must be given to the vexing issue of land-based missile vulnerability. But one must avoid the mistake of pursuing the chimera of counterforce nuclear war by trying to prolong the life and invulnerability of land-based missiles. What would deter the United States from attacking Soviet cities in a crisis is not the new phenomenon of Soviet heavy missiles and throw-weight superiority, but the old fear of retaliation against American cities. This vulnerability is mutual. On the other hand, scenarios of protracted counterforce nuclear war sparing cities are inherently dangerous: the more accurate each side's missiles become, the greater the enemy's incentive to preempt. Ultimately, the choice for both superpowers will be between developing expensive mobile systems that may not guarantee invulnerability (and could seriously complicate the verification of arms control) and gradually phasing out intercontinental ballistic missiles (ICBMs) altogether. Since the Soviet arsenal consists so largely of ICBMs, the predicament will hit them much more than the United States. This should allow for negotiations.

Another issue is that of theater nuclear forces in Europe. Leonid Brezhnev's 1979 offer to reduce the number of medium-range nuclear weapons deployed in the western part of the Soviet Union—on condition that no new ones be introduced in Western Europe—showed that for Moscow to be willing to negotiate limits on the deployment of their new middle-range missiles, it was necessary for the allies to begin moving toward deploying missiles capable of hitting the Soviet Union in Western Europe, but it was not necessary for them to wait until these weapons had been deployed. The Soviet offer does not invalidate the arguments for these deployments, but it should be greeted as a first move in a bargain, rather than dismissed as a trick for dividing and delaying the allies. In fact, it is both. Moscow stresses that its new weapons merely replace older ones; the North Atlantic Treaty Organization (NATO) could offer to retire some existing forward-based systems while proceeding with the plan to deploy, and to negotiate about, new intermediate weapons.

But the level of the NATO's ultimate deployment ought to be clearly linked to the level of Soviet forces. This will be a difficult negotiation, since the Soviets will want to include not only all the American theater nuclear forces, but also the British and French strategic nuclear forces. But the Soviets have realized that they had no chance of exploiting the political resistance that exists in Western Europe to new NATO efforts unless they offered concessions of their own.

Whatever their scope, nuclear arms control agreements should be dealt with on their own merits. The idea of linking explicitly such agreements to Soviet "good behavior" does not deserve serious consideration. It suggests that such agreements are somehow more in the Soviet than the American interest, which is false. It also suggests that they are so much in the Soviet interest that the United States could use them as a lever and short cut to obtain Soviet acquiescence to the U.S. concept of international stability and moderation. It is hard to believe that a power that has never given up the effort to tilt the world "correlation of forces" in its direction would suddenly do so in exchange for mutually beneficial arms restraints. Moreover, the United States would not like to give up the pursuit of unilateral advantages, for instance in the Middle East peace process or in relations with China, and it would object violently to any Soviet attempt to link strategic arms control or Soviet cooperation in nonproliferation efforts to a condition that the United States behave according to Soviet-defined conditions. Kissinger, who had come to office with firm ideas about linkage, later became the most convincing exponent of the view that a mutual interest in arms control precluded any effort to link SALT to other matters. There is, in any case, an implicit linkage: if the Soviets rock the boat too vigorously, they will find it impossible to get the U.S. Senate and public to endorse arms agreements that seem incompatible with such behavior.

A second realm is that of economic relations. There is much to be said for the argument that was made in the early 1970s: the Soviets try to preserve as much autarky as possible and to preserve the autonomy of their political decisions; but even so, the more East-West ties grow—and dependence in areas such as grain, technology, and even oil deepen—the more difficult such control becomes. It is up to the Soviet leadership to make the difficult choice between the uncertain costs of further involvement and the tangible benefits it entails. If, and as long as, the involvement spreads, it could lead to greater moderation in political and military behavior abroad. Attempts at explicit linkage may well fail, since the Soviet Union, under threat of economic sanctions or in explicit exchange for Western technology or grain, is not likely either to change its domestic practices or to forgo a political opportunity abroad. But the desire to expand commerce, to receive credits and technology, and to fill gaps in its own production may incite Soviet leaders to pursue competition in ways that do not risk exposing them to economic retaliation. The advantages provided by trade or credits from the United States might suggest a more subtle and less provocative pursuit of local gains. Self-restraint, or self-linkage, could work.

Opponents to such a course argue that in exchange for a mere hope of moderation, the West would be actually building up the Soviet economy and providing Moscow with means for diverting more resources toward the military contest. However, there is much distance left to travel before U.S.-Soviet trade and American credits to the Soviet Union reach such levels as to justify these fears. And while the United States may go far enough to reach the stage where Soviet self-restraint begins to make sense, it is unlikely to go so far as to vindicate the anxious, given the lack of sufficient Soviet exports and and Moscow's own desire to preserve the semi-autonomy of the Soviet system. Moreover, years of relative autarky did not deter the Soviets from competition, which was at its fiercest when the Soviet

Union was economically weakest. An influx of outside technology is more likely to exacerbate the contradictions of the Soviet economy than to smooth the path of its leaders. (Why would Western trade and aid be any less destabilizing there than in any other developing economy?)

The third realm is that of regional conflicts. It is the most delicate and the one most conducive to pessimism. Both superpowers are vulnerable to manipulation by clients or proxies. Whereas crises have been avoided in areas of direct contact, such as Europe, where the potential for escalation is visibly great and the margin of error small, the biggest peril lies in gray areas, where uncertainty may exist about the scope of one superpower's commitment to an ally or friend and about the other's likely response. This danger exists in the Middle East, where the dynamics of the energy problem, the potential for social unrest, and the unresolved Arab-Israeli dispute may drive the superpowers deeper into the whirlpool; in southern Africa, especially if Cuban involvement persists; and, above all perhaps, in East Asia, given China's relationship to Cambodia and hostility to Vietnam, the Soviets' commitment to Vietnam, and America's desire not to see China weakened.

Another peril is partly economic, partly political. The United States is the inevitable target of powers and forces that want to achieve emancipation from pre-existing dependency or to overthrow a tyrannical regime, but meet American resistance or obstacles created by U.S. presence or aid to their foes. This has already been witnessed in Iran, Ethiopia, Central America, Chile, and in part of the Palestinian movement. The world is full of potential candidates for such a challenge. It is here that the opportunities for Soviet exploitation are great.

There is also the danger of nuclear proliferation. Most of the current candidates for nuclear status—Pakistan, India, South Africa, South Korea, Brazil, Argentina, and Taiwan—are on the Western side of the East-West divide. The spread of nuclear weapons to such states (or to others, for example in the Arab world) would mean further regional fragmentation and instability, since the conditions that have kept the balance of terror stable between the superpowers do not exist everywhere. It would also mean a further loss of control and influence by the United States; this in turn could lead American leaders to dangerous reactions, especially if the Soviet Union should try to fish in those troubled waters. But nonproliferation policy itself is not primarily a Soviet-American issue, since cooperation in that area has been good.

IV.

In looking at regional conflicts, one must distinguish between the areas where Soviet and American interests genuinely conflict and those where they do not.

DEAD ENDS

In the Far East, the great U.S. achievement of recent years—reconciliation with and recognition of China—is also a source of risks and predicaments. Americans have reached the point where they must choose between two very different directions: a worldwide alliance against the Soviets of the kind the Chinese leaders would like or a delicate balancing game between Moscow and Peking. The aim ought to be the latter. The former policy could not fail to be seen as intensely and intentionally provocative by Moscow. To say this is not to plead for appeasement. But such an anti-Soviet alliance would throw away the chances that now exist for "cooperative competition" between Washington and Moscow.

It is neither required by nor in proportion with the kinds of challenges the United States faces from the Soviet Union. It would artificially provoke Sino-American solidarity and identify American policy with Chinese objectives far beyond what is wise or necessary. It is not in America's interest to embrace all of China's designs or to encourage China to escalate hostility toward Moscow.

The problem with a policy of balance is that so many factors seem to push Washington into the policy of alliance. The United States has a stake in protecting and developing bilateral relations, painfully reestablished after so long an interruption. It does share a concern about Soviet behavior, an interest in keeping Moscow from attacking China, and Hanoi from expanding further. It wants to encourage Chinese leaders to continue their tolerance of Taiwan. The Association of South East Asian Nations is so worried about Vietnam that it has pushed aside traditional fears of China and encouraged Washington to tighten the bonds with Peking. Also, China is capable of creating situations that push the United States into closer ties than it should want to have—either through direct action (such as strikes against Vietnam) or through subtle blackmail (such as talks with the Soviets).

In fact, the United States may well need to steel itself against manipulation by China. One could argue that this is precisely what happened in 1978: the timing of Peking's acceptance of a formula for recognition that had been hatched much earlier served the double purpose of interrupting the American dialogue with Hanoi just as the Vietnamese had dropped their insistence on economic reparations and of delaying SALT II.

Mathematical even-handedness is not required. If the criterion of the Jackson-Vanik amendment—free emigration—is met by China but not by the Soviets, it is difficult to deny China most-favored nation trade status just because the Soviet Union cannot benefit from it. But the United States must exercise enormous prudence. Washington must give Peking more than an expression of nonapproval for operations against Hanoi. It must stress that such actions only strengthen Hanoi's dependence on Moscow and that

Peking should not count on Washington to rescue it if Chinese moves provoke Moscow to act against China.

Another issue is military assistance to China. The present policy is a wise one, and the United States should not encourage its allies to provide such assistance, except in the form of strictly defensive weapons. The risk of Western military assistance to China is a greater deterrent to a Soviet attack on China than the rearmament of China itself would be (a deterrent which, however, might cease to operate if China moves massively against Vietnam and obliges the Soviet Union to choose between military action and a drastic loss of face or power). What has kept the Soviet Union from threatening China has been the combination of this deterrent and China's ability to inflict heavy damage on Soviet cities. China's nuclear forces are limited, yet capable of partially surviving a first strike.

China has an interest in playing the America card. But America has no interest in playing the China card. It should not encourage the Chinese to expect more than it can deliver. To do so would lay the groundwork for future Chinese resentments against dependence or against the kinds of social dislocation that Western-style modernization breeds. Washington and Peking have no identical interests in Southeast Asia, where some other U.S. friends may clash with Peking over offshore resources. Washington certainly has no interest in provoking further Soviet arms build-ups or in reinforcing hawks within the Soviet leadership through U.S. ties with Peking. A Soviet-Chinese rapprochement is not about to result if the United States fails to give China enough support. There are enough sources of discord between Moscow and Peking to prevent a return to the days of alliance. But if there should be a defusing of Sino-Soviet border disputes, mutual political restraint, and eventually even arms control understandings, Washington should applaud them—especially if it strives at the same time to increase the density of its own links with Moscow.

In the Middle East, Africa, and Latin America, while Soviet and American objectives remain antagonistic, some degree of cooperation ought to be possible. For the United States, the best way of limiting Soviet influence is to help create conditions in which local actors will not be inclined to turn to Moscow; in that event, it will be in Moscow's interest not to stay out, so as to preserve some possibility of influence. And the American reasons for formally excluding Moscow from U.S. diplomatic efforts will be much less compelling; it will be in the U.S. interest not to provide the Soviets with excuses or opportunities for undermining U.S. efforts.

Precisely because the Soviet-American rivalry is only one aspect of various local conflicts or of an internal turmoil, the way in which the United States handles the conflict or reacts to the turmoil must be determined by local circumstances; it should be guided by the importance of its own stake.

To be sure, Soviet (or Cuban) involvement is never in the American interest, but it should not be enough by itself to turn what may be an area of little concern into a major arena of contest. Above all, Washington must avoid the temptation of supporting automatically whatever regime or faction is opposed by Soviet arms or advisers. A policy of supporting all who claim to fight communism would put the United States on the side of doubly unattractive clients—unattractive in terms of American values (such as the Somoza regime in Nicaragua or the South African regime) and in terms of the prospects for success. Some groups that call for Soviet or Cuban aid, such as the Palestine Liberation Organization or Zimbabwe's Patriotic Front, are not thereby forever lost to Western influence. Nor are they forever incapable of pursuing their own course, as Washington discovered, for example, in relations with the late President Neto of Angola, and earlier with President Siad Barre of Somalia. Moscow can give them the arms they need to become necessary participants in a process in which they may still hope to gain American political consent and, should they prevail, economic assistance. Nor should the United States be guided by the facile division of regimes into moderates and radicals; many are difficult to label because their external behavior may not be the same as their internal practices or because their foreign policy varies over time.

Thus, a strategy to contain Soviet influence in the Third World must be a pre-emptive and indirect one. Obviously, the United States must be vigilant about Soviet efforts at subverting fragile political and social systems or exploiting internal troubles (in the Persian Gulf area) or at encouraging clients (such as South Yemen, Ethiopia, or Angola) to subvert or attack neighbors. But these problems do not require any great new undertaking, beyond the strengthening of U.S. military capability to intervene quickly against aggression. Overt attacks by Soviet satellites can best be dealt with by a combination of U.S. military assistance and regional defense measures. As for the subversion of weak regimes, it cannot be solved by the use of American forces. Washington must incite its own allies and clients to fight corruption, open their political systems, and improve their social policies while there is still time. And Washington must learn to loosen its ties to a particular regime if it remains blind, deaf, and therefore excessively vulnerable. This is the task that requires the greatest skill, because Washington is ill-equipped for it, given the concentration on military threats and the daily tasks of economic development, and because Americans are reluctant to intervene by giving such advice. But is precisely because a U.S. presence or assistance (whether military or economic) often creates social dislocations or cultural alienation and helps focus political turmoil, that Washington must become more alert and less timid. The same indirect strategy makes it necessary for the United States to develop friendly relations with new regimes that may appear leftist—what regime that has overthrown an authoritarian tyranny can fail to appear leftist—yet whose foreign orientation will be shaped to a large extent by American behavior.

V.

The guidelines suggested here differ both from the erratic course of the Carter administration in U.S.-Soviet relations and from Kissinger's détente policy. One should have no illusions about the great powers' ability to dampen or settle regional conflicts, about their willingness or ability to forgo unilateral advantages in international affairs, about the wisdom of explicit linkages, and about the success that a complex manipulation of rewards and sanctions could have in shaping Soviet behavior according to American notions of stability. However, the emphasis here is on the conditions Washington would have to meet to make this strategy possible.

It requires a political climate that certainly does not exist today. And it also requires consistency. Even paranoids have real enemies, and the United States should avoid feeding Soviet paranoia, because the whole purpose of the proposed policy is to make international affairs somewhat more predictable—to minimize risks, if not to maximize control—for the superpowers. Only if the United States is consistent does it have a chance of affecting the ways in which its rival uses its power abroad, and perhaps even the outcome of internal Soviet debates. While it would be naive to suggest that America should offer the Soviets a global deal, it should indicate to them that it has an overall policy that is less contradictory than Carter's initial assumptions, less disjointed than his later course, less Bismarckian than Kissinger's, and less hostile than Reagan's.

Another requirement is the burial of obsolete attitudes and the dispelling of nostalgia. Regret for lost supremacy, illogically accompanied by an itch for showdowns and by false memories about the good old days when America "prevailed," will not help. Nor is it useful to treat the Soviet Union as a genuine power only in the military realm, both because military might casts a political shadow and because American economic predominance is not an unmixed blessing. It is a source of constraints, a sum of assets and ties that others can manipulate, and a focus of envy—indeed a target for attack when the United States fails to use its wealth in ways that less privileged nations could approve.

One more popular attitude that will have to be discarded is the overt use of human rights as an instrument of policy against the Soviet Union. It is not that Americans endorse the Soviet system or believe that the domestic performance of a regime cannot be an international concern. But the key question for a genuine human rights strategy (as opposed to rhetoric or ad hoc lurches), is, in every case: how can one, from the outside, best help to promote human rights and to curb violations? If the systematic application to the Soviet Union of a human rights test could in any way help dissidents, Jews, or other victims of the system, then one might argue that the costs— in terms of opportunities for collaboration lost or heightened tensions— might be worth paying. But this is not the case. Direct linkage does not improve anyone's condition. While cooperative competition cannot guarantee that a more humane regime will emerge, a return to propaganda wars and a policy of sanctions is most likely to harden the Soviet regime. There will always remain an implicit linkage, as in the case of economic relations. And private individuals and organizations (such as scientific associations) may be much more effective—through direct pressure or even occasional boycotts—than the U.S. government. In any event, there is no contradiction between concern for human rights and a policy of cooperation. Peace is a human right, and only if there develops comity and communication among states is there a chance for successful human rights efforts.

The most difficult requirement is to pursue a dual policy, to wage both cooperative competition and confrontations at the same time, and to do so even when, at a given moment, the United States seems faced by more challenges than collaboration. It is in these moments that the arguments against cooperation are likely to seem most persuasive, that the proponents of the policy advocated here will be most easily thrown on the defensive—accused of naiveté, reminded of Munich, and summoned to use such traditional tools of power as sanctions, boycotts, and linkages to redress the balance. It will not be easy to convince the public and Congress of the wisdom of a dual policy, since the ultimate rewards of cooperative competition are either negative (the reduction of risks) or delayed (greater restraints on the way the Soviets play their game). They are bound to appear limited in any case, since the Soviets will still be playing their own game, not the American one.

Thus, once again the question must be raised of the compatibility of U.S. institutions and expectations with the waging of a complex and long-range policy. In the short run, heroic poses or, at best, discontinuous and easily popular cooperative moves (such as the test ban of 1963 or the first SALT agreement) are safe bets for American leaders. The policy suggested here is much harder to pursue and, indeed, to sell. And yet one dreams of a president who would be willing to explain to the American public why such a strategy makes sense, why no spectacular results should be expected, and yet why it is superior to the alternatives. Nixon oversold his détente policy. Carter has alternately neglected to educate the public and just stitched together conflicting statements offered by competing aides. Better luck next time?[3]

NOTES

1. Robert Legvold, "The Concept of Power and Security in Soviet History," *Adelphi Paper 151* (London: International Institute of Strategic Studies, 1980), pp. 5-12.

2. Leslie H. Gelb, "A Glass Half Full," *Foreign Policy 36* (Fall 1979): 21-32.

3. This essay incorporates part of my SALT II testimony presented to the Senate Foreign Relations Committee on September 10, 1979.

CHAPTER 7

THE NEW ORTHODOXY: A CRITIQUE AND AN ALTERNATIVE

I.

AMERICAN FOREIGN policy since the end of the Second World War has gone through two full cycles—that of the Cold War and that of détente—and three strategies, those of containment, Kissinger, and Carter. Today we are apparently back at square one. But the similarities between our immediate postwar predicament and our present situation are misleading. America's condition at home and abroad is troubled. We face a difficult choice in trying to devise a new foreign policy. We can either rely on the magic of old formulas and act as if a return to the policies that worked in the days of American supremacy would ensure success, or attempt to tailor our diplomacy to the requirements and dangers of the very different world of the 1980s. The mood of the country seems to favor the first alternative. This makes it only more necessary to explain why the second one should prevail, and what its main features ought to be.

During the Cold War, our priority was the containment of Soviet power, and of the power of those communist forces we deemed dependent on or allied with Moscow. It was pursued with a unique blend of *Realpolitik* and crusading idealism, and rested on a strong national consensus. Its biggest mistake, (which led to its demise), the war in Vietnam, was a result both of misapplied idealism—protecting a small country from aggression—and of what Raymond Aron (writing about FDR's wartime policy toward Stalin) once termed "wrong realism"; it was also the product of the stolid consensus.

DEAD ENDS

After the election of 1968 began the second cycle, that of détente. It differed from the first in three ways: we tried to shift our relationship with the Soviet Union from a predominantly adversary one to a mixed one; the national consensus was never restored; and we went through two very different phases. The strategy of Henry Kissinger was still essentially bipolar, almost, indeed, obsessively so; but it was far more complex than the containment diplomacy which he criticizes so forcefully in his memoirs. He added to the old arsenal of containment an array of incentives aimed at inducing self-containment on the part of the Soviets, and he introduced a third player, China, into the game. Moreover, the policy was pursued with a penchant for secrecy and "unsentimental" realism that reflected both the personalities in charge, and the influence of long reflections on European cabinet diplomacy. But it failed, partly because of a revolt against its style, partly because of disillusionment with détente, and partly because of what might be called the revenge of neglected issues.

The election of Jimmy Carter opened a second phase, which consisted of an attempt to continue the search for a mixed relationship with the Soviets (and for a triangular game), but also of an effort to move away from a bipolar vision of world affairs, and to concentrate on global issues and multilateral relations. It appealed, once more, to the enthusiasms always latent in American idealism, but it tried, this time, to channel those energies away from the bipolar confrontation, toward, one might say, world humanitarian causes. This policy also failed, for reasons that I have described elsewhere,[1] and which concern the style, the strategic deficiencies, the economic weaknesses, and the political ineptitude of the Carter administration.

In 1980, the climate in which Americans were discussing foreign affairs reminded many observers of that of 1947. Then as now, a new resolution was rallying those who had long hesitated, or who had hoped for a more cooperative relation with Moscow. Then as now, a tough mood grew out of a sense of frustration, a fear of having been duped, a belief that the time had come to stop "babying" the Soviets. Then as now, there appeared a militant interpretation of Soviet behavior, linking disparate elements into a global scheme, as well as a consensus on the need for a strong, worldwide American response. Then as now, the Soviets acted as catalysts, with moves that seemed to vindicate those who thought that a firm policy of containment was long overdue.

Indeed, in the public and in the foreign policy elite, there seems to be wide agreement on five propositions:

First, that priority must be given to redressing the military balance (in the strategic nuclear realm, in Europe, and in conventional forces generally) and to shoring up with military means the dangerous situation in the Middle East.

122

Second, that relations with Moscow offer only the perspective of "containment" and "confrontation," that is, that there are few opportunities for renewed cooperation and that the benefits of past cooperation have gone disproportionately to the Soviets.

Third, that Soviet behavior is intensely threatening to Western interests because of a combination of internal weaknesses and external hubris, reflected in and reinforced by a new capacity to project military power globally, and, more specifically, because of ominous strategic doctrines that envisage waging and winning nuclear war and are backed by the ability to try those doctrines out.

Fourth, that "linkage" between different foreign policy issues is not only inevitable but indispensable as a tool of policy.

Fifth, that our allies must be made to understand our sense of urgency, to share our vision, and to play their part in carrying out the policy.

And yet we are not in 1947. Neither the United States nor the world looks as it did then. Then, we were not only the most powerful, but the most prosperous, indeed the only healthy political economy among the actors on the world scene. Today the contest between Washington and Moscow seems, in the words of Pierre Hassner, a contest in "competitive decadence." It is therefore much more dangerous.

When a nation faces a crisis there are often two possible responses. (We could think, for example, of the case of France in the late 1930s and the 1940s.) One response can be called "fundamentalist"; the other one one constructive. A fundamentalist response tries to find remedies in old verities: not in the spirit that led to past success, but in the mythified recipes that worked before, in the rituals of national celebration, and in the rationalizations that attribute troubles or temporary decline to internal dissolvent forces or evil men and ascribe recovery to a rediscovery of traditional ways. A constructive response aims at mobilizing all the reserves available for innovation and at using all that remains healthy and hopeful in order to master the challenge imaginatively. The first approach may make people feel temporarily better, because it not only provides an explanation for discomfort and disorientation but assures that what will work now is the familiar. However, it rests on denial—it denies that there is something radically new to be faced, and that something equally new may have to be invented. France tried this remedy, or rather this poison, with the Vichy regime. The result was disaster. It tried the second approach after the liberation—not without excesses, trials, and errors. But the effects have been remarkable.

American reactions since the beginning of the crisis, in the mid-1960s, have been mixed and varied. The electorate shows a great deal of pragmatism—it repudiates whatever did not appear to work. But with each such disappointment the sense of betrayal gets deeper, the faith in "the system" becomes less ardent, and the tendencies, if not toward extremism, at least toward withdrawal, become worse. And the fundamentalist instinct gets stronger.

Carter offered a fascinating but unsuccessful mélange of fundamentalism and innovation. He wanted, he said, a government as good as the American people, and he appealed to the idealistic and humanitarian components of American internationalism. But he offered neither a vision of the future nor a coherent strategy, at home or abroad. And the electorate moved on to what appears like fundamentalism pure and simple: the "City on the Hill," America as the chosen people, and free enterprise as the solution both to inflation (budget cuts) and to stagnation (deregulation and tax advantages for business). This is a disturbing evolution, because it shows not only a kind of collective inability to cope with complexity, but also an unwillingness to examine our present predicament seriously.

II.

In the past, students of American foreign policy began with a verdict on the state of the world, followed by prescriptions; they rarely bothered to diagnose America itself. Today we must begin with a look at ourselves. The picture may not be quite so grim, the patient so run down, as the friendly and subtle French sociologist Michel Crozier suggests in his *Le mal américain*.[2] But there is an American sickness. What is striking are the similarities between its domestic and its foreign policy manifestations.

Both show, in the first place, a divorce between Americans and their environment. Two elements reinforce each other. One is a crisis of complexity. Since the 1960s, this country has had to face simultaneously problems of enormous magnitude. The drama of the Johnson years, well recounted by Crozier, was a glut of ordeals: a major unintended war, a domestic revolution of rising expectations—the blacks, the poor, the students. Abroad, we have, in recent years, had to contend with the same kind of overload. At home and abroad, the crises of complexity can be given another name: the end of deference.

In the past, as writers as different as Samuel P. Huntington and Michael Walzer have reminded us, the good functioning of American democracy at home rested on the general acceptance, and on the perpetuation, of certain exclusions, on the unquestioned acceptance of established authorities—in other words, on the self-restraint which Tocqueville thought essential for the compatibility of democracy with freedom, which requires an intelligent elite and a prudent people. And so we had the confident rule of the Wasps, and the seniority system in Congress, and a managed process of presidential selection. We had a system of mass public education, but residential segregation created its own school hierarchy. All of this was challenged and changed.

Abroad, the end of deference has taken the form of an assault on American authority: witness the relentless growth of the Soviet Union, whose arms build-up did not stop when it reached parity with us, and whose self-restraint in the Third World—after the Congo crisis and the Cuban missile fiasco—ended quite spectacularly in the mid-1970s. At the same time there has been increasing restlessness among our allies, whose willingness to question American initiatives and interpretations has extended far beyond the old Gaullist enclave; and of course the revolt of the developing nations, whose most devastating expressions have been the oil embargo of 1973 and the policies of OPEC. We thus face, at the same time, a major security challenge and a major international economic crisis; in the case of oil, the two issues are intertwined.

The second element of this divorce is a crisis of possibilities. Our domestic system has worked on the assumption of unlimited resources (allowing both for experimentation and for waste—including the waste of human resources, as in the quick and often heavy layoff of workers in recessions); and it was uniquely geared to technological innovation—in a country where labor was expensive but energy and raw materials were abundant and cheap. In the post-war world, the United States acted as the universal pump primer, with its Marshall Plan aid, its Point Four program, its training of others in matters of management and productivity, its faith in the do-it-yourself of economic development.

The new discoveries of the 1970s were grim: the limits of growth—both the material ones heralded by the Club of Rome (temporarily at least vindicated with respect to energy), and the social ones so incisively analyzed by the late Fred Hirsch—and the growth of limits. These include the mounting resistance of our allies to accepting our dollars, the need to take domestic measures in order to shore up our position in the international economy, and the loss of our quasi-monopoly of innovation as others, particularly the Japanese, began to use the recipes that had worked so well here. Being more dependent than we were on the outside world, they also turned out better at scanning it in order to understand and meet the needs of their clients.[3]

In the second place, the domestic and the external troubles are also the product of a severe crisis of the American polity: our own policies have powerfully contributed to our difficulties, and we have shown ourselves rather inept at adjusting to a world that is no longer favorable. Here again, we find two components. One is the inadequacy of traditional solutions. In domestic affairs, we have had roughly two traditions. The liberal one, in favor since the Great Depression, relied, for a mix of Keynesian and political reasons, on the virtues and effectiveness of federal spending for the solution of social problems. But, as we have also often discovered abroad, in our foreign aid programs, and our flings at "nation-building," when the obstacles to change and progress are built into the structures of economic and political power, "throwing money" at problems is not only futile but ruinous. Our welfare mess and urban debacles testify to this.

Liberalism also relied on change through law—the law handed down by a judge or drafted by Congress. But in the new conditions created by the end of deference, and by fierce resistance to it, the law, far from being an instrument for orderly change—a way of avoiding turmoil or revolution—can become a source of chaos, a tool in the hands of all the parties. What has happened with respect to the participation of the poor ("maximum feasible misunderstanding," in Daniel P. Moynihan's words), to affirmative action and quotas, to school integration, shows that legal reform, not supported by radical policies of economic and social change, can backfire.

While liberal methods have done much to promote social integration and to increase prosperity, they also ended up adding not one but two patterns, or "games" as Crozier would call them, to the preexisting two that were characteristic of the American polity. We already had the model of the market and of free enterprise, and that of the political system, based on bargaining, log-rolling, compromise, and sometimes corruption. We then added the bureaucratic model, based on regulation and on technocratic rationality, and a model of "participatory democracy" which Johnson tried to establish in social affairs by bureaucratic means (with dreadful results) and which was later extended to the electoral process (with very mixed ones). All these games had different rules, whose flaws combined, or fought each other, into paralysis.

The other tradition that is inadequate is the conservative one. To get the state off our backs is a good slogan; it appeals both to the instinct to find scapegoats and to the legitimate irritation created by the excesses of bureaucracy (even if it conveniently forgets that many of these merely enshrine, or encrust, popular demands for protection). But when a nation faces a major crisis of its economy, the automatic pilot of laissez faire does not work. The policy aimed at overcoming the crisis and the strategy for redirecting the economy toward competition at home and competitiveness abroad both require imaginative public guidance. Deregulation and tax benefits may not suffice to encourage oil production, or the development of alternative sources of energy. Deregulation and budget cuts may make public services even more ineffective, and replace a taxpayers' revolt with a users' rebellion. A policy of industrial relocation and (as the French would say) redeployment is urgently needed; but, everywhere, free enterprise—especially in an economy of giant corporations—leads not to a smooth adjustment to a new international division of labor but to strong pressures for protectionism.

In foreign affairs, our policies pushed us into our present predicament. Our response to challenges was to maximize our power, and to spend our resources. In the 1960s we launched a huge new nuclear arms program; this, when combined with the Cuban missile fiasco, determined the Soviets to prevent any possible repetition of such humiliations, and to begin a long-range effort of nuclear and conventional rearmament that became a nightmare in Washington during the later 1970s. Our oil import quotas policy of the 1960s "stimulated production levels that eroded domestic reserves"[4] and led to an increase in our dependence on imported oil. Our butter-and-guns economic policy in the Johnson years led to the deterioration both of the American economy and of the international monetary system: to the dissipation of political and economic resources, in Robert O. Keohane's words.[5]

In the new conditions of internal constraints and an undeferential world, we can no longer use so freely and abundantly the two great instruments of power we used in the past—military assistance and economic aid; choices have to be made. Our experience in recent years shows that neither grand designs—détente, the Nixon or Carter doctrines, the quest for reliable allies, such as the shah, in each region—nor mere incrementalism, in such areas as in energy policy, arms control, NATO, have been very effective.

Of our historical traditions, one—isolationism—is so obviously ruled out by the very scope of American interests and commitments, as well as by the realities of strategic interaction and economic interdependence, that only a handful of people abroad (often, strangely enough, in France) still worry (or hope) about a possible reawakening of the urge to cultivate one's virtues alone and apart. The other grand tradition, internationalism, is split by the rift between those who want it to be tough and emphasize military power and the United States as the world's policeman, and those who want it to be evangelical, problem-solving, and enlightened. The present world fits neither variety of internationalism. Indeed, we have learned that when we throw either our weight or our virtues around, and gain neither respect nor results, a formidable backlash rises at home.

The inadequacy of traditional solutions is compounded by that of traditional institutions. Clearly, one of the most hallowed—American enterprise—suffers from serious flaws, such as the tyranny of short-term financial results, caused by the dependence of firms on the market for funds, and resulting in risk avoidance and managerial sclerosis. The political system of

DEAD ENDS

checks and balances has also frequently led to paralysis. The presidency often looks like a huge beached whale: the bigger it has grown, the more difficult the problems of executive coordination have become, and the more pathetic it appears when it is stymied from within or, by Congress, from without. The decline of the parties and of traditional structures of authority in Congress, combined with the reassertion of congressional initiatives and the increase in the Congress's ability to control policy, has made its own contribution to the domestic and foreign policy crises. And while pressure groups, and even single-issue pressure groups, are not new, their effects are far more crippling in an undeferential society, at a time of economic trouble, when economists discover that we have become a zero-sum game society, and when there is neither (as there was in the 1930s) agreement on what the dominant issue is nor a clear recipe for dealing with it.

American institutions are aimed at thwarting excessive authority by one man, excessive influence by any one faction, excessive power by the majority of the people. But they function well only when there is an underlying consensus. The trouble is that such a consensus tends to fragment and disappear when there is no single, overriding goal. And when it is replaced by division, or by skepticism, the president has much less freedom of maneuver. When there is a consensus on a strategy, an occasional failure—say, the Bay of Pigs—can be overcome: it can be presented as a fumble along the way, and balanced against the wisdom of the overall design. In the absence of a consensus, pressure for immediate and recurrent successes becomes much more ferocious. And we have been caught in a vicious circle: complex policies have evoked more skepticism than support, and skepticism has made the development of long-range policies more difficult.

This has been the drama of détente. Quite apart from the fact that the U.S.-Soviet détente rested on two opposed gambles that could not *both* be won (but which each side feels it lost), the success of the American gamble on Soviet self-restraint presupposed a consensus on mixed relationships, and on patience in managing them. It was inevitable that "rewards" for Soviet "good behavior" would be attacked by the right, and the application of punishments denounced as proof of failure.

Today, insofar as there is a new consensus at all, it is extremely narrow. It really deals with only one slice of reality—the contest with the Soviet Union—and with one issue—the decline of American prestige or of respect for America.[6] It seems to envisage only one remedy—muscle. But there is no consensus on what kinds of arms should receive priority or on what to do with those arms. There is a furious desire to win somewhere—preferably where it can be easy and cheap, and thus have a "demonstration effect" at low cost. But an attitude, or an itch, is not a policy. A commitment to "victory" in El Salvador certainly does not amount to a policy for El Salvador, or similar cases. And therefore we are left with a double quandary: a "fundamentalist" view of our relation to the outside world may be thoroughly inappropriate, and thus provoke wrong policies; but on many essential issues, it does not even suffice to define policies, and it presents us with an inadequate range of choices—such as the choice between the "moderate containment" advocated by Robert W. Tucker[7] and the far more ideological line that can be associated with others who write in *Commentary*. Clearly, while we are *not* in 1947, we had better start from scratch, or rather from reality.

III.

Power has become the catchword of the new orthodoxy proclaimed by Reagan and his publicists. This is what it holds: it is the decline of American power that must be reversed; it is power that the Carter administration was afraid to use; it is power that the new administration must rebuild; it is power politics that is the name of the game of nations. It is therefore power that we must begin with.

The new orthodoxy often seems to suggest that power comes in two packages. One is military might, the other is the American ideology of anticommunism or antitotalitarianism. This will not get us very far. Military might is a precondition for effective diplomacy, and a most important instrument for deterrence (although it can turn out to be unnecessary—when there is no threat—or insufficient). It is also a tool to be used against attacks on our security. But we must remember that a nation that has to resort to force not only as a last but as a first or early resort is a nation in trouble. As Britain demonstrated in the eigthteenth and nineteenth centuries, a successful great power is—to use Clausewitz's vocabulary—one that does not have to pay cash, or to face truth at every moment.

To be sure, a state that has no or few other instruments for spreading its influence can cause enormous problems to its neighbors and rivals; which is precisely why they need military power of their own. But the rivals are not condemned to a symmetrical poverty of means. Indeed, in the nuclear age nothing would be riskier than a policy that would imitate Soviet reliance on might, which reflects in part historical experiences, in part serious internal weaknesses, and in part the traditional need of multinational empires (or heterogeneous communities) to use the army, along with the schools, as a means of integrating a divided society.

It has become fashionable in some circles (for instance, with reference to the grain embargo) to say that we must show the Soviets our willingness to shoot ourselves in the foot, at times, in order to demonstrate the seriousness of our resolve to stop them. (Why the Soviets should mind it, instead of being delighted, as long as they remain intact, I fail to understand.) But to shrink tangible power to its military components would mean shooting ourselves in the head. It testifies to a curious discounting of our economic and technological power, and to an even more curious distrust of diplomatic power—the art of forming coalitions, of striking bargains, of building international arrangements and alliances and understandings that serve the interests of many, help reduce uncertainty, and allow for the sharing of risks.

The demand for such arrangements increases with the number and seriousness of the issues that states have to face. They are the alternative either to the hegemony of a single power that provides both the norms of behavior for other states and the incentives for these states to adhere to such rules, or else to chaos. If we assume that even with a much increased military force the era of American hegemony is over, then such diplomatic power becomes essential. (The example of the protracted Conference on the Law of the Sea—whose conclusions have now been rejected by the new administration—comes to mind.) Successful diplomatic power requires American expertise about other countries, and in many past crises we discovered that it did not exist. Developing such expertise requires more, not less, federal aid to higher education, which may turn out to be more useful than the same amount of money spent for arms.

The new orthodoxy ignores the fact that security policy is only one aspect of foreign policy; security issues—the core issues of the bipolar contest—are not separable from the others. This does not mean that all world affairs can be reduced to the contest between Washington and Moscow: Richard Nixon's "real war" is a gloomy fantasy. On the contrary, it means that our ability to manage problems of security depends on our skill in coping with other problems. A mismanagement of the world economy, indifference to nuclear proliferation, neglect of the demands presented by developing countries, laxity in dealing with regional conflicts such as the Arab-Israeli dispute or that of Namibia, a right wing disdain for human rights, all could create opportunities for the Soviets that would intensify our security fears.

Moreover, the definition of our security interests is not self-evident. It is a political definition, not a scientific one. We are, as Robert W. Tucker points out,[8] condemned to some sort of containment in the coming years (as we have been ever since 1947). But to declare containment the purpose of American power is no substitute for defining the criterion of what is essential containment. Not every position in the world is either defensible or worth defending against every kind of potential threat. For instance, the new orthodoxy does not make it clear whether only the extension of Soviet (or Cuban or Vietnamese) military power is to be resisted. Or are we to resist the establishment of regimes that "enter into a relationship with the Soviet Union that resembles the relationship with Cuba"? Or should we also resist the establishment of any regime supported by Moscow and Cuba? Tucker adopts the middle position, but it is a difficult one: can one know in advance? The new administration prefers to assume that any forces that receive "enemy" aid are likely to create a new Cuba. But this would, in effect, blur the distinction that Tucker wisely wants to maintain between a concern for the internal regimes of states and a concern for their strategic behavior.

Containment, even when it is limited to protection against the expansion of the military power of Moscow and its allies, can never be successful with military means only. The United States and its allies will continue to find it difficult to match Soviet conventional forces, and arms transfers by the United States to third parties can create more problems than they solve when these arms go to shaky rulers, or are used by them for purposes other than containing Moscow (the Soviets are having a parallel experience with their aid to Iraq). Nor is even successful military containment a substitute for an integrated policy, either toward the Soviet Union or toward the countries of the Third World.

It would also be self-mutilating to restrict American ideological power to anticommunism. First, there are, strange as it may seem, other sources of misery and repression than communism in the world. A great power that concentrates on only this one is likely to find the response abroad more cynical than enthusiastic, unless it shows a willingness to deal also with the causes of human blight that lie in its own sphere of influence.

Second, the attempt to connect all revolts against injustice and oppression with Soviet plots and Soviet-sponsored terrorism—even when there is evidence of Soviet weapons, or of weapons coming from Soviet allies—is unlikely to be convincing abroad. No one should have illusions about the machinations of Soviet or Libyan secret intelligence; but for the guns to be sent, there have to be people there to want and to get them, and it is a great error to assume these people are all essentially the same. If the reasons for their revolt are genuine, rooted in institutionalized patterns of political and economic inequity, no amount of documentation showing communist external support is likely to stop others from asking whether the mere suppression of dissidence will be enough to prevent new revolts as long as conditions are not radically changed, or whether the only alternative to such a change is not permanent repression and state terrorism (as in Guatemala). American counterintervention is often likely to push the domestic politics of the country in trouble further to the right, a result that is politically dangerous and can be morally repugnant.

Third, the attempt to distinguish between "moderately repressive" friends and totalitarian enemies flies, as Tom Farer has shown, in the face of realities, since it rests on a dubious comparison between the milder of our repressive clients and the more ferocious of our foes.[9] To contrast the shah and Pol Pot may be good polemics. But Somoza and Kadar? Some radical regimes may turn out to be worse for some human rights than a corrupt, conservative, anticommunist dictatorship (as in the case of Castro versus Batista). But a radical regime may well be the only legacy that a supposedly "reversible" authoritarian dictatorship may allow, as it kills off the democratic opposition. And at what cost in blood is it worthwhile, for American values and reputation, to prevent the coming to power of radical regimes? Don't some repressive regimes, in our spheres of influence, survive not because they correspond to local political cultures but because of the support we lend them?

Indeed, when we deal with ideological power, let us remember that its effectiveness depends on a modicum of consistency in behavior—that is, we must be willing to protect and promote wherever we can the values whose destruction are alleged to cause our hatred of our opponents. Moreover, if we stand as the champions, not of anticommunism, but (as Mr. Moynihan preferred to put it) of democracy, then again our chances of being heard depend on our success in actually enhancing democracy, that is, in pushing "friendly" oligarchs and tyrants beyond mere repression, and on recognizing that political democracy is unlikely to flourish unless certain economic and social rights are acknowledged as well.

At a time when handwringing about the decline of American power continues, and before credit is claimed by members of the new administration for having restored this power, the distinction between available, usable, and effective power must be clearly understood. Our available power remains immense, and can be increased, but we face two kinds of problems. One is the growth of the power of others—Soviet military might, German or Japanese exports, OPEC's monetary reserves. We can neither, in the first case, prevent our rival from trying to match our own exertions, nor, in the others, weaken their power without seriously wounding ourselves. Second, we have current vulnerabilities (the decline of American productivity, our low rate of savings and capital investment, our lagging domestic oil production, the situation of the automobile industry, the so-called "throw-weight gap," the prospect of Minuteman vulnerability, the condition of the volunteer army). Most of them can be remedied, but only at considerable cost (and therefore with difficult tradeoffs), and over time.

Even available, even greatly increased power is often unusable. Military power is of little use either when the objectives we try to achieve are economic or when the threat to our economic security could be worsened by sending the Marines or the rapid deployment force. Nor can we use it when the result would be thoroughly disproportionate to the goal (say, to help the Poles with arms should the Soviets invade). Nor, above all, can we deploy power as we would like when the very states we want to protect resist our presence. Thus there is a major difference between the case of our alliances with Western Europe and Japan and the alliances we are trying to work out in the Persian Gulf. Nor can we use power, for example to help Afghan rebels, if the country that would have to be the base, Pakistan, demands so exorbitant an economic and political price as to make it counterproductive. In other words, we depend on frequently unfavorable external opportunities which are either beyond our control or can be shaped favorably only by the wise resort to other forms of power.

The use of economic power abroad, however, is increasingly inhibited not by bad conditions overseas but by political prejudices at home. We suffer from the combination of a shrinkage of available resources owing to stagflation and of a philosophy, or rather an ideology, that denounces foreign aid as useless at best, nefarious at worst, and tells developing countries to count almost exclusively on their own efforts and to rely on private foreign investment (least likely to go to the most needy places). This is why the United States often appears as having little to offer and little to threaten with.

Even usable power may turn out to be ineffectual. In Vietnam, we learned that the employment of immense power assured no victory if we respected domestic and external restraints on even bigger efforts that would be capable of annihilating the enemy. Such efforts were risky abroad, too divisive at home; yet anything less (even if it was huge) turned to dross, given the weak and rotting political base from which, in South Vietnam, our power was being exerted. And in wartime the dynamics and requirements of the military enterprise make it difficult, if not impossible, to concentrate on achieving what is the precondition for ultimate success: political and social reform.

More recently, all of America's might in the Indian Ocean and Persian Gulf probably could not have brought America's hostages back from Iran alive. Here too, we had to rely on events—the Iraq-Iran war—and diplomatic skills. We had used huge amounts of power to build up and shore up the shah of Iran. Had we used more to save his throne, we might well have failed.

That success is at the mercy of local circumstances is thus one unquestionable lesson of Vietnam and Iran. Should we use military and economic assistance to "stop communist advances" in El Salvador, ultimate success would depend on internal reform. But what incentive would the ruling junta, or the military elements that partly threaten and partly control it, have to share power and overhaul the social structure if they think they have already won and have our support? And what enthusiasm and competence for such reform could be expected of current American officialdom, which believes that it is always either too litle or too late for reform, or shows toward events beyond our own national experience the kind of understanding that Louis XVI evinced toward the events of 1789? Success without internal reform would depend on setting up a repressive protectorate, a move that could cost us far more than it would be worth.

Often, usable power, when used, boomerangs. We have experienced it in our economic policy aimed at pushing West Germany and Japan toward economic expansion in 1977-1978, only to find ourselves outpaced by them both. Military deployments in some regions—the Middle East, Central America—could provoke the opposition of friends, and if not a deeper armed involvement of the Soviets and their allies, at least a commitment on their part to making our life more difficult and our engagement yet more costly.

In sum, power is needed—if only because any great nation needs a reputation for power; but power is about politics. This means, first, as Robert W. Tucker recognizes, that it is not really an independent factor: it is, or ought to be, tailored to the purposes we pursue. He rightly claims that one of our important purposes is "extended deterrence," that is, the ability to protect allies and clients from enemy attack in areas where we have vital interests. This, he says, is incompatible with our acceptance of nuclear parity with the Soviets. But if the return to nuclear superiority is impossible or highly unlikely, as clearly seems the case, the conclusion—which he fails to draw—is that we should try to provide extended deterrence by means other than American military and nuclear might alone.

Second, we must, in shaping our power for our goals, make every effort to analyze political reality correctly. Here Professor Tucker and I also differ, for instance, when we consider the Persian Gulf. His narrow equation of power with military might and his partly normative, partly traditional view of the hierarchy of states lead him to describe the region as a power vacuum into which, inevitably, the superpowers are being sucked and which one or the other will fill. But not every power vacuum in history operates as a magnet. On the contrary, some operate as repellents, as long as all the major outside actors stay out, or at the fringes; it is the intrusion of one that may attract the rivals. In today's world, furthermore, the independent actors of a given area are most likely to make it difficult for outsiders to "fill the vacuum" quite so mechanically and completely.

Once again, we must study the political terrain before preparing the military ground. And this, in turn, means beginning with a clear view of the possible threats (among which, in the Persian Gulf, a Soviet invasion is but one and not the most likely). We must go on to ask which of these threats could be deterred, deferred, or met by American military forces in the region, and which ones could actually be made worse by such forces. We should end by asking what the political obstacles and preconditions are to an American military presence, insofar as it would be useful at all.

Those who lack enthusiasm for that presence may do so, not because, as Tucker says, they can't face the prospect of difficult relations with Moscow, but because they are acutely aware of these preconditions—such as dealing with the Palestinian issue—and unconvinced that the Soviet threat of aggression, against which American ground forces might have a credible trip-wire effect, is so urgent that the benefits of deploying them would outweigh the costs. Those of the new orthodoxy who analyze the world almost solely as a contest between Washington and Moscow, and who concentrate on the giants without perceiving the costs and inhibitions the giants face, and the stilts on which the pygmies stand, risk stumbling into another disaster.

IV.

What kind of strategy would respond to the international situation many Americans find so ominous today? A few guidelines, at least, can be useful, first about preconditions for effective policy, then about priorities.

One precondition is the need to minimize discontinuity. The American system of government, with its concentration on the president, and the absence of a permanent bureaucracy at the top is always prone to sudden changes of course. When presidents do not make it to a second term, the risk of hairpin turns increases. When a new president also is of a different party from his predecessor's, and there is a big shift in Congress, the temptation to repudiate the past and to put Creation in the present is overwhelming. But nothing is more destructive of confidence abroad, more dangerous, and ultimately more confusing at home. It is a way both of raising excessive hopes in the electorate, and of telling many voters to burn what they once adored.

In the not so long term, this aggravates the voters' distrust of politics and politicians, and injects cynicism where trust should be, apathy where what John Stuart Mill called "the invigorating effect of freedom" ought to be felt. Many of the new initiatives, announced not because they are part of a well thought through policy, but because they demonstrate the desire for novelty and symbolize the new priorities, are likely either to backfire (remember the early Carter pressure on Bonn over the German-Brazilian deal, or Carter's first proclamations about human rights), or to go out of control (would even Mrs. Kirkpatrick and Mr. Lefever be happy with a perfectly likely epidemic of right wing coups aiming at establishing or at hardening regimes that practice an "average" rate of torture?).

Allies and adversaries alike are unhelpfully upset; insofar as one of our goals is to induce more predictable behavior from our foes, our own unpredictability entails a change of signals, the throwing of new wrenches into the negotiations (as in the case of the Law of the Sea Conference), the raising of new conditions, and the failure to pick up dangling threads (as the sad story of SALT II since 1972 shows). Allies keep worrying about the wondrous new initiatives we will invent, the new slogans we will float, and above all the new demands we will make. Two months after the inauguration of the new president, we have already had a flap over the neutron bomb, turned the tiny country of El Salvador into a "litmus test" of alliance solidarity, been told that we should not exaggerate its importance, and failed to respond clearly to the allies' own concerns about the direction of the relations between Washington and Moscow.

A frequent consequence of this urge to be different is the unproductive detour. Carter's attempt to exorcise the weighty ghost of Henry Kissinger led to the doomed March 1977 arms reduction proposals to the Soviet Union, and to a clumsily improvised search for a comprehensive Middle East settlement. In each case, we had to return to the previous path. Will the Reagan administration, after much internal arguing, return—overtly or in disguise—to the SALT II treaty its members have so frequently denounced? Will it rediscover the Palestinian issue, which it now professes to find less important than meeting the Soviet threat in the Middle East, as if Soviet opportunities and American difficulties there did not largely flow from the failure to pursue the Camp David approach with energy, and indeed to go beyond it? Will it revert, in El Salvador, to the view for which Ambassador White was fired—that only a political solution, establishing a democratic coalition of civilians, has a chance of bringing peace and reform to this unhappy country?

A second proposition is that an effective foreign policy presupposes solid domestic underpinnings. It requires, on the one hand, an economic basis. This means a gradual reduction of inflation, allowing for a return to steady growth. A mere injection of money into the economy, by worsening inflation, would once more lead the government and the Federal Reserve authorities to put on the brakes and to provoke a recession. But a strictly monetarist attempt to break inflation by shock therapy followed by several years of recession and high unemployment would be unpalatable politically, at home and abroad. Second, it means an energy policy that reduces American dependence on imports from the Middle East, and thus decreases the imbalance of bargaining power between producers and consumers, reduces the weight of oil prices for developing, oil-importing countries, and thus helps to save them from increasingly more staggering indebtedness and falling rates of growth. It means, in the third place, a policy of industrial reconversion, to avoid, instance after instance, the bleak choice between bankruptcy and bailouts, between collapse and protectionism.

It is too early to say if the Reagan economic program will provide such a basis, but there are reasons for doubting it. The proposed budget applies the brakes and the tax program pushes on the accelerator simultaneously, in the hope of lowering inflation and fostering growth. But will a tax cut promote savings and investment, or produce an inflationary spending binge, to which the size of the budget deficit and the vast increase in military expenditures would contribute?

The hypothesis that attributes inflation largely to the size of the federal budget, and therefore prescribes cuts in nonmilitary expenditures as the remedy (along with an increasing supply of goods)—and yet keeps the size of the deficit quite large—may turn out to be more ideological than scientific. Is a stern management of the money supply, designed to curb inflation, compatible with optimistic projections of growth? Won't the imperative of a return to growth and a reduction of unemployment—indispensable for success at home and abroad—lead to more relaxed money supply guidelines, and higher inflation? Wouldn't Lester Thurow's suggestion of tax cuts on investment but tax increases on consumption make more sense?[10] The worst outcome would be a continuation of stagflation, and this is certainly not ruled out.

As for energy, a policy unconcerned with conservation, relaxed about alternative sources, and confident in the effect of deregulation and tax cuts on domestic production seems naive. With respect to industrial adaptation, the commitment to market economics seems both unwise and untenable. To request "voluntary" restraints from the Japanese on their car exports to this country solves neither the domestic nor the foreign policy problems of adaptation.

A sound domestic political basis is also necessary. It entails, first, a reorganization of the executive, which makes the State Department the clear center of decision, negotiation, and execution. We have been promised that this would be the case, but—apart from the fact that such promises have been made before—there are still reasons for skepticism. While the National Security Council staff and its head are currently underground, physically and effectively, this may not last forever, in view of the greater concentration of hardliners and activists in its ranks. If Mr. Richard Allen stays anonymous, clearly the president's adviser to whom Mr. Allen reports, Mr. Meese, is both visible and audible, even on matters of foreign policy.

We need, in the second place, more of an effort to include important members of Congress, from both houses and parties, into the policy process, from the start. And we need, above all, a president keen on educating the public. The new president is, in the words of Mr. Meese, excellent as a "management communicator." To be a good educator, he would have to be a bit more: he would have not only to inspire confidence, to be lucid in spelling out goals and priorities, but above all to be able to make Americans recognize and accept the reality and effects of complexity. He would have to see to it that their legitimate thirst for respect, their concern for honor and pride do not degenerate into the kind of machismo that, at best, is no more than posturing but, at worst (especially when rationalized by slogans, wrapped in spite or paternalism, and acted out by a mix of ignorance and arrogance), could make some Americans far more ashamed than proud. In this respect, the president's fondness for American exceptionalism, displayed in his inaugural address, does not bode well.

V.

The goal of American foreign policy ought to be not merely the containment of Soviet expansionism but the management and steering of inevitable change. Not all changes are welcome, nor are all changes irresistible or unavoidable. But what is utterly unrealistic is a Metternichian attitude that equates stability with the status quo; what is almost as unrealistic is one that tolerates only the kind of peaceful, orderly change that not even Americans have always experienced in their history.

A few things appear certain, even to one whose skepticism about waves of the future, necessary trends, and philosophies of history is total. Complete and permanent repression is not a safe method of government. Even in countries with very old traditions of iron rule, expert in insulating their peoples from contamination and contact, the spirit and the contagion of criticism and ethnic assertiveness may be felt. Indeed the Soviet Union is probably, along with South Africa, the society whose present "formula" is, in the long run, the most unworkable. Nations such as Chile and Brazil, in which formidable inequities, extreme contrasts of poverty and wealth, rapid growth without benefit for the poor are maintained only by police methods and the control of all organizations by the state, face a stormy future. Countries such as Taiwan and South Korea, with increasing prosperity and rapidly expanding middle classes but no political safety valve, risk having the lid blown off—as happened in Iran. New countries such as Zaire, Ethiopia, or Uganda, whose precarious unity can no longer be assured by the battle against foreign masters, which are wracked by every kind of internal heterogeneity and ruled by small and greedy cliques, are breeding grounds for rebels and tempting preys for meddlers.

Many of the potentially most unstable countries happen to be clients or allies of the United States—they range from Guatemala to Pakistan and the Philippines, from Haiti to Morocco and Egypt, from El Salvador to Saudi Arabia and Indonesia. Our twin worries, in years to come, will be to prevent explosions in such places from becoming manifestations of anti-Americanism and opportunities for Soviet influence; and to prevent explosions and disruptions in the Soviet universe from leading to general war. The one thing we will not be able to do, however hard we try, is to prevent explosions. Rather than direct aggression, it is the exploitation of revolutionary conditions, either through subversion or through encouragement of local revolutionary groups, which is the most likely form of Soviet expansion. In Afghanistan, indeed, it was such exploitation that, having been a failure, led to aggression.

In other words, the key issue—for the rest of the century—is the issue of revolution. And it so happens that, of all major powers in history, we may well be among the least well-prepared to cope with it—since our only revolutionary experience was national not social, and since it is against the excesses and local incrustations of capitalism that many revolutions are likely to occur. To try to "co-opt" change by rhetoric, à la Brzezinski, will not get us very far. To excommunicate it will get us nowhere. In some countries, such as the Dominican Republic, democratic governments have survived with U.S. encouragement. But to try crassly to manipulate other societies in a quest for progressive moderates, for benevolent centrists, has become a depressing ritual, since in many places such centrists are either ineffectual or the first victims of the contending extremes, and since nothing weakens their legitimacy more than an ardent embrace by us.

If we see in every revolution in which there is a trace of Soviet involvement a test between us and Moscow, we will stagger from one self-fulfilling prophecy to another in the worst possible conditions—we will either face endless military quagmires (or "pacification" campaigns), or risk dangerous escalations in order to "win" on more favorable ground, or fail. To see in every place where there is an opportunity for our opponents a deliberate target already chosen by them would also be self-defeating because it would allow them to divert attention, through propaganda, from their own exactions; and because it would radicalize large numbers of people, even in countries friendly to us. It is the United States, not the Soviet Union, which would appear as the greatest threat to the independence of Third World countries, should our interventions on behalf of the status quo turn us into heavy-handed protectors of shaky regimes, and should we behave as self-appointed geopolitical policemen.

Obviously, in a world of 170 countries, sweeping generalizations are of little use. But a valid guideline would be, wherever we are closely associated with a regime, to encourage timely reform (by this I mean not only economic and social measures, such as land reform, by which we tend to get hypnotized, but above all the sharing of political power, which is what most discontented groups want, since political power conditions their future); for what is destabilizing is not such reform, but immobility. And we should distance or dissociate ourselves from a regime when it resists reform and dooms itself to upheaval, thus becoming a burden to its people and a liability to us.

In all cases where we are not particularly close, we should give no encouragement to regimes that trample the human rights for whose defense we stand (such as the current regimes in Argentina and Chile). And we should—as Carter did in Nicaragua and Zimbabwe—accept ungrudgingly radical new regimes, even if some of the groups that fought for power received support from "unfriendly" sources, as in Angola or Mozambique. We should then use our resources, our influence, and our skills to protect our main interests, to encourage these regimes to have normal relations with us, and to make it clear that it is to their advantage to avoid vicious treatment of internal opponents. When we treat such regimes from the outset as delinquents, and try to quarantine or to "destabilize" or to starve them, we foster both unnecessary hostility and the kind of internal reaction that strengthens extremism, paranoia, and repression.

What about Saudi Arabia, some will say? I see no reason to make an exception in that case. The United States has to take account of the current regime's legitimate needs for arms and to have cooperative relations with it; but it must also quietly anticipate the possibility that through revolution, or mere succession, a new regime may appear, which will decide to cut down oil production for purely Saudi reasons. (Note that this case has to be distinguished from that of a deliberate effort, by the Soviet Union or by a coalition of Middle Eastern states, to "strangulate" Western economies.) The United States would be in a tragic position if it had to choose between economic disaster and a military intervention that could be economically futile and would be politically catastrophic. The Saudi sword over our heads is an added, powerful incentive for a combined energy policy of the United States, its European allies, and Japan. It is not a reason for abandoning these guidelines.

VI.

In the world as it is, American foreign policy will have to be complex and to take advantage of complexity. This has several implications. The first is the end of unilateralism. The diffusion of power, in the Third World as well as among the industrial countries, the appearance of new regional actors, the ability of the lesser ones either to combine their interests in a variety of groups and bodies, or to appeal to their bigger neighbors or to distant powers for protection against outside threats—all of this makes it impossible for the United States to impose its own concerns (or obsessions), so to speak, from above and outside, and to assume that it is in the higher interest of others to share and to heed them. In this sense, the battle over the Panama Canal treaties was highly symbolic; it was a battle about accepting the end of the colonial era.

If we face major threats in parts of the world we deem essential—the Persian Gulf, Central America—we have no other recourse than to enlist the support of the main states in the area. If we want them to give priority to the threat of invasion or subversion by the Soviets or their proxies, and to make sure that our own military assistance does not end up supporting the local ambitions and grievances of the states we assist, we must also cooperate with the countries of each area in order to help them resolve intraregional disputes. We can have a unilateral Central American policy only at the cost of antagonizing not only Mexico (a nation of growing importance for our future) but Venezuela, the other democratic republics of the area, and of Latin America—and even some of the authoritarian ones, whose distaste for radicals is matched by their dislike for the big stick of Washington. To be sure, in a case such as that of El Salvador, the countries in the region may disagree on the best solution. But most of them agree on what would be the worst one—American military intervention—and we could do far worse than enlist their cooperation in the search for a political compromise.

In the Middle East, we have found that even Arab countries divided over Camp David agreed in their reluctance to provide us with bases—not because of the decline of our power, but because of our failure to use it in the one case, the Arab-Israeli dispute, that concerns them all. After the Israeli elections, unless Israel comes forward with an initiative that could lead to a breakthrough comparable to Sadat's in 1977, it would be in our interest to enlist the support of our European allies (many of whom have good contacts with Israel's Labor Party, the likely winner) as well as that of all the nonrejectionist Arab states in the search for a solution of the Palestinian issue.

In the case of southern Africa—Namibia, the future of South Africa itself—the cooperation of European states, especially Britain, and of key Black African countries will be indispensable; any rapprochement with South Africa will be shortsighted.

What this requires is a willingness on our part not merely to share the burdens and divide labor in a task defined by us but to devise a policy together. This does not mean encouraging selected allies whose own designs could prove deeply divisive in a given part of the world (as Iran did under the shah, as the King of Morocco tends to be because of his Western Sahara adventure). It does require regional efforts aimed at coping with local threats—that of the Soviets in the Persian Gulf, that of Qaddafi in Central Africa—and providing such groupings with assistance, rather than shortcircuiting them with our own forces. Insofar as these would be needed, as against a Soviet threat of invasion in the Middle East, to have available a quickly deployable force stationed outside the area would be preferable to the permanent stationing of ground forces in it. The theoretical advantage in deterrent and war-fighting power permanent ground forces might enjoy would be smaller than the political costs of stationing them in so unstable an area where the winds of nationalism are so strong.

The first inclinations and initiatives of the new Reagan administration with respect to unilateralism are far from reassuring, although one of the most important issues—a common strategy with Western Europe and Japan to deal with Soviet influence outside the NATO area—has not yet been addressed. In El Salvador, the Reagan administration's decision to increase its military assistance to the government was made without anyone in the region, including, it seems, that government, asking for it.

Another implication of complexity is the need for selectivity, because of the limits on American power. The United States must have both "power politics" goals—to preserve from aggression the territory of its allies and to preserve access to vital natural resources—and "world order" goals—to preserve chances for a humane and reasonably prosperous world. But, especially if America's economy does not recover speedily, the means at our disposal will have to be used intelligently. A worldwide crusade, stretching the meaning of security to extend to the internal order of states, or making of "friendly" states an essential ingredient of a tolerable international milieu, is clearly beyond our means, as well as likely to be counterproductive. But a policy of accommodating change and accepting revolutions, while more modest in its goals, still ought to make use of varied incentives to promote such important objectives as nonproliferation, the protection of human rights, and the improvement of economic conditions in developing countries.

VII.

With respect to security, selectivity means concentrating our resources on improving the state of readiness and the equipment of our conventional forces, at the cost of returning to a peacetime draft if this appears necessary

THE NEW ORTHODOXY

to build up adequate reserves. We need, also, more abundant means of air and naval transportation for the rapid deployment, reinforcement, and supply of our conventional forces. The navy needs antisubmarine protection and air defense against Soviet attack submarines and planes, and more ships for the Persian Gulf; but vulnerable supercarriers and revamped old battleships with cruise missiles are a dubious investment. All this is far more important than strengthening our nuclear forces. Our main problem there, the vulnerability of Minuteman missiles by the mid-1980s, is significant far less for its military effects—as an incentive for a Soviet strike, or a military disaster should Moscow strike—than for its psychological ones, the effects on our own perceptions and on those of our allies. And it can be dealt with by several possible policies.

First, we could try to negotiate a new agreement with Moscow to allow missile site defense, at a time when Soviet missiles are likely to become vulnerable to American strikes also. This would make sense only when ballistic missile defense is technically safe, and if there is an arms control agreement limiting the number of warheads each side can use to overwhelm the other side's defenses. In any case, it may not be to our overall advantage, since it would protect a far greater portion of the Soviet nuclear arsenal than of ours (land-based missiles constitute only one-fourth of ours, but four-fifths of theirs).

We could, alternatively, make Minuteman missiles mobile, underground, or, should this prove to be financially and politically too costly, on submarines near the coast. Neither the MX nor a new strategic bomber is necessary. It is more important to deprive the Soviets of the one advantage their alleged war-fighting strategy can theoretically count on than to increase or improve our own nuclear war-fighting capacities beyond our regular program, which includes already air-launched cruise missiles and more accurate missiles on Minuteman and on our nuclear submarines. The latter, as well as most of our planes, would in any case survive a Soviet attack on Minuteman.

It may be argued that deterring a Soviet conventional attack on our European allies, or in the Persian Gulf area, requires an American ability to strike first with nuclear weapons, which would be aimed at Soviet military targets. But, on the one hand, there are many other targets besides Soviet missiles; and on the other hand, technological progress is going to make Soviet missiles vulnerable anyhow, without the MX or a new strategic bomber. We already have, and will increasingly have, counterforce capabilities, and while the Soviets may have a temporary advantage, it is neither decisive (given the formidable risks the Soviets would incur if they attacked our land-based missiles) nor irremediable.

What we surely need is "crisis stability," which means forces neither so vulnerable as to tempt the other side to strike first, nor "so provocative to the other side as to induce the attack it seeks to deter."[11] An American policy of piling up the MX, a new strategic bomber, cruise missiles, middle-range missiles in Europe, and perhaps ballistic missile defenses, would be provocative. Moreover, to concentrate on strategic rather than on conventional forces would put the main burden of conventional rearmament on Bonn and Tokyo, with disastrous results, including bitter and divisive reactions both within Germany and Japan and from neighboring powers. To go for both a conventional and a strategic arms build-up would put an enormous burden on the economy and divert resources from other forms of power and other policies.

A selective policy means, above all, a new attempt at establishing a mixed relationship with Moscow. The preconditions are clear: First, we need to improve the military balance in Europe, with respect to NATO's conventional and middle-range nuclear forces. There is no justification for a doomsday view of the current conventional balance in Europe, but the trends of the 1970s are disturbing. The Warsaw Pact forces have a considerable lead in artillery, armored vehicles, attack helicopters, and offensive chemical warfare; their equipment is standardized; they have shorter lines of communication, and the number of long-range aircraft available to them has increased. NATO forces have an advantage in precision-guided munitions, anti-tank weapons, and tactical aircraft. But they can no longer expect to compensate for their quantitative inferiority with qualitative superiority, in view of Soviet progress in quality; and above all, they must try to overcome their opponents' current advantage in being able to build up their forces much faster. NATO needs more "prepositioned" stocks in Europe, quicker reinforcement capacity, and increased reserves.

As for middle-range nuclear weapons capable of hitting the Soviet Union, their need arises from the rapid deployment of the mobile and precise Soviet SS-20 missiles, and from the Soviet construction of the Backfire bomber—weapon systems unmatched so far by NATO. The purpose of these Soviet weapons seems to be to make it possible for the Warsaw Pact countries to wage a purely conventional war in Europe, in the hope that the United States would be deterred from the first use of its strategic, long-range nuclear weapons against Soviet territory by the fear of Soviet retaliation on the United States, and that NATO would be deterred from resorting to its own short-range nuclear weapons (most of which could not reach the Soviet Union) by the ability of new Soviet missiles and bombers to destroy NATO's military objectives, including troop concentrations and nuclear installations. The NATO decision, in December 1979, to deploy 108 mobile middle-range Pershing missiles and 464 ground-launched cruise missiles capable of reaching the Soviet Union means that the Soviet Union would, in invading Western Europe with conventional forces, expose itself to nuclear attack launched from Europe on its own territory; and the burden of initiating a strategic, intercontinental nuclear war would then rest on Moscow, not on Washington.

A second precondition is a Soviet willingness to move toward a generally acceptable solution in Afghanistan; one that would include withdrawal of Soviet troops. Large-scale, overt American arming of the Afghan resistance, untied to any diplomatic offer of a political solution, is likely to be counter-productive: it would incite the Soviets to dig in (and help justify their fake rationale for invading), and it would require a commitment to the Pakistan regime that could harm both our relations with India and our nonproliferation policy.

The French president has suggested a conference of neighboring countries, regional powers, and permanent members of the Security Council dealing with the end of external interferences and aiming at the withdrawal of foreign forces and a neutralization of the country. This leaves aside the crucial question of the Afghan regime. It is unlikely that the Soviets would withdraw all their forces as long as the regime seems incapable of surviving by itself. But some indication of their interest in the French proposal or some Soviet initiative that would go beyond their ritual statements of the past twelve months would be needed, even if this marks only the beginning of a long bargaining process. Such a new position would have to be less equivocal than Brezhnev's offer, at the recent Party Congress, linking Afghanistan to the Persian Gulf.

A third precondition would be Soviet restraint in the aggressive use of force in other parts of the world—no more Afghanistans, and no invasion of Poland.

The objectives of a new relationship with Moscow cannot be the same as those of détente in the 1970s. Then, we hoped for a swift reduction of the burden of armaments, and we hoped to convert Moscow to our notion of international stability. Moscow hoped to bring about a reduction of America's presence and influence in the world, and to obtain a kind of political condominium. But we can no more prevent the Soviets from trying to affect the "correlation of forces," by exploiting opportunities in the Third World, or by trying to drive wedges between the Western Europeans and ourselves, than they can prevent the reassertion of American influence and the resistance of Americans and others to the Soviet dream of a world run by the two superpowers together. In other words, each side had excessive expectations; and each one should learn from the experience: the Soviets, that the tilt in the "correlation" can go either way, and that political condominium is beyond their reach; we, that agreements with Moscow mean neither ideological demobilization on their part nor a Soviet endorsement of the status quo. However, neither the mutual disillusionment of recent years, nor the new American mood of confrontation, nor the change in the military balance makes a revised policy of détente (under that or any other name) unadvisable or absurd.

As I have suggested before, the aim of foreign policy ought to be to make it possible for each of the two powers to play its own game, in such a way as not to violate the vital interests of the other. What is involved is not a fading away but a taming of the competition; not an explicit code of conduct demanded of the other side, but a change in the means and intensity of the contest, and a clear understanding both of what each side deems intolerable and of what measures it would take against the other if the intolerable should occur.

The immediate objectives are also clear. One would be to preserve the gains that have been achieved, by our allies, through their own détente process. The West Germans have, with some shrillness, pointed out the importance of these gains: improved contacts between families in the two Germanies, and between Western and Eastern European countries; military "confidence-building measures" between the two alliances; above all peace in Berlin; and a variety of economic deals, thanks to which Western Europe, in a difficult period, has found export markets as well as means to diversify its energy imports.

But these gains also created problems for both sides. They have been accompanied by new developments heightening the underlying tensions in Eastern Europe. While Eastern Europe was never stable, as the eruptions of 1953, 1956, 1968 and 1970 in East Germany, Hungary, Poland, Czechoslovakia, and the huge exodus from East Germany in 1960 and 1961 have shown, dissidents there can now invoke the Helsinki agreements and will probably continue to do so, notwithstanding the imprisonment of forty-five Helsinki monitors in the Soviet Union. The economic ties Gierek sought with Western Europe only worsened the plight of Poland's economy, helping indirectly to produce the Solidarity movement, with all its potential both for deep reforms and for serving as the target of another Soviet invasion—possibilities that hang in the balance as this is written.

Conversely, Western European business deals with Moscow can also lead to contradictory results. First, they provide the Soviets with technology that can be used for military progress, or can facilitate the transfer of the Soviet Union's own resources to the military sector. Second, Western European dependence on Middle Eastern oil may be compounded rather than relieved by dependence (soon to be as high as 30 percent) on Soviet natural gas. Even if, as the West Germans argue, the Soviets might hesitate to embargo such supplies of energy in a crisis, since their clients would retaliate, it is not clear that the losses would be even; and above all the economic ties between Western Europe and the Soviets expose our allies not so much to outright blackmail as to the risk of showing themselves too accommodating on political, strategic, and human rights issues in order not to jeopardize their economic benefits. The Soviets find it much easier to pursue a two track policy of political and strategic advance and economic cooperation, since both tracks serve their overall purpose—the increase of their power and influence. Nevertheless, until now, there have been mutual gains and they deserve to be saved, even if it is time for the allies to discuss in common the desirable scope and limits of economic cooperation with Eastern Europe and the Soviet Union.

It is true that France, in recent months, has moved closer to Washington. This is partly because the French president, in his reelection campaign, faces more of a foreign policy challenge from the Gaullists than from the Socialists; partly because the French, who have their own nuclear deterrent and took no part in NATO's decision in December 1979 on middle-range nuclear forces, are more skeptical than the West Germans about arms control for nuclear weapons in Europe; partly because of their intense sympathy for the Polish freedom movement; partly because they feel that their past gestures of friendship toward Moscow have not been rewarded; partly because they hope to occupy the mythical position of moderators-friends of Washington, abandoned by an immoderate Mrs. Thatcher and a not-so-friendly Helmut Schmidt.

But, especially after the presidential election, France can be expected again to give priority both to the Paris-Bonn connection, without which the European Community or European political cooperation—Giscard's grand designs—would not function, and to its own freedom of maneuver, which requires that tensions between the superpowers remain low, American strength be undeniable yet not overbearing, and relations with Moscow promising.

A second objective is the pursuit of arms control. Recent statements by Brezhnev suggest a possibility of incorporating the main provisions of SALT II into a SALT III treaty that would go beyond them in dealing both with limits on the deployment of new classes of submarines and with short- and middle-range nuclear forces in Europe. He has, indeed, incorporated into his basket of flowers several proposals of French and West German origin (although with thorns that have been grafted on by him). This makes it more difficult for us to reject them as mere propaganda, and several are worth exploring.

The present reaction against arms control in this country is a typical example of the tendency to throw away a tool because it has failed to do a job we were probably quite wrong to expect it to do—whether it is restraining competition in the Third World or stopping the Soviet build-up—rather than appreciating what it can do. The fact is that without a limit on the number of warheads each type of missile can carry, the threat to our land-based missiles

DEAD ENDS

would become far worse, and it would be futile to invent schemes to make land-based mobile missiles: the more holes we would dig, the more warheads Moscow could aim at.

Bringing about strategic arms limitations and a comprehensive test ban soon would make the future arms race both more predictable and more restricted. It would allow us to concentrate, in our military efforts, on the more serious problem of conventional forces. It could provide the basis for the negotiation of serious discrete issues arising in the near future. These issues include: ballistic missile defense; antisatellite weapons; land-based missile vulnerability; verifying the number of mobile land-based missiles (should their increasing vulnerability, on both sides, lead each power to seek solace in such mobility); and curtailing ground- and sea-launched cruise missiles.

In building cruise missiles, we may repeat the mistake we made when we failed to push hard for a curb on MIRVs at a time when we were ahead. In the long run, unlimited cruise missiles may become a curse for us, if the Soviets should multiply conventional as well as nuclear cruise missiles. Arms control could save both sides from a costly and dangerous drive for superiority.

Moreover, negotiating limitations on or reductions of both strategic and middle-range European-based nuclear weapons is a political prerequisite for the acceptance by the West Germans of the new NATO missiles I have described above. The NATO program of December 1979 needs both a military rationale and a political base. The willingness to negotiate is the only way of containing the wave of nuclear pacifism that has spread over part of the British and West German left and over the smaller Western European countries, where the new American emphasis on counterforce war (for instance in the 1980 Presidential Directive 59) and the ominous rise in mobile and precise nuclear weapons in the two alliances that face each other in the middle of Europe have reawakened the latent fear of a nuclear war fought over Europe.

A last objective in our policy toward Moscow would be a renewed search for agreement on matters of mutual benefit. Economic cooperation can be one of them, especially with respect to the development of Soviet energy resources. The pursuit of a joint nonproliferation policy is another. There may be a joint interest in political cooperation in the Middle East, an area from which it is impossible to exclude either great power, which neither one can dominate, where each one finds its clients either troublesome or unreliable, and where the risks of confrontation far exceed the advantages of stirring the pot of troubles.

We face two Soviet threats. One is military—capacities for aggression (neither unlimited nor universal) and the ability to provide arms to groups

148

and governments supported by Moscow. The other is political—the ability to exploit or exacerbate revolutionary tendencies or conflicts in the Third World. But the Soviet Union has little to offer to countries in quest of economic development and political self-reliance. Its control over its Eastern European satellites is shaky and costly, its influence over distant clients is often temporary, and it suffers from political and economic rigidities that could cripple its effectiveness as a superpower or oblige it to sink its energies into drastic, painful, and unsettling internal reform. Against the Soviet military and political threat, against a Soviet temptation to find in external adventures a diversion from the domestic problems, we must follow a multiple strategy. We should combine defense measures, preventive diplomacy, and policies aimed at increasing the capacity for national and collective independence of other countries. We should also preserve possibilities of mutual arrangements with Moscow, given the waste of resources the arms race entails, the perils of confrontation, the fact that a large number of issues require some cooperation, and the Western ability to affect Soviet choices.

We should not let ourselves either be obsessed by Soviet strengths or lulled by Soviet weaknesses. The former are manageable. The latter are real, but not less serious than the present economic weaknesses of the noncommunist world in general and of the United States in particular (such as the decline of American productivity). And we could make our own economic weaknesses worse if, emulating Lyndon Johnson's mistakes in the mid-1960s, we combined vast military expenditures with tax cuts and if our nonmilitary industries were obliged either to hide behind disastrous protective barriers or to succumb to the competition of countries that invest fewer financial and human resources in defense.

The directions suggested here are not those which our new leaders are inclined to follow. But they may find that their own analysis—which makes of the Soviet-American conflict the omnivorous issue of our time, and attributes past difficulties with allies and clients to our earlier failure of will and power—is far too simple-minded. They may come to see that the projection of a bipolar grid on regional disputes and internal turbulence all over the world is unsuccessful; that their neonationalism and their emphasis on military power antagonize more nations than are impressed; that their dislike of North-South bargains is putting the United States at a disadvantage; that their view of Soviet expansionism is too militant to be widely shared by those who also deem Moscow dangerous. Then, perhaps, a chance would come for a more constructive approach.

The twin perils of the 1980s are a mismanagement of our contest with the Soviet Union, which may occur if its leaders feel altogether confident in its might, trapped by an unreformable and creaky system at home, and

DEAD ENDS

entirely cornered and surrounded abroad; and a mismanagement of the world economy, which the risks of a prolonged recession in the West and the shaky condition of the international financial and monetary systems might well provide. Against these dangers, the fundamentalist reaction that now prevails in the United States has little to offer; it may indeed contribute to them. The hard crust of confidence, however, may be thinner than it appears.

ADDENDUM TO CHAPTER 7

This essay was written in February 1981. Since then, a number of things have happened. As I had suggested, the Reagan administration did indeed discover the virtues of SALT and the urgency of the Palestinian problem. Contrary to what I had believed, the Labour Party did not win the Israeli elections of the summer of 1981: Mr. Reagan's apparent support of Mr. Begin, and the latter's shrewd moves, such as the bombing of the nuclear reactor near Baghdad, helped consolidate the power of the Likud and its allies. It is also quite obvious that the Reagan administration does not share my belief in the existence of a joint Soviet and Western interest in developing the energy resources of the Soviet Union.

Finally, concerning my misgivings about the economic program of the Reagan administration, what can be said as of January 1983 is that, despite these misgivings, inflation has largely been defeated—but mainly through a recession. There is no economic recovery yet, and unemployment has reached its highest figures. This is partly the result of the very high interest rates that prevailed until recently, and which in turn resulted partly from the Federal Reserve Board's policies and reflected the bankers' and businessmen's dismay at the size of the budgetary deficit. It is not clear yet whether the recent fall in interest rates (a consequence not only of the drop in inflation, but also of the falling demand for credit in a depressed economy), the buoyancy of the stock market, and the new tax increases voted by Congress in order to reduce the deficit, will suffice to ensure recovery in an economy in which the deficit stays huge, productivity remains low, many businesses and financial institutions appear to be quite shaky, and consumer demand is not particularly buoyant.

NOTES

1. Stanley Hoffmann, "The Perils of Incoherence," *Foreign Affairs, America and the World in 1978* (Special Issue, 1978):463-491; and Chapter 4 of this book.

2. Michel Crozier, *Le Mal américain* (Paris: Fayard, 1980).

3. Raymond Vernon, "Gone Are the Cash Cows of Yesteryear," *Harvard Business Review* (November/December 1980):150-55.

4. David A. Deese and Joseph S. Nye, *Energy and Security* (Cambridge, Mass.: Ballinger Publishing Company, 1980), p. 392.

5. Robert O. Keohane, "Hegemonic Leadership and U.S. Foreign Economic Policy," in William P. Avery and David Rabkin, eds., *America in a Changing World Political Economy* (New York: Longmans, 1982), pp. 48-76.

6. Daniel Yankelovich and Larry Kaagan, "Assertive America," *Foreign Affairs 59* (1981):696-713.

7. Robert W. Tucker, "The Purposes of American Power," *Foreign Affairs 59* (Winter 1980-1981):241-74.

8. Tucker, "The Purposes of American Power," p. 272.

9. Tom Farer, "Reagan and the Dictators," *The New York Review of Books* (March 19, 1981):10-16.

10. Lester Thurow, "The Moral Equivalent of Defeat," *Foreign Policy* (Spring 1981):114-24.

11. Carnegie Panel on US Security and the Future of Arms Control, *Challenges for US National Security* (Washington, D.C.: Carnegie Endowment for International Peace, January 1981), p. 56.

CHAPTER 8

REAGAN ABROAD

I.

IF AN ideology is a set of beliefs about the state of the world, about how it got to be that way, and about what should be done to change it, the Reagan administration came to power with an ideology of foreign affairs. The lesson most observers have derived from the first year of Reagan's foreign policy is simple: an ideology is not a strategy, a set of attitudes is not a policy. Moreover, insofar as the view of the world was plainly wrong, the divorce between convictions and realities puts policymakers in a dilemma. Either they act on their beliefs, with potentially disastrous effects; or else they merely express and trumpet their beliefs, which may be enough to scare or antagonize others; or else they try to close the gap and to adapt to reality, always a slow and painful, and often an incomplete, process for true believers.

The Reagan ideology was shared by all the factions that had come together under Reagan's leadership: his old California associates; Republican moderates whose own preferred candidates had bitten the dust; Henry Kissinger, whose Canossa had been the Republican convention in July 1980; the neoconservatives who had deserted the Democratic Party. It could be summed up in a decalogue.

1. Carter's foreign policy fiascoes resulted from incoherence, itself the outcome of conflicting world views; a unity of views must be restored.

2. Insofar as there had been a dominant world view under Carter, it had entailed an almost criminal neglect of American power, a drift into and an acceptance of weakness; the first imperative of the new policy is the restoration of American strength.
3. The Soviet Union is on the march; its expansionism has entered a new phase, the most dangerous yet for the West, because of both new Soviet military strengths and growing internal Soviet problems; America must contain and confront the adversary.
4. The Soviet Union is the key factor in most of the world's disputes, because it either initiates conflict and subversion, or exploits troubles at the expense of the West. The United States must, in coping with regional affairs, give priority to removing or neutralizing the mischief caused by Moscow and its proxies.
5. It should be the policy of the United States to mobilize as many states as possible against the Soviet danger.
6. Carter's problems with the Allies (as well as with the Soviets and with many nonaligned countries) were caused by a lack of will. If decisiveness is restored, if Washington leads again, the Allies will stop bickering with us or among themselves and be grateful for clear leadership.
7. The next few years will be particularly dangerous because of the "window of vulnerability"—the vulnerability of America's land-based missiles, and that of military targets in Western Europe to the SS-20 and the Backfire bomber; these imbalances must be eliminated as fast as possible.
8. The United States should cease being always on the defensive, allowing Moscow to pick the ripest opportunity; Soviet expansionism could be checked by an American strategy aimed at exploiting Soviet weaknesses, and particularly at retaliating against Soviet puppets and clients.
9. The solution to the problems faced by the countries of the Third World will be provided mainly by their own efforts, and residually by foreign assistance, but in both cases private enterprise is the key, capitalism is the answer.
10. The American people, tired of humiliation, weakness, and decline, are eager for a policy of strength and decisiveness.

If coherence and consistency of views were the only conditions necessary to produce an impressive foreign policy, this new orthodoxy would deserve the highest marks. But this ideology—the views of the Committee on the Present Danger—has, not surprisingly, proven to be better as a ram against the rather flimsy diplomacy of Jimmy Carter than as a compass in the jungles of the real world. It has turned out to be utterly deficient as a strategy because it fails to address many real problems, it aggravates others, it provides no priority other than the anti-Soviet imperative, and precious little guidance even in connection with the new Cold War.

II.

The policies followed during the first year of the Reagan administration fall into four categories: those for which the principles of the original decalogue have turned out to be wrong or insufficient; those cases where the attempts to apply the decalogue have been actually dangerous; those cases in which it has become necessary to adjust to reality and to give up the initial assumptions; and those policies which show signs of schizophrenia because of the conflict between the ideology and the need for adaptation.

In the first category, one finds the excruciating troubles of foreign policy-making in the Reagan administration. Whatever happened to the promise of coherence made by Secretary of State Haig at the beginning of 1981? Clearly, a common philosophy has not sufficed to restore harmony and smoothness in the process of making decisions. There are many reasons for this, but two are of special importance. When there is a shared world view (as there was not under Carter), subtle differences of personality and temper, past experiences, and separate career patterns can become inflated factors of opposition. Nuances are elevated into barriers, since the normal instinct of bureaucrats in fragmented bureaucracies is to splinter; small divergences in perspective (or, sometimes, retrospective ones) substitute for philosophical splits. Indeed, the fiercest struggles for power often are the pure ones (maybe pure isn't the word: I mean, those in which the contest for preeminence is untouched by ideas, and different world views play no role at all as fig leaves in a battle of naked bodies).

Moreover, a common philosophy provides no principle of organization. Indeed, it has not been enough to distribute faithful believers in the decalogue at various key points in the government. A system in which foreign policy is run neither by a strong secretary of state, nor by the president aided either by a secretary of state whom he fully trusts (as in the Eisenhower-Dulles team, or in the Nixon-Kissinger team in 1973-1974) or by a powerful national security assistant, is a recipe for trouble—whether trouble comes in the form of the Vance- (or Muskie-) Brzezinski split under Carter or in the more bizarre Reaganesque form. What we have had is a weakened national security adviser, a secretary of state regularly contradicted by other officials, a secretary of defense with his own views on foreign affairs, a White House triumvirate concerned above all with protecting the political power of the president and looking after his domestic base of support, but uninformed about external affairs, and a genial president who spends most of his energies on economic issues and intervenes in foreign matters more as a rescuer *in extremis* than as a constant leader. But in the AWACS rescue a great deal of capital had to be spent, and in the weeks preceding Reagan's November 18, 1981 speech on arms control in Europe, a great deal of capital was lost.

The second article of the decalogue—the restoration of American strength—has, alas, proven to be an inadequate guide to action. To be sure, the defense budget has been increased even beyond what Carter proposed. But there remain two major ambiguities. One is the compatibility of the armament effort with Reagan's domestic priority, economic recovery. Only supply-siders still seem to believe that there is no conflict here, that it is possible simultaneously to spend much more for defense, to reduce taxes considerably, to tolerate a vast budget deficit, and to expect both a drop in the rate of inflation and a new wave of investments.

So far, the tax cut and the deficit, as well as the anti-inflation priority of the Federal Reserve, have, because of the high interest rates, led to a serious recession. If the budget deficit—which recession will worsen—and the inflationary effects of military spending should first slow down the decline in interest rates that results from the recession, and later produce a new increase of these rates (should, in other words, the anticipated recovery not occur), Congress will have to choose between highly unpopular further cuts in the civilian budget (cuts which would, this time, affect the voting middle classes, and not merely or primarily the nonvoting poor), higher taxes, and cuts in the defense budget.

The other ambiguity concerns military priorities. More of everything is not a policy. Neither between conventional and strategic forces nor within each category have clear choices been made yet. The quarrel between those who believe that the greatest risk of military imbalance between the United States and the Soviet Union lies in the erosion of American nuclear superiority and those who think that the conventional advantages enjoyed by the Soviets in Europe and on the periphery of the Middle East are far more dangerous has not been settled or even confronted.

Concerning conventional forces, the pressure toward more sophisticated weapons systems (including vulnerable battleships and aircraft carriers that need whole fleets to protect them) seems once again to have prevailed over more mundane concerns such as improving the state of readiness of existing forces. Nor has a choice been made among the various conceptions of the Rapid Deployment Force, which range from a mere air and naval presence to an army actually stationed in the Middle East. Neither in the conventional nor in the nuclear realm has the administration offered a strategic doctrine that would provide a rationale for the catalogue of measures it has announced.

But no article of the decalogue has proven to be more defective than article five—the search for a global anti-Soviet strategic consensus. In the Middle East, to take the most acute example, the new American team had to rediscover what Carter had already found out—that Israel, in the near future, deems its Arab enemies more dangerous than the Soviet Union; that Saudi Arabia fears too close an American embrace, and deems the disruptive effects of the Palestinian issue more theatening than Soviet machinations; and that even Egypt won't provide bases for the Rapid Deployment Force as long as the Palestinian issue remains unsettled.

Even more numerous are the cases in the second category—those in which the attempt to enforce the decalogue has been dangerous and counterproductive. The mere declamation of articles of faith has sometimes sufficed to sour relations between the United States and other countries. Concerning North-South relations, Reagan has proclaimed the merits of private enterprise and "the magic of the market" to countries many of which are actually too poor to attract foreign capital and have very important economic sectors (sometimes including their entire "infrastructure") that are rarely profitable enough to interest foreign investors. For such countries, capitalist development, uncorrected, may lead to serious economic distortions, social inequities, and, often, external dependence.

Reagan's advice to these countries is not the best way of winning friends, even (indeed, especially) if it is right to emphasize the need for domestic measures of self-help, to criticize the failures of "command economies," and to warn against entrusting all negotiations to the General Assembly of the UN at the expense of specialized agencies.

More significant even is the effect of the Reagan rhetoric on the NATO allies. The shrill anti-Soviet statements made in the first eight months of the administration by the president, Haig, and Weinberger, combined with all the talk about restoring military superiority (or a "margin of safety") and about the need for a nuclear "war-fighting" strategy, and aggravated by the president's decision to produce neutron bombs, have been largely responsible for the growth of the antinuclear movement in Western Europe.[1]

The strident and sometimes contradictory pronouncements of the administration put several allied governments in a very difficult position—squeezed between a sizable fraction of their public and their 1979 commitments to NATO. The planned deployments of Pershing II and cruise missiles were intended to make it impossible for the Soviets to believe that if they launched a nuclear attack on NATO's military forces, or a conventional war in Europe, their own territory would be immune from nuclear retaliation because the United States would hesitate to use strategic nuclear weapons and because NATO would not have enough theater nuclear weapons capable of reaching Soviet territory. In other words, the deployments of new missiles, scheduled to begin in 1983, were obviously aimed at "recoupling" Europe's security with the strategic nuclear arsenal of the United States, and thus at strengthening deterrence. (They were also viewed as bargaining chips in a negotiation for mutual reductions of those nuclear weapons left unregulated by SALT II, whose imminent ratification was expected at the time of the NATO decision.) That they should nevertheless have come to be widely interpreted in Western Europe as steps toward making possible a nuclear war limited to Europe would be largely incomprehensible were it not for clumsy American statements suggesting precisely that possibility.

Beyond mere rhetoric, it is the attempt to carry out the initial ideology that has caused trouble, or risks being very dangerous, in three different sets of cases. In the first place, the sale of weapons to clients and friends whom the Reagan administration considers threatened by the Soviets and their allies risks embarrassing Washington whenever the beneficiaries of our solicitude happen to be one another's enemies, tempted to use weapons not against Moscow but against one another—or whenever one of our clients is engaged in a dispute with a state which it is in our interest to keep friendly, or whenever our military support of a friend endangers an important negotiation.

Again, the most acute case is that of the Middle East: the promise of AWACS to Saudi Arabia, a kind of substitute for a Middle East policy and a step toward the elusive strategic consensus, obliged the administration to try to reassure Israel by acceding to a deal of strategic cooperation with Begin. This in turn obliged Washington to try to assuage the Saudis by an all-out commitment in the AWACS fight, by an attempt at minimizing the significance of the agreement with Israel, and by saying a few kind words about the Saudi peace plan. This, of course, angered the Israelis, who reacted by annexing the Golan Heights. Reagan's decision to suspend the strategic accord with Israel and Israel's own reaction to this have exposed both the hollowness of the strategic consensus and the incompatibility between, on the one hand, the kind of military support of Israel which the accord symbolized and, on the other, sustaining a peacemaking process to resolve the Israel-Arab conflict.

Similarly, campaign commitments to Taiwan and the later promise to help China arm have displeased both sides. Indonesians and Indians worry about possible American supplies of arms to China, even though no such agreement has yet been completed, and relations between Beijing and Washington are cooler than at any time since 1971, even though nothing has yet been decided about Taiwan. America's new arms sales to Pakistan, justified by the Soviet threat on the borders between Pakistan and Afghanistan, are of a sufficient scale to worry India and reinforce Delhi's ties with Moscow.[2] The Reagan administration's enthusiasm for the military junta in Turkey has made relations with the new Greek government very difficult indeed. Its support for the Duarte government has collided with its attempt to negotiate a *modus vivendi* with Nicaragua and, as under Carter, its military aid to Morocco hinders a negotiated settlement of the Western Sahara dispute.

In the second place, the attempt to put pressure on states considered to be secondary troublemakers or proxies for the Soviet Union has often led to two bad results. It has either functioned as a self-fulfilling prophecy or conferred a kind of Robin Hood prestige on our targets. Denouncing the Cubans' aid to revolutionary forces in Central America and the Sandinistas' drift toward authoritarianism and repression has not helped the United States gain much support from Latin American countries (not even from those, like Venezuela, who support the Duarte government in El Salvador). And it has neither stopped the Cubans nor deterred the Sandinistas. Asking for the repeal of the Clark amendment and staging meetings with Savimbi won't exactly persuade the Angolan government to throw out its Cuban protectors, just as persisting in supporting Pol Pot will do nothing to loosen Hanoi's ties with Moscow. The recent campaign against Libya has not been endorsed by America's allies, and it makes it more difficult for the Arab moderates—who fear and loathe Qaddafi—to act against him. For a great power to put smaller ones into the headlines in the Reagan manner is to elevate their nuisance value into might and to provide them with a kind of vicarious glamour.

In the third place, in El Salvador as in the Middle East, the United States has committed itself to supporting regimes of dubious solidity, and it is not always clear (as in the case of the president's vague and blanket promise not to allow Saudi Arabia to become a second Iran) whether we plan to defend them against external threats only, or also against domestic ones. Egypt, the Sudan, Saudi Arabia, and Pakistan are all countries whose regimes face a host of internal and external dangers. The problem with the broad but vague commitments the administration has been making is double: they exceed our means and they are sure to give a needlessly anti-American impetus to domestic opposition forces. They make the United States appear both as the champion of a frequently ugly status quo (as in El Salvador), and as a kind of neo-imperial bully—or sheriff—that extends its heavy protection even to some who didn't ask for it. This is a perfect recipe for becoming, in effect, the dependent of a reluctant client, whom we must keep helping so that he remains obliged to us.

III.

There is a more reassuring side: a process of adaptation to reality has been intermittently noticeable. Two major discoveries explain it. First, the administration has been obliged to recognize that axioms five and six, about the readiness of others to follow us in our new crusade, were plainly wrong. It found itself caught, therefore, in a contradiction between what it thought its mandate meant, and the need to safeguard America's alliances and friendships. Second, American politicians, eager not to let America be pushed around any more, and keen about a stronger defense, nevertheless turned out to be far less enthusiastic about either the Carter MX basing mode or the participation of American forces in wars abroad: strength is fine, as a way of not having to use it.

The public's response to the original campaign raising alarms about El Salvador was negative, and part of the coolness in the press and in the opinion polls toward the AWACS sale came from the memory of arms sales to the shah. In other words, the "Vietnam syndrome" has left some traces: axiom ten, positing an eagerness to display national strength, was only partly true. It is perhaps not surprising that the State Department should have been particularly sensitive to the dismay of allies and friends abroad, as the Defense Department and the White House were to the coolness of the public here.

Indeed, it is the State Department that has initiated a return to reality in two matters where other countries had manifested their displeasure. One is Namibia. While some in the Pentagon and White House saw in South Africa a rich potential ally against Moscow, Haig and Assistant Secretary Chester Crocker, impressed by Lord Soames's achievement in Zimbabwe and by the arguments of our European partners, and aware of the need for support from the black African states that protect and promote the South West African People's Organization (SWAPO), have tried to find a solution that entails some concessions to Pretoria but no sacrifice of essential principles. It is too early to know whether the attempt will succeed, and whether, here also, the friendly attitude of the Reagan administration toward the South Africans, which has encouraged them to raid their neighbors repeatedly, will not prove incompatible with a settlement for Namibia; but clearly, so far, realism has prevailed over dogmas such as the division between good moderates and dangerous radicals.

The other matter is the theater nuclear forces in Europe. The administration's tepid endorsement of the arms control part of the December 1979 NATO decision to deploy new weapons had to be turned—when the advice of European leaders could no longer be ignored—into a ringing endorsement of arms control in Reagan's November 18 speech. The United States has thus temporarily regained the diplomatic initiative: "option zero" happens to be exactly what many of the Western European demonstrators— and their governments as well—would like. Moreover, in the process, Washington has given up its original, disastrous, intention of linking arms control negotiations to Soviet good behavior generally.

The White House and the Pentagon have also been eager to accommodate American political opinion in such decisions as the abandonment of the mobile MX scheme and the lifting of the grain embargo, and through repeated assurances that ground forces would not be sent to fight in Central America.

However, at the end of Reagan's first year, one is struck by two facts. The first is the frequent incoherence that results from the tug of war between ideology and reality, between assertion and accommodation. The second is the absence of a genuine foreign policy in a number of important spheres, because of the wide gap between Reagan's dogmas and the world.

Part of the incoherence in the foreign policy machine results from divisions between those (often in the White House and the National Security Council or in the Defense Department) who resent our allies' independence and recalcitrance and remain true believers in something like an American crusade, and those (often in the State Department) who are willing to take into account the scope of our allies' worries and fears and who are aware of the gap between the way in which the allies see their own interests and the way in which the decalogue assumes they must define these interests.

A policy toward the Soviet Union that is based on a particularly alarmist view of Soviet behavior yet avoids reestablishing the draft, despite the stated magnitude of the threat, and lifts the grain embargo, despite the absence of any Soviet concession or retreat, is not very impressive. Nor is a military program that provides for a B-1 of questionable usefulness and for a vulnerable MX placed in existing silos—just threatening enough to tempt Soviet preemption, yet incapable of coping with the fatuously proclaimed "window of vulnerability," although satisfying the citizens and politicians of Utah and Nevada.

The administration also proposes the construction of cruise missiles to be put on submarines, perhaps because of an expectation that the ground-launched cruise missiles planned for deployment in Europe will either not be deployed or will be reduced by arms control agreements; but this plan thereby gives a powerful and valid argument to demonstrators who deny the need for the ground-launched missiles, and who consider them to be far more dangerous for Western Europe (which they are supposed to protect) than sea-based cruise missiles. And it makes the arms control negotiations more difficult.

Nor can much be said for a policy in Central America that is just blustery enough to discourage Duarte from negotiating with his adversaries, as well as to reinforce the suspicions or paranoia of the Sandinistas about American intervention or subversion. (We have, after all, canceled economic aid, asked for specific ceilings on the Nicaraguan army, and allowed enemies of the Sandinistas to engage in military training in the United States.)

DEAD ENDS

Yet this policy is not capable of either stopping the flow of arms to the left in El Salvador or helping the Duarte government to win its war and stop the terror of the right wing paramilitary forces. Nor is there much to be said for a policy that praises the Saudi peace plan just enough to harden the Israeli position during the last phase of the Camp David process and to encourage the Saudis to submit a doomed scheme for settlement to their Arab friends, rivals, and foes. Especially after Israel's strong reaction, the U.S. endorsement was so weak it ensured the failure of the Saudi plan at the Arab summit in Morocco. The episode was a miracle of bad timing, both in Washington and in Riyadh.

Coherence and clarity do not characterize the Reagan policies on human rights and nuclear proliferation either. On human rights, adaptation to reality has begun, with the appointment of an official in the State Department more plausible than Mr. Lefever, and with the recognition that a human rights policy cannot either be superseded by the fight against international terrorism or simply ignore the crimes of "merely authoritarian" systems friendly to the United States. The famous distinction between unchanging totalitarianism and perfectible, limited authoritarianism has been badly battered by reality. A regime's brutality cannot be inferred from its "essence"; in Poland, we have seen a would-be totalitarian government having great trouble in its struggle to control society and to prevent change. The vicious current attempt at "normalization," that is, at wiping out not only Solidarity's gains but also the other liberties tolerated in the 1970s, results less from the essence of the Polish regime than from the pressures of the Soviet Big Brother and the intimidating role of the Red Army. Without these pressures a weak and demoralized Communist Party of Poland would probably have succumbed to the popular wave for freedom and renewal, and not entrusted its own survival to the Polish army. On the other hand, some authoritarian regimes, such as Argentina's, continue to remain beyond fundamental reform.

Moreover, the purpose of a human rights policy is not to change a regime, but to ensure a basic floor of rights for all. As long as the main purpose of the policy remains one of crudely showing up the Soviets and as long as the policy is treated as a cold war propaganda instrument, it is difficult to figure out what it will amount to, especially when security assistance and loans continue to be granted unconditionally to "friendly" governments engaged in violations of human rights.

Indeed, having made of effectiveness as anti-Soviet propaganda the criterion of its policy instead of effectiveness as an instrument for change or a price imposed for intolerable wrongdoing, the Reagan administration found itself caught short when the Polish tragedy took the form not of an invasion but of a ruthless assault on human rights by the Polish army and

162

police. For no thought had been given in advance to the kinds of measures that ought to have been taken in order either to induce the military dictatorship to restore essential freedoms or to punish it for not doing so, or to the need to coordinate such measures with the allies. (The government's embarrassment, or the paucity of effective measures, should of course not stop private citizens, professional associations of every sort, and the press and television from expressing their outrage and their solidarity with the Polish nation.) Effective or not, the sanctions applied to Poland and the Soviet Union point up the difference between the treatment of the Soviets or their allies and the lenient attitude toward delinquent friends.

As for nonproliferation, it was the Israeli raid on Iraq that gave the administration the necessary push to define a policy—against creating new weapons facilities—after its initial indifference (and criticism of Carter's zeal). But in the case of Pakistan, a test case par excellence, the decalogue has prevailed.

The most disturbing conclusion concerns the almost complete absence of a coherent policy to deal with several major issues. There is no satisfactory policy toward the economic demands of the countries of the South. Dogma has been maintained here in toto—and has led to American demands for a revision of the draft treaty on the law of the seas, at the request of mining companies (and despite the protests of the Pentagon, whose interests the draft safeguards). While the economic conditions in the advanced nations make concessions to the demands for a "new international economic order" unlikely, many of America's allies, both among the developing and among the industrial nations, are unhappy with America's lack of response and its apparent belief that the market, or existing international financial mechanisms, will be able to cope with the formidable problems caused by the slowing down of growth in the industrialized countries and the financial plight of many of the developing countries.

The failure to consider the internal or regional causes of conflicts—as in El Salvador and Guatemala—and the tendency to concentrate on the cold war aspects—except in Namibia—have also helped to produce the present crisis with Greece (because of the long-festering and long-neglected Cyprus dispute) and above all to a complete policy vacuum in the Arab-Israeli conflict. To put it bluntly, American policy in 1981 has consisted of trying to gain time through questionable weapons sales, and through Philip Habib's excellent management of the crisis over Lebanon in the summer.

But the time thus gained has not been well used. The administration has not tried to give some meaning and chances to the only process to which it is committed—Camp David—by appointing a successor to Mssrs. Strauss and Linowitz and by seeking to obtain from the Israelis an autonomy scheme for the West Bank that could appeal to the Palestinians who live there (one sine qua non being an end to Sharon's settlements policy). Nor has it prepared a new plan for the period after April 1982, when all the fruits of Camp David will have been consumed, and when Egypt will probably try to build bridges to the other Arab states.

In a sense, Sadat was a casualty of an American policy that both contributed to increasing the strains of modernization and to raising excessive expectations of prosperity within Egypt, and failed to help him with his gamble on the momentum of peace abroad. Begin's annexation of the Golan Heights showed the lengths he is prepared to go to test and embarrass the Egyptian government as well as to take advantage of the Reagan administration's passivity toward peacemaking. His moves actually make it more obvious than ever that the Camp David process cannot go beyond the restoration of peace between Israel and Egypt, more certain than before that Egypt will, after April, seek to rejoin the Arab side, and more likely that the Arabs will try to overcome their divergences. Creating a more promising policy is of the highest importance. It would have to be prepared in cooperation with the so-called moderate Arabs—the Saudis, Jordanians, and Egyptians—and, through them, with the PLO, as well as with the Western Europeans. And it would require a willingness to confront Begin—not only to stop him from impeding peace but also to push him toward a settlement. There is no trace of any such preparations so far.

The biggest void remains where it was under Carter—what I once described as the hole in the middle of the doughnut: a long-range policy toward the Soviet Union. Reagan, in the beginning, seemed to offer only two prospects—confrontations in the near future (given the axioms about Soviet expansionism and American determination) and, in the long term, a Soviet acceptance of "moderation," caused by successful containment and the costs of the arms race to Moscow. This was exactly the vision of Acheson and Dulles. But it was a utopia, not a policy; the Soviets have often demonstrated their refusal to endorse our concept of stability, and their ability to leap over (or sneak under) the barriers of containment and to embarrass Washington by exploiting crises in which the United States finds itself on the losing side, on the wrong side, or incapable of acting.

Moreover, while American economic resources far exceed the Soviets', a game of chicken over armaments is a risky one for us: just as—despite Herman Kahn's predictions—we cried "ouch" before the North Vietnamese did, the Soviets' ability in peacetime to squeeze consumers and to shift resources to the military is far greater than that of the United States. Unlimited arms races, like deflationary policies, provoke the anguish of the voters long before the promised success materializes.

The need for a policy has never been greater. A vista of recurring confrontations provides no inspiration for American allies—eager as they are to preserve a mixed relationship, not a purely adversary one, with the Soviet Union—or even for the American people. West German resistance to a policy of pure confrontation, Japanese resistance to American pressure for a greater defense effort, and the American public's own continuing support for arms control show this very clearly.

Moreover, the evolution of nuclear armaments is exactly as disturbing as George Kennan tells us.[3] The distinctions that made arms control agreements possible and reliable—between strategic and tactical, conventional and nuclear, weapons—are getting blurred. The coming vulnerability of land-based missiles will force both sides to choose (in the absence of arms control) between costly, internally disruptive, and fanciful (or nightmarish) attempts at mobility and the kind of jitters that lead to thoughts of preemptive strikes. The coming proliferation of cruise missiles will heighten insecurity all around. We will be living increasingly in an absurd world, in which there will be too many uncertainties to be sanguine about the ability to keep war limited if nuclear weapons are used, and in which this danger is likely to keep such weapons from being used even though conflicts, armed and unarmed, will persist. The accumulation of nuclear arms will thus be both a huge waste and a potential calamity.

Finally, political and economic conditions in this world, and particularly in many of the countries that are currently our friends or clients, in Africa, Latin America, or Asia, are such that some understandings with our chief rival about the management and limits of the competition will be essential. Indeed, it is only if such understandings develop, and if the tone, level, and nature of the contest get milder, that those armament measures that are in fact necessary (such as the strengthening of command and control procedures) will not also appear as threatening,[4] and that ultimately some liberalization of the regimes in Eastern Europe might be achieved.

A future filled with confrontations means a choice between another increasingly less plausible game of chicken—preventing Soviet advances and offsetting Soviet conventional advantages by threats of nuclear war—and the grim prospect of conventional wars all over. The incipient retreat of the administration from this ghastly prospect in November 1981 has been partially reversed by the Polish crisis, and the sum of the administration's acts does not yet amount to a policy.

The administration's hypnotic concentration on external uses of force by the Soviets and their clients—and the preparations it therefore made in case of a Soviet invasion of Poland—meant that when martial law was imposed by General Jaruzelski at the instigation of, or under threat from, Moscow, we found ourselves with inadequate means of reaction. Improvised economic sanctions against Poland risk, if they concern loans and credit, hurting the Western creditors who have engaged in a somewhat

165

mindless, and dangerously unconditional, expansion of loans to Poland in recent years. And if they concern food, sanctions risk hurting the Polish people themselves. (Indeed, can we starve the Poles while feeding the Soviets?)

As for economic sanctions against Moscow, however justified, they are being resisted or resented by our allies, whose cooperation is indispensable to the success of restrictions on the sale of industrial products or technology, and they risk leaving us without any further political instruments to use in the event of Soviet military actions in Poland (except for a total ban on trade, which would have little effect, and for one more suspension of arms control talks, which would be contrary to our interests). Never has the need for a coordinated, long-range economic policy of the Western Alliance toward the Soviet Union and Eastern Europe been greater. But it cannot be adequately defined in emergencies or case by case, for each case will then bring forth the reluctance of the Western Europeans, especially the Germans, to end the benefits they derive from their considerable trade with Eastern Europe and the Soviet Union (and also, in Bonn's case, from the Berlin agreement). But their willingness to arrive at a common policy that would provide the Soviets both with incentives for political restraint and with the certainty that intolerable acts will incur sanctions cannot be separated from a long-range political and arms control strategy acceptable to the allies, as the sharp dissonances at the end of 1981 have shown.

Whether "option zero" in the theater nuclear talks is the beginning of a bargain, or the kind of not-so-clever trick, used before, that consists of proposing something we know the Soviets will reject in order merely to demonstrate their wickedness, is also unclear. Even at best, the negotiation will be difficult, both because our bargaining position is weak and because the technical issues (especially the distinction between so-called intermediate nuclear forces and others) are formidable. The Soviets are unlikely to accept the dismantling of their intermediate missiles unless NATO agrees not only to cancel the deployment of new ground-launched missiles but also to reduce either some of its forward-based systems aimed at the Soviet Union (which we do not want to include in the current talks) or some of the planned sea-based cruise missiles which we define as strategic, not intermediate, forces.

While we are committed to resuming talks on strategic weapons, moreover, Eugene Rostow, as head of the Arms Control Administration, has made a sweeping repudiation of past efforts. He is enthusiastic for "deep" cuts, some of which—where the Soviets have an advantage—may be immensely hard to negotiate and some of which may not be to our advantage. He insists on stricter methods of verification but has not shown these to be truly necessary. Such an attitude leaves one, again, wondering whether the administration is trying to define a policy or to prove its ideological points.

During most of 1981, the Soviets' behavior was relatively prudent. They had difficulties within their own system—in Poland, in the economy, in the leadership. They were skillful rather than crude in exploiting the opportunities provided by cracks in NATO. They were evidently concerned to reassure the Islamic world after Afghanistan and not to tempt Washington to move from rhetoric to action. They continue to suffer from the intellectual rigidity that makes a new, postdétente rationale for Soviet diplomacy hard to find as well; they continue to cling to the residual hope that the Americans might climb down a bit. All of this argued for some restraint, but as we have seen in Poland, restraint in form can be deadly in substance; and even the form may not last. If opportunities for a less risky relation between the United States and the Soviet Union are not seized soon—particularly in arms control where, for instance, much could be established by a comprehensive test ban—the danger of serious crises between the superpowers, and of a widening gap between Washington and our main allies, will grow.

IV.

The reason why the administration is finding it so difficult to turn a pose into a policy is simple: no sane policy can be derived from the original decalogue. Kissinger had criticized the architects of containment for having failed to blend force and diplomacy. This is even more the case today. Either diplomacy is missing, or it tends to be the continuation of the (cold) war by other means. For a blend to succeed, the Reaganites would need first to abandon some of the most cherished assumptions that had been so useful to them on the road to power, and then to replace a simplistic view of the world with a more sophisticated one.

They would, in particular, have to replace a demonological view of the ambitions and objectives of the Soviet Union outside its sphere of imperial control—not, of course, with a Panglossian one that ignores the brutalities of the Soviet regime and of Soviet rule in Eastern Europe, but with a conception close to the balanced and by no means idealized or overindulgent view recently presented by George Kennan.[5] They would have to recognize both that a policy of military build-up and lavish arms sales creates more problems than it can ever solve and that a curtailment of arms would not, by itself, be any more a substitute for patient diplomacy dealing with the local causes of conflicts than is a policy that relies on military measures alone.

They would also have to curb the urge, so strong in this administration, toward grand unilateral action, which makes them take bold initiatives that offend or dismay the very friends and allies without whom, in the world of the 1980s, no American policy has any chance of succeeding. This is a doubly dangerous urge, since the reluctance or annoyance of our friends then gets interpreted as evidence of cowardice, blindness, or cynicism on their part, and feeds a rather ugly and illusory belief that we could somehow punish them by leaving them to their own resources and by taking care of our interests all by ourselves. Finally, the administration would have to realize that the restoration of power is only a beginning, and that the reassertion of will can be a dead end (or merely a way of making oneself feel good); for if there can be no international politics that is not about power, power is about politics, and will without the skill to use it is either foolish or dangerous.

ADDENDUM TO CHAPTER 8

Several months have gone by since this chapter, taking stock of the first year of Reagan's diplomacy, was written. What has happened since?

The resignation of Secretary of State Haig seems to have resulted from two factors. First, he appeared to have an overall conception, which was not his own, but was Kissinger's of the 1970s: he aimed at a mixed strategy toward the Soviet Union (containment and negotiations, particularly over nuclear arms); he wanted to give priority to the preservation of America's main alliances; and he wanted to oppose, by force if necessary, even limited challenges by "radicals" (for instance, by the left in El Salvador or by Nicaragua's new regime), in accordance with Kissinger's principle that one has to show oneself implacable at an early stage, even when faced by an unimportant threat, rather than allowing things to get worse. Second, he supported Israel and did not want to go beyond Camp David, if only out of hostility to the PLO's "radicalism" and Moscow's support of it. Many of these stands were in perfect conformity with the new orthodoxy's decalogue. But others were not. Haig had clashed with Reagan over the embargo of the export of gas and oil technology to the Soviet Union. Moreover, the absence of a coherent policy in the White House seemed to annoy the irascible general. And above all, he was irritated and tired out by his inability to be recognized as the "vicar" of American foreign policy. Checkmated by the new head of the National Security staff, Judge Clark, on bad terms with Mr. Reagan's chief advisors, engaged in disagreements with Mr. Weinberger and Mrs. Kirkpatrick, too eager to protect his own turf, he threatened to resign once too often. The reasons for institutional confusion have not disappeared with the arrival of George Shultz, as the firing of Eugene Rostow shows.

Substantively, the process of adaptation to reality has continued, but often in a bumpy way. It has been continuous in one case only—those already mentioned in Chapter 8: the return to nuclear negotiations in Geneva. In the case of China, a compromise Chinese-American communiqué dealing with Taiwan, which is full of ambiguities and could lead to dangerous misunderstandings and opposite interpretations in the future, has only been reached after a perfectly needless increase in tension between Washington and Peking (the time when American policy seemed to risk going too far along the road of an alliance with the Peoples' Republic of China—something I was afraid of in Chapters 4 and 6—seems to have been replaced, not by a policy of balance between Moscow and Peking, but by a policy of hostility toward Moscow and a cooling off toward Peking). The Peking-Moscow move toward a détente thus appears as a slap at Washington.

In the Middle East, the United States has finally given up both the luckless priority given to the quest for a "strategic consensus" that would line up Israel and "moderate" Arab states, and the futile attempt at being merely a mediator between the increasingly incompatible positions of Egypt and Israel in the suspended enforcement of the Camp David provisions that deal with the West Bank and Gaza. President Reagan has finally condemned Israel's annexationist policies in those areas, and clearly defined America's position about the outcome of the autonomy period, which Camp David had left dangling. It was the failure of the Carter administration to obtain a freeze on Israeli settlements and the openendedness of the autonomy process that led to the refusal by Jordan and by representatives of West Bank Palestinians to join in the process.

However, this belated recognition of realities came only after a disastrous period in which, absent any American strategy in the area, the implacable duo of Begin and Sharon imposed its own will. They had been able to exploit Reagan's basic hostility toward Soviet clients and PLO "terrorists" in order to neutralize a possible negative reaction of the United States to the invasion of Lebanon. This invasion was a double blow to American interests and policies. It meant the collapse of the precarious peace that Washington's negotiator, Philip Habib, had succeeded in shoring up, and it also led, in an otherwise divided and impotent Arab world, to collective indignation against America's passivity. As long as the United States had no other policy for the Palestinian problem than the myth of Camp David (what had been positive in it had been systematically destroyed by Begin and Sharon's policies in the occupied territories), Reagan swallowed the Israeli argument according to which the PLO's elimination from Lebanon would make a final settlement of the Palestinian problem possible.

Washington now appears to want to seize the moment, but in a direction entirely different from that of the Israeli government. Success in this attempt would be very difficult at any time, given Arab splits and Israeli obstinacy. But Israel's military victory over the PLO, its hardened policies in the occupied territories, and its occupation of much of Lebanon, are likely to make it even more unwilling to yield to America's new line. Almost four years have been wasted since the conclusion of the peace treaty between Egypt and Israel. The Reagan administration's supporters can argue that no pressure on Israel over the Palestinian issue was conceivable as long as the Sinai had not been fully returned to Egypt; this did not happen until the end of April 1982. However, the absence of any audible American protest against the Begin policies on the West Bank, and Washington's susceptibility to his anti-Soviet arguments must have encouraged Begin into believing that the invasion of Lebanon would seal the fate of the occupied territories. If the United States had made its position clear earlier, and taken its initiative immediately after the evacuation of the Sinai, the martyrdom of Beirut, of innocent Palestinians, and of much of Lebanon might have been avoided. Having waited so long, the administration had no better alternative than a public stand on most of the major issues, of the kind that inevitably produces desperate Israeli resistance, and incites the Arabs to formulate a plan of their own, different from Washington's.

In this area (as in the case of Argentina, in which many were encouraged by Mr. Reagan's "sympathy" into believing that the United States would not oppose an attempt to seize the Falkland Islands) the original ideology of the new orthodoxy has led to misunderstandings and calamities that must now, in more difficult circumstances, be overcome. The biggest obstacle now lies not, as some of the defenders of Israel's policies have said, in the extremism of the common Arab position defined at the Fez summit meeting. It would have been foolish to expect the Arab states to give up the call for an independent Palestinian state and to deprive the PLO of its status as the recognized representative of the Palestinian people (even moderate West Bank leaders recognize that this is indeed the case). The American position is, on the face of it, elastic enough in its reference to Palestinian self-government and to an association with Jordan, and firm enough in its new definition of the meaning of autonomy, to make it theoretically possible not only for Jordan to enter negotiations, but also for the PLO to allow its supporters in the occupied territories to participate in these negotiations. Nothing of this sort has been ruled out in Fez.

The real obstacle lies in the policies of Begin and Israeli Defense Minister Ariel Sharon. At present, the real dividing line is between them and the Arab consensus, the United States and its allies in Western Europe. Whether this consensus will persist and a bargaining process will develop that is acceptable to both Jordan and the PLO depends on Israeli politics, and on the firmness and dexterity with which the United States pursues its new policy.

Vagueness about the future role of the PLO in the peace process may disturb the Israeli government, but too categorical an exclusion would harden Arab reticence. Excessive pressure on Israel could consolidate Begin's power and reestablish a common front between him and American Jewish organizations whose support for him has been shaken first by his intransigence and next by the unspeakable horror of the Beirut massacre—a massacre for which the descendents of centuries of victimization created all the conditions leading to the brutal victimization of innocent and homeless Palestinians.

The king of Jordan has no incentive to negotiate over the Palestinian issue without either the consent of the PLO, or the endorsement of respected and representative West Bank leaders. The latter have no incentive to give their endorsement as long as Israel's policies in and about the occupied territories remain unchanged. Only a clear and reasonable persistence by the United States in its balanced but belated proposals, a willingness to appeal to the Israeli public (increasingly troubled by its government's excesses and increasingly tempted to accept the idea of exchanging territory for peace with security), and a determination to use pressure whenever the Begin government endangers both American long-term interests and Israel's own, will give the president's peace plan a chance, help produce a change of policies (or government) in Israel, and prove that Washington's adaptation to reality is more than momentary or verbal.

A beginning of an adaptation to reality seems also to have taken place with respect to our relations with the developing countries. The United States has, in the summer of 1982, helped Mexico avoid financial bankruptcy, and announced a somewhat reluctant willingness to allow the quotas of the International Monetary Fund (IMF) to be increased. However, it is still difficult to take seriously the pretenses of a new human rights policy and of a new antinuclear proliferation policy. In both respects, the administration's laxity continues. Countries that violate human rights still receive blessings, or have their leaders praised by and invited to Washington. The new antiproliferation policy has given up the requirement that European countries and Japan obtain a case-by-case approval for the reprocessing of fuel supplied by the United States; Washington has approved sales of nuclear materials and of sensitive equipment to South Africa and Brazil, and partially lifted the ban on the exporting of reprocessing technology.

The conflict between ideology and reality continues to plague American policy in Central America. After the right wing victory in El Salvador's elections, conflicting signals have appeared in Washington; appeals for a nonmilitary solution in El Salvador and for a dialogue with Nicaragua coexist with strong pressures and threats against the Sandinista regime, acquiescence to the policies of the Salvadoran one, and disregard of Cuban overtures. The same conflict risks affecting the administration's arms control policies. The initial proposals are obviously unacceptable to Moscow. The zero option for Europe asks the Soviets to eliminate their deployed weapons in exchange for an American decision not to deploy weapons that have already met technical difficulties and political resistance in Western Europe. In the START negotiations, we demand drastic reductions that would paradoxically leave Soviet land-based missiles vulnerable to new American weapons (the MX and Trident II), oblige the Soviets to reduce the number of warheads on their ground-launched missiles drastically (while the United States could increase slightly the number of warheads on its own), and force them to scrap almost twice as many ballistic launchers as the United States. Moreover, we maintain intact the theoretical vulnerability of America's Minuteman (the very reason for making such demands of the Soviets).[6] It is not yet clear whether these proposals are opening gambits or insurmountable obstacles.

The attempt to impose the original decalogue has led to a major political and legal crisis with the West European allies and with Japan over the sale of pipeline technology to the Soviets—a crisis resolved only by an American retreat under a face-saving formula that entails no concessions by the Allies. American unilateralism and a fundamental difference in evaluating both the effects of the deal and the function of economic relations with Moscow— the Allies want to use them for mutual gains, the Reagan administration wants to use them as a weapon in economic warfare—have led to the bizarre situation of an American government penalizing American firms, as well as Western European enterprises and workers, in a vain attempt to force the Soviets to change the Polish situation. Uncertainty concerning arms control, the conflict over oil and gas technology coming so soon after the shaky verbal agreement on an economic strategy toward Moscow at the Versailles summit meeting, Washington's indifference towards the economic effects of America's monetary policy on Europe, and the resurgence of protectionism in the case of European steel exports toward America, all have exacerbated interallied tensions. And this, in turn, affects American policy toward Moscow: without allied cooperation, the Reagan administration's hope to force the Soviet *system*—not just Soviet *behavior*—to change, by withholding economic supplies that would allow it, in a period of declining growth, to meet both its civilian and its military objectives (a dubious hope in the best of the circumstances) does not stand a chance. Indeed, and above all, there still exists no coherent strategy toward the Soviet Union.

President Reagan has renewed, for one year, the grain agreement, but imposed sanctions on oil and gas technology transfers. He has observed the SALT II provisions and called for a massive reduction of the nuclear arsenals, but also for an ideological crusade against communism; the arms build-up continues, and America's START proposals aim at obliging the Soviets to restructure their nuclear forces drastically in order to meet our conception of crisis stability, which requires the elimination of Soviet heavy land-based missiles and of much of Soviet throw-weight (but not of American cruise missiles or countersilo weapons, for instance). He appears torn between his deepest convictions and the desire to reassure the allies as much as possible, and American opinion above all. Indeed, on the eve of the midterm elections, in a country where economic recovery has not started, not only do the farmers' votes matter, but the sudden antinuclear movement provoked by too many official statements about waging and "prevailing" in a nuclear war has taken the administration by surprise and obliged it to sing the praises of arms control negotiations. This movement, kindled by books that are often more terrifying than solid, has been launched not by politicians, but by average citizens: lawyers, doctors, scientists, housewives. The ultimate direction of the administration's Soviet policy may well be deeply affected by the staying power and resourcefulness—or by the dissipation and division—of this popular surge, and by the extent to which it will be reflected in the new Congress.

As Mr. Reagan assured the legislators that human rights have improved in El Salvador, Guatemala and Chile, reassured the country that clashes with the Europeans are a mere family quarrel, explained to Arab countries that Washington does not control Israel, and proclaimed that the Soviet Union is a decaying society, one had to remember Pierre Hassner's witty remark about the competitive decadence of the superpowers. Even though today, under George Shultz, the United States is moving away from the simplistic ideology of 1980-1981, no new coherent design has appeared. What prevails is a kind of conservative pragmatism that coexists and tries to accommodate itself with the new orthodoxy's original ideology, and which reminds one of the latter part of the Eisenhower administration. But Eisenhower had a coherent view about U.S.-Soviet relations, whether it was entirely adequate or not, and very definite opinions about military "sufficiency." This is not yet Reagan's case.

Finally—and perhaps most importantly—the inability of the administration to define an economic policy that could put an end to the recession results in a gradual deterioration of the world economy: the developing countries which are deep in debt cannot pay for it with exports to the industrial countries, whose own markets are depressed and whose policy of protectionism rises; and the whole international banking system—private as well as public—is threatened by the peril of multiple defaults. The most essential adaptation to reality is the one that must take place at home.

DEAD ENDS

NOTES

1. For a more detailed analysis also in *The Nuclear Delusion* (New York: Pantheon, 1982), pp. 192-200 and Chapter 11 of this book.

2. See Selig Harrison's analysis, "Fanning the Flames in South Asia," *Foreign Policy 45* (Winter 1981-1982):84-102.

3. George Kennan, "On Nuclear War," *The New York Review of Books* (January 21, 1982):8-12.

4. John D. Steinbruner, "Nuclear Decapitation," *Foreign Policy 45* (Winter 1981-1982):16-28.

5. Kennan, "On Nuclear War."

6. See Leon S. Sigal, "Warming to the Freeze," *Foreign Policy* (Fall 1982):54-66; and Jan M. Lodal, "Finishing START," *Foreign Policy* (Fall 1982):66-81.

PART III

THE WESTERN ALLIANCE IN TURMOIL

T HE THREE essays in this section examine the difficulties in relations between the United States and Western Europe since the end of 1979. They emphasize the divergences toward the Soviet Union: disagreements in evaluating Soviet behavior and disagreements over policy. They also study the area that has, in the past, always been the most contentious—nuclear weapons placed in Europe for the deterrence of Soviet aggression or of Soviet political pressure. The issue of new NATO deployments of inter-mediate nuclear forces remains, potentially, one of the most explosive.

Concerning the first theme, what is at stake is the future possibility of détente. For a while, Western Europe seemed to cling to its own détente with the Soviet Union with almost excessive energy, and some blindness. This was partly due to a certain parochialism, and partly to a reaction against the equally abrupt and excessive American repudiation of any sort of mixed relationship with the Soviet Union. This particular conflict is still very much with us, despite some estrangement between the West Europeans and the Soviet Union (largely because of the sinister events in Poland in December 1981) and despite the Reagan administration's gradual accep-tance of arms negotiations with the Soviet Union. The predictable bone of contention remains the nature and range of economic relations between the Soviets and the West Europeans, although, in this area, the United States offers a singular example of inconsistency, given its persistent grain sales to Moscow.

Concerning the antinuclear movement in Europe, the proclamation of martial law in Poland, which came shortly after my essay on nuclear weapons for NATO was written, has dampened the fervor of the demonstrators. The American decision to negotiate with the Soviet Union and to propose the removal of all Soviet SS-20s in exchange for cancelling the planned deployments of NATO has also contributed to this. A shift to the right in Holland and West Germany, where Helmut Schmidt's coalition has disintegrated, may also appear to have helped the supporters of NATO's 1979 position. But the antinuclear movement is far from dead and might be revived both by internal developments, if—especially in West Germany—the nuclear issue becomes a dividing line between pro-NATO governments and the opposition (rather than one that divides the government itself) and by external developments, should the INF negotiations get nowhere before the end of 1983, when the deployments are scheduled to begin.

Two questions concerning the future of U.S.-European relations are dealt with implicitly in these esssays. First, are the difficulties of the alliance radically new by comparison with the innumerable troubles of the past? It is clear that the scope of disagreements has gotten much bigger in recent years, partly because of the increased importance of conflicts outside of the geographical area of NATO—conflicts over which Washington and the allies disagree—and partly because there are now serious divergencies concerning what can be called the heart of the alliance: defense and economic cooperation. It is also clear that the methods of the Reagan administration have exasperated Western Europe: the "benign neglect" of the effects of America's financial and economic policies on Europe's recession, as well as the unilateral imposition of embargoes in a vital area of Soviet-West European economic cooperation, pressure against Europe's farm policies, and the protectionist measures affecting European steel exports. Commentators in Western Europe can be forgiven for writing that the Reagan administration has been waging economic warfare against its allies as well as against Moscow—by pursuing an internal economic strategy that seems calculated to force European governments to choose between adopting a similar one or else facing ruin, by attacking the European Economic Community's policies, and by trying to impose its theories about East-West trade. On the other hand, the closeness of the economic links across the Atlantic and Western Europe's continuing need for an American nuclear and conventional commitment to its defense suggest that the alliance will survive.

Second, what is the ability of the Europeans to increase their own cooperation, partly in reaction to the new American assertiveness? In the past, American pressure has often succeeded in preventing the various nations in Western Europe from coalescing. For instance, the United States succeeded to a large extent in isolating de Gaulle by consolidating its ties with West Germany. There has never been perfect coordination of the foreign policies of the main countries in Western Europe (this has been seen time and again in the Middle East); and, of course, domestic cooperation within the European Community during the years of recession has been extremely disappointing. However, in the case of America's pressure against the construction of the pipeline that would link Western Europe to the Soviet Union, there has been a remarkable convergence between the main Western European countries whose economic interests and political analysis were being challenged by Washington. In a recent book, James Goldborough describes a new assertiveness in Western Europe and, above all, new habits of cooperation that make the often divided members of the community into much more of an entity than in the past.[1] He may well be right, and America's opportunities for splitting Western Europe will be smaller than in the past. On the other hand, there has been no progress at all toward a substantial discussion by the Western Europeans of the possibilities for a common defense system in Western Europe, and the political developments in various European countries might once again lead to estrangement rather than to closer cooperation. Neither question can be answered decisively.

NOTE

1. James Goldborough, *Rebel Europe* (New York: Macmillan, 1982).

CHAPTER 9

THE CRISIS IN THE WEST

I.

SIX MONTHS after the Soviet invasion of Afghanistan, and seven months after the seizure of American hostages in Iran, American foreign policy is faced with a protracted, often acrimonious crisis with its European allies, and stuck in a deadlock with its chief rival. And the choices that confront the United States seem to be either more of the same, or far worse.

The Atlantic alliance has never been smooth. Its structure alone generates trouble. It is an alliance between one preponderant state and a number of middle and small powers, several of which are engaged—on the side, so to speak—in an experiment in economic integration and political cooperation of their own. Consultation has always been a headache; it works best when all are in agreement, that is, when it is least necessary. Let us only remember the interminable inter-allied battle over West German rearmament, which derailed European integration, and the Suez crisis.

There are substantive reasons for trouble as well. Dependence on the American nuclear guarantee and on the presence of American forces in Europe breeds as many doubts and fears as it gives assurances. Separated from the United States by an ocean, from the Soviet Union merely by an iron curtain, the Western Europeans have always been anxious about American intentions and actions. They have oscillated between the fear of being drawn into a world war by American imprudence and the fear of being abandoned, or—worse still—of being "defended" in a conventional war that would destroy Europe while sparing the two superpowers.

DEAD ENDS

The economic recovery of the Western European half-continent has pointed up the sharp contrast between European success in industry and trade and European military dependence on the United States; the intense economic interdependence between Europe and the United States has created mutual dissatisfaction over monetary practices (remember America's indignation toward de Gaulle's conversion of dollars into gold, and more recently Bonn's anger against Carter's failure to stop the decline of the dollar in 1977-1978) and over economic policies (each side counting on the other for the preservation of a high level of growth).

Finally, Western Europe's dependence on Middle Eastern oil has contributed to the alliance's troubles, both because it has introduced an element of economic dependence on the United States' behavior—America's rising oil imports and the slide of the dollar having strengthened the hand of OPEC and led to new price increases—and because it has made the Europeans more sensitive than Washington to the political desiderata of the Arab countries.

To these permanent sources of tension, new ones have been added by three sets of recent changes. The first is the evolution of the foreign policies of Paris, Bonn, and London in the 1970s. The "big three" of Western Europe have sought a foreign policy that would give them the best of all possible worlds. West Germany has moved from total reliance on Washington for defense and diplomacy, and dependence on its Western European partners for moral rehabilitation, to the successful liquidation of its own special Eastern problems (Berlin, the Oder-Neisse line, the issue of partition) and to a preponderant financial position in the European Community. France has moved from de Gaulle's fierce pursuit of independence from Washington (under the American nuclear umbrella) to a complex policy of military autonomy with collaboration with NATO, détente with activism in Africa, Middle Eastern oil deals with a coherent national energy policy. Britain has moved from its "special relations" with Washington and the Commonwealth to contentious membership in the European Economic Community.

These shifts have had two results. In Bonn and Paris, the link with Moscow has become a major factor both in foreign (and foreign economic) policy and in domestic politics—not because of "Eurocommunism," which never existed in Germany or in France where the communist range of policies extends only from pro-Soviet to chauvinistic, but within the governing coalitions themselves. In Bonn, Paris, and London, there has been a certain detachment from the United States. In the case of Bonn (remember when a distinguished American economist talked of German-American "bigemony"?) this is because of dismay at Washington's economic policies and the absence of a consistent détente strategy. In France's case, it is because of traditional suspicions as well as new irritations (Carter being deemed too passive and soft in Africa, too passive and slow in the Middle East); in the case of Britain, because of the need to prove itself a "good European."

But there are also reasons for estrangement which exist on both sides of the Atlantic. One is a change in generations. The trans-Atlantic elite that governed in the days of John McCloy, Robert Bowie, Jean Monnet, and Walter Hallstein is gone, replaced by men who, on the European side, are much busier dealing with one another than with Washington, and on the American side have lost their early enthusiasm for or faith in European integration.

The second common reason is mutual exasperation with one another's political system. The Americans find it hard to deal with allies who are, simultaneously, crotchety separate states and partners in a formidably complex community-building enterprise—one in which foreign policy coordination and economic (including foreign economic) policy integration are handled separately. As for the Europeans, they have been watching the American political scene with increasing bewilderment. The cascade of interrupted or failed presidencies, the rivalries within the foreign policy-making process in the executive branch, the revolt and frequently destructive interventions of Congress, the dismal spectacle of the presidential campaigns, the apparent mediocrity of the political personnel, the broad swings of public opinion, have been deplored, but neither perceptively analyzed nor understood.

A second set of changes consists in the increasing importance, for the alliance, of crises that arise outside the geographical zone covered by the North Atlantic treaty. Such affairs—with the exception of the Cuban missile crisis—have always spelled trouble: Korea, Suez, Vietnam, the October war, and so forth. But these were discrete events, or—again with the exception of the Cuban missile crisis—at least they did not threaten to turn into major superpower conflagrations (by 1973, for instance, Washington and Moscow had learned how to defuse the Arab-Israeli war). In the Persian Gulf, where the two current conflicts have broken out, the Europeans fear that their two biggest nightmares might merge: the nightmare of a cutoff of oil supplies and the nightmare of a Soviet-American armed struggle into which they would be dragged. Thus, the peril is much greater than before. Here is a region of vital interest to the West and to Japan, yet equally important to the Soviet Union—just like Europe; but unlike Europe, it is also a region in which the Soviet Union enjoys enormous military advantages, and where what might be called the NATO formula—compensating for a conventional imbalance by a clear link between the West's conventional and its nuclear forces—would not be a sufficient deterrent, since the Soviets also enjoy opportunities that do not depend on military aggression, but consist in the exploitation of social unrest, ethnic conflicts, and political instability —opportunities entirely absent in Western Europe.

And yet the alliance's machinery simply does not work well for such extra-European predicaments. In 1958, Eisenhower rejected de Gaulle's idea of a French-British-American directory to define policies and strategy outside the NATO sphere, and Washington has never since been any more eager to share decisions, while frequently calling for a sharing of burdens (as in Kissinger's famous "Year of Europe" speech in April 1973).

A third set of changes lies in what could be called the alliance's crisis of pluralism. In the 1960s, de Gaulle could snipe at American power and try to deflate it a bit; there was no doubt about Washington's preponderance both in the alliance and—after the Cuban missile crisis of October 1962—over Moscow. Before the missile crisis, de Gaulle, always watchful of the world balance of power, had been more "hardline" toward Khrushchev than the Americans had been. But there has been a change both in the respective power positions and in the respective interests of the Americans and the Europeans.

Concerning power, America's predominance has declined (with respect to the Soviets, to OPEC, and, economically, to Western Europe and Japan); and America's still considerable power cannot be said to have been brilliantly managed by the Carter administration. Western Europe, on the other hand, has broadened its concerns, and begun to behave more like an entity; there is now a common foreign economic policy, an important series of agreements with many developing countries in Africa, the Pacific, and the Caribbean, and an incipient common foreign policy. In the Sixties, except for the French, the other Europeans always consulted Washington before taking diplomatic stands (and they abstained from taking any when Washington disapproved). This is no longer the case. Western Europe also has some impressive leaders. Yet it cannot replace the United States as the dominant power in the alliance because of a lack of military resources, dependency on oil imports, and the persistent imperfections of cooperation among the members of the European Community (shockingly illustrated by Britain's recent aboutface on sanctions against Iran, a result of Parliament's revolt, and by Giscard's futile journey to Warsaw, in flagrant contradiction to his own goal of fostering greater foreign policy unity among the Europeans, in May 1980).

The deepest reason for Europe's inability to lead is, however, a certain habituation to dependence, a cozy belief that the risks and responsibilities of world politics belong to Washington alone, a failure of will and a shrinking of ambition that create a gap, not, as Kissinger once said, between America's "global" interests and Europe's "regional" ones, but between Europe's world-wide concerns and its timidity of ambition. Thus there is a

182

formidable crisis of leadership: Washington's is handicapped, Western Europe's is reluctant or absent. The European habit of criticizing America still flourishes; but recriminations are now more destructive, given the change in power and the divergence of interests.

This divergence is manifest precisely in the two nightmare realms I have mentioned. One is East-West relations. The United States and its allies have all practiced détente, but the Europeans have traveled on a different road. On the one hand, the Europeans have gone much farther in the direction of economic and humanitarian exchanges, as in the reuniting of Eastern Europeans with their families in West Germany. Détente has thus created a network of interests, tying the Western Europeans not only to Moscow but also to the Eastern Europeans (and in Bonn's case, particularly to the East Germans). It has also given both the Western Europeans and several of the Eastern European countries some greater leeway, either in world affairs or in domestic politics, alleviating the burden of their respective Big Brothers' preponderance, and allowing the EEC countries to pay more attention to North-South relations. Hence there is on the part of most of the Western Europeans a strong desire to protect their newly won turf and to limit whatever damage the eagle and the bear could inflict on it.

As the Allies' decision to increase their military budgets and to deploy new theater nuclear forces, and the determined French effort to increase France's military power show, this desire has much less to do with a craven wish to accommodate the strongest, with a resurgence of the Munich atavism, than with a yearning to preserve material but also spiritual and political gains. This may appear short-sighted or naive to Americans, yet it is perfectly honorable in its inspiration, Walter Laqueur notwithstanding. On the other hand, the Western Europeans, who have not taken serious steps toward arms control yet, see in arms control the best insurance against a disastrously escalating arms race, and are utterly dependent on the superpowers' willingness to keep this road open.

As for the Middle East, there too a divergence of interests has appeared. Largely for domestic reasons, none of the Western European countries has the peculiar relationship with Israel that exists between Tel Aviv and Washington. Committed to the survival and security of Israel, they are much more likely to see in Israel's own policies toward the Palestinians, or toward Lebanon, the main threat to its ultimate security than has been the case in the United States. Moreover, within the Arab world, Washington and its allies have developed different clienteles: Washington has been relying increasingly on Egypt, and now on Oman. The French have relied above all on Iraq, and more recently on Algeria—regimes that are altogether more radical in ideology, more anti-American, and hostile to the Camp David approach. As for Iran, while all the allies had supported the shah, the Western

Europeans never had with him the intense military and advisory relationship that led to the sweeping Americanophobia of the Khomeini revolution; and they tend to look at the Iranian drama as America's problem.

II.

This is the background of the present crisis in the alliance. What follows is, inevitably, an oversimplification. There are in Western Europe differences among countries, along familiar lines. For example, the German-American defense ies are far tighter than those between Paris and Washington; British diplomacy is more anti-Soviet, at least in rhetoric; the French insistence on independence and excommunication of "blocs" is as noisy as ever, and so forth. And there are differences within each country: between government branches (Lord Carrington is less strident than Mrs. Thatcher, the Quai d'Orsay is not of a single opinion), between parties, within parties, and so forth. However, one can describe a kind of average Western European view, and compare it with American opinions.

Interestingly enough, the Western European view of the Soviet Union is not too different from the average American one (vintage 1980). Europeans and Americans recognize a change in the world situation. There is now nuclear parity; the Soviets have carried out a military build-up that has aggravated the regional imbalance in Europe, especially in tanks and long-range theater nuclear forces; and turbulence in the Third World provides Moscow with tempting opportunities. The Soviet Union is seen as a source of great dangers. It now has the ability to project its power far from its borders, and it has shown its readiness to destroy what had seemed to be one of the accepted rules of the game by sending a large invasion force outside the "zone of Yalta." It may be eager to tilt the "correlation of forces" in the world in its direction again by the use of armed might, or by setting up regimes that will call for Soviet forces—and, unlike Sadat, will neither want nor be able to throw these out later.

Moreover, the 1980s may be a period of difficulties for a Soviet Union that will face a succession crisis (or two), a slowdown of its economic growth, and perhaps a shortage of oil. This might tempt Soviet leaders even more to play their one and only strong card, the military one—and to seek in foreign successes a diversion from domestic tensions.[1] Especially in view of current claims to the contrary, it is important to point out that there is little evidence, in Western Europe, of a benevolent view of the Soviet Union, outside the French Communist party.

THE CRISIS IN THE WEST

However, the average Western European view is different from the average American one, on a number of central issues. First, with respect to the diagnosis. Americans and Europeans agree on the implications of the Soviet presence in Afghanistan for the Persian Gulf region—for Pakistan and Iran in particular. But Americans seem more willing to attribute to the Soviets the intention of pushing beyond their present prey; and many American officials believe that the Soviets did not miscalculate in Afghanistan—that they expected the immediate American reaction to be strong, the Western alliance to be strained, and Third World countries (and some of America's allies, as well) sooner or later to reconcile themselves to the fait accompli. The Western Europeans are less willing to accept the worst-case hypothesis, more likely to see in the invasion a local (if "unacceptable") affair, and to believe that Moscow misjudged the resilience of Afghan resistance and the effect that the spectacle of Soviet brutality and lack of swift success would have on Soviet influence abroad.

Second, there is a difference in prescriptions for the short run. American politicians and diplomats tend to believe that sanctions were necessary even if they weren't going to get the Soviets out of Afghanistan, because they would show the Russians that we care enough about their aggression to inflict pain and costs on ourselves. The Europeans believe that sanctions that do not much hurt the Soviet Union but hurt us (especially in the case of SALT II) are likely only to exacerbate the Soviets' national pride, to make them less, not more, accessible to reason or moderation, to limit the margin of maneuver of the Eastern Europeans, and to worsen the position or change the disposition of that segment of the Soviet elite that has an interest in closer relations with the West.

Moreover, for the reasons given earlier, our allies are eager to declare détente divisible and to protect the net of European-Soviet agreements, which, they say, should be endangered or sacrificed only if the Soviets move in Europe or mount a major assault on détente elsewhere. Like George Kennan in this country, they argue against overkill—what sanctions will remain available in a major case if the United States exhausts its supply in this instance? This stems from prudence, not cowardice. However, the Americans reply, not without justification, that the European case is tantamount to ruling out sanctions over Afghanistan altogether, that an unwillingness to take risks can only incite the Soviet Union to more salami tactics, and that the Western Europeans—but not the Soviets—have become hostages to their network of deals.

On the other hand, the Europeans are eager for a negotiated solution leading to a Soviet withdrawal from Afghanistan. Lord Carrington's proposal for such a solution, endorsed by his European partners, was launched without consulting Washington, just as Washington had initiated the Olympic boycott without consulting its allies. The Americans are skeptical of negotiating in a region where the balance of power favors Moscow, and fearful that any bargain struck in such circumstances would legalize and legitimize the puppet regime of Babrak Karmal.

Third, and most importantly, there is disagreement over long-term prognosis and prescription. With respect to the Persian Gulf, while the Europeans recognize the seriousness of the military situation and the need to inject more military power, they remain skeptical of the Carter doctrine approach, which they deem militaristic and simplistic in two ways. It seems to demand of all countries in the area that they align themselves with Washington once again, that is, to impose a strict choice between East and West, instead of recognizing that it is nonalignment that should be bolstered because it constitutes the best obstacle to Soviet advances. And the American approach neglects all the factors and forces, other than the military balance, that explain the predicament of the United States in the Persian Gulf and can be neither suppressed nor superseded by force alone, such as the Arab-Israeli conflict, or the internal weaknesses of the Saudi regime, or the Iranian internal turmoil.

With respect to East-West relations, the Western Europeans, on the whole, remain convinced of the mutual benefits of trade, and reject the current American view that transfers of credit, trade, and technology only build up the Soviet war machine. And they remain far more convinced than the Americans of the possibility of influencing Soviet behavior, and perhaps even the conflict of factions within the Soviet leadership, by contacts, exchanges, and negotiations—whereas Americans seem to have reverted to George Kennan's view of thirty-four years ago that Moscow is "inaccessible to considerations of reality in its basic reactions" and can be stopped only by barriers of containment.

The gap can best be described by referring to the game of historical analogies. Each side mentions 1914, but not in the same way. Americans compare Soviet Russia and Imperial Germany—each one a power with world-wide ambitions, a determination to be accepted as co-equal of Number One (the United States and Britain respectively), and a brutal policy clumsy enough to antagonize those whose friendship it claimed it wanted, and to provoke the encirclement it feared. Europeans compare the two camps of today and the two alliances of 1914—each one fearful that things would get worse unless it acted now, and each one complacently convinced that the other side should find it easier to back down.

To the Europeans, Washington's view of 1914 suggests that war is the only way to curb Moscow, just as it was the only way to cut down German expansionism. To the Americans, the Europeans' view of 1914 means that

—as in the 1930s—they are in effect willing to appease Moscow's expansionism; they forget that appeasement only leads to conflagration in ever more disadvantageous circumstances. To the Americans, if the Europeans failed to react strongly to as clearcut an aggression as the recent Soviet one, what are the chances of their standing up in cases that may well be more ambiguous (say, a Soviet intervention at the request of an Iranian government)? To the Europeans, if Americans overreact in this instance, aren't they going to push the Soviets onto a collision course that could still be averted by a wider policy?

In Washington, it is common for experts to see signs of Finlandization and marks of "Euro-neutralism." The Europeans deny the charges, but blame Washington for wild zigzags and short-sightedness. Indeed, at the heart of the present crisis we find not merely different conceptions of how to deal with the Soviet problem but profound European exasperation with the Carter administration, its inconsistencies, its lack of a sense of priorities, its insensitivity both to allies (as in its economic policies, or in its nonproliferation drive, or in some aspects of its human rights campaign) and to its chief rival (as in the handling of SALT and of the "China card"), its inability to step out of the triangular cage it had built at Camp David with Begin and Sadat, and its wide swings of policy over the American hostages in Iran.

III.

What are the prospects for better American-European cooperation? They depend, essentially, on the choices the United States will make concerning the Soviet Union.

In the short run, there is no cause for optimism. On the one hand, the Carter administration has, here also, locked itself in its own cage. By linking the ratification of SALT II to Soviet behavior in Afghanistan, Carter has made it very difficult for himself to follow Cyrus Vance's pressing advice in his admirable Harvard 1980 commencement speech. In order to bring the treaty back before the Senate, he would have to reverse himself and to look as if he retreated before Moscow's will (as in the foolish case of the Soviet brigade in Cuba in 1979); moreover, even if he did, or if Muskie persuaded him to do so, it is unlikely that the Senate would comply. The economic sanctions having also been tied to Afghanistan, a redefinition of our economic relations with Moscow cannot be undertaken now either. As for the enforcement of the Carter doctrine, it remains impaired, not so much by the absence of the famous Quick Deployment Force as by the

187

failure of the Camp David process, the interminable crisis with Iran, and the rejection by Pakistan of America's offers of assistance.

On the other hand, a resolution of the Afghanistan crisis, which is the necessary prerequisite to an improvement in U.S.-Soviet relations, is exceedingly hard to envisage. The Soviets, in some respects, are as stuck as the Americans were in Vietnam. They seem to have three bad choices available. They can stay there, fighting a long guerrilla war and destroying the country, along with the chance for better relations with Washington or with Moslem countries. They can try (like the French at Suez during the Algerian War) to crush the Afghanistan rebellion by attacking its bases outside Afghanistan, for instance in Pakistan, thus widening the war in the mistaken belief that the resistance has no indigenous bases. Or they can negotiate a way out. But they have made it clear that they want to leave behind a safe and "friendly" regime, and yet the longer the war lasts the smaller is the possibility of finding a "Finnish" solution: all those who are not pro-Soviet will be anti-Soviet, and no pro-Soviet regime will be able to stay in power without the presence of the Red Army.

If the Soviet formula for a political solution is a "broadening" of the Babrak Karmal government comparable to the notorious "broadening" of the Lublin regime in Poland after Yalta, few Afghan patriots will be attracted; yet there are no signs so far of Soviet willingness to accept a regime that is not dominated by communists (as before April 1978). And Washington can neither accept the Karmal formula of May 1980—which essentially demands the end of all foreign aid to the resistance and the recognition of its own legitimacy by its neighbors—nor try to defeat Soviet policy by escalating aid to the rebels.

For here the resemblance to Vietnam ceases; Pakistan is not a "sanctuary" comparable to North Vietnam, and any attempt by us to treat it as if it were would run into huge obstacles. Pakistan is a weak country with a shaky regime, and it could disintegrate if we tried to turn it into a kind of bastion. Its leader is reluctant—for his own good reasons—to let us do so, and has raised conditions that would jeopardize both our relations with India and out antiproliferation policy. Afghanistan, while not vital enough for the United States to run such risks, will be considered important enough to the Soviet Union for any such American attempt to provoke a violent Soviet reaction, which we are not in any position to fight without a major escalation; and this would be, once more, the wrong war in the wrong place at the wrong time.

After the American 1980 elections, the new administration will therefore find all the deadlocks unbroken. The choice is between two presidential candidates whose policies are unlikely to please the Europeans. To put it bluntly, it is a choice between two politics of nostalgia: an *apparent* return to the

Sixties versus an *apparent* return to the Fifties. The Carter foreign policy promises containment plus arms control. Carter's case for arms control rests partly on the fact that mutual interests in control do indeed exist (divergence in strategic doctrines makes it only more, not less, essential), partly on the need to accommodate the Europeans (whose endorsement of the deployment of Pershing II and cruise missiles in Europe is tied to the pursuit of arms control beyond SALT II), and partly on the belief that in the 1980s the Soviets may at last have to choose between guns and butter and will have a bigger stake in reducing their arms burden.

However, his Philadelphia formula remains simplistic. What are the long-term views of the administration on U.S.-Soviet relations? Can arms control by itself restrain Soviet competition sufficiently to prevent it from turning increasingly more bitter in various parts of the world? Unless there are other restraints as well, and kinds of cooperation, will the Congress and the public support arms control in the first place, and won't the competition turn into repeated confrontation? Lyndon Johnson was inching toward SALT when the invasion of Czechoslovakia blocked the path; it is only when it became part of a broader détente policy that arms control proceeded. Nor is there any guarantee that a second Carter administration would avoid the internal battles between its two foreign affairs agencies in the White House and the State Department that have marred the past four years. Diversity of advice is fine when the president can produce his own synthesis, or stick to his own choice. It is disastrous when he vacillates from one course to the other, or tries to straddle two paths that go in opposite directions.

What a Reagan foreign policy would be remains difficult to imagine. Presidential candidate Reagan's statements are a mixture of the fuzzy and the foolish. Sometimes, he and his advisers sound as if they wanted to go back to the good old days of Eisenhower and Dulles—America the wise leader of the worldwide alliance against communism (not just the Soviet Union). Sometimes, there are echoes of a far more aggressive and chauvinistic nationalism, à la John Connally. Between global commitments against the spread of evil, in cooperation with allies, and a fortress America mentality, there is a huge margin. However, some points emerge clearly from Reagan's statements. One is a much more militant and alarmist interpretation of Soviet behavior than that which could be called the average view of the Carter team. First, "the Soviet Union underlies all the unrest that is going on"[2] (back to dominoes, and to what the former British ambassador to Washington calls "bad regionalism")[3] and second, Moscow is likely to take advantage of the "window of opportunity" provided in the early 1980s both by the "arc of crisis" and by the vulnerability of our land-based missiles.

A second point is the need for an intensely militant response: a huge increase in the military budget (while cutting taxes!), a crash program to close that hideous window—an attempted return to superiority. A third point is a neglect of, even contempt for, diplomacy, as shown by Reagan's remarks about the Arab-Israeli conflict, his sympathy for Taiwan, his attitude toward Third World problems and crises (surely some of the new money for arms would come from the dwindling sums for economic assistance), his lack of interest in any dialogue with the Soviets (except for the kinds of substitutes for SALT II which they already rejected in 1977, and which an American drive at regaining superiority is unlikely to make more acceptable).

A fourth point is a dangerous fallacy about America's alliances. Reagan and his advisers seem to believe that the behavior of the allies is caused only by the absence of American leadership, and that as soon as America gets strong and bellows orders again, the allies will fall into line, with gratitude. It is true that they are used to American leadership, and annoyed when it lapses, but they don't want just any kind of American direction. The worldwide alliance against Moscow that Reagan offers does not tempt them at all; and in any case, instant obedience is out of the question. How a Reagan administration would react to the discovery that the alliances are not unconditional—by going it alone, which would be self-defeating, or by wise retreat, but into what?—remains unclear. Nor is it clear at all that, despite the new anti-Soviet consensus in this country, the public would support a policy that would shift resources from domestic needs to foreign priorities, that might either allow for disastrous reversals as long as we have not "regained our strength" or, more plausibly, invite confrontations everywhere and appear dangerously provocative to Moscow, where it would feed (and be taken as vindicating) the most paranoid and hardline views.

At this stage, whether in its simplistic homely form, as recited by Reagan, or in sophisticated pseudorealistic form as rationalized by Robert W. Tucker,[4] the Reagan view of the world is a rhetorical attitude, not a strategy, an act of faith, not a political design. It is what I have elsewhere called the Popeye fantasy, with military force substituting for the old sailor's spinach. Power as an alternative to skill, military power as synonymous with power, an obstinate unwillingness to acknowledge, in Vance's words, that "increased military power is a basis, not a substitute, for diplomacy," and "a pervasive fallacy that America could have the power to order the world just the way we want it to be"—these are the hallmarks of global calamity.

IV.

What can be done to avoid it? On the American side, while nothing is less conducive to long-range thinking than an election campaign, there are some vital imperatives. First, all those who have doubts about the implications of the present course, misgivings about the present choices, and, especially, disagreements with the more systematic, oversimplifying, and hysterical interpretations of Soviet behavior—those interpretations which simultaneously describe the Soviets as ten feet tall, as manipulating countless forces in countless countries, as devilishly clever, scheming, and successful, and *also* assert that a simple overpowering display of military might would drive all our troubles away—must speak up and engage their adversaries. Our Vietnam experience should have taught us not only (Vance's words again) "that the use of military force is not and should not be a desirable response to the internal politics of other nations," but also that an unexamined national consensus can drive us into our graves.[5]

A second imperative is for us to think through what will remain one of the two dominant issues of world politics (the other one being the issue of revolutionary change in the Third World): what kind of Soviet-American relation do we want? It is a vexing problem, for two main reasons. One is that thirty-five years after the end of World War II each of the superpowers remains indifferent to the effect of its moves on the other, and eager to blame the other for all that goes wrong.

The Carter administration has not paid sufficient attention to the effect on Moscow of its divagations, and above all of its proclaimed, and unenforceable, determination to relegate U.S.-Soviet relations to secondary importance in its diplomacy. The Soviets have given no signs of understanding that their post-1975 thrusts in Africa and around the Middle East, plus their military build-up, were seen by Americans not as a discrete series of tactical moves but as a pattern of deliberate expansion and increasing provocation, and therefore hardly compatible with the improved relations the Soviets said they wanted. It is in the nature of competitions, moreover, that even situations in which one side's gain is not simply the other side's loss—Angola, for example, has been a costly client for Moscow, and a reasonable economic and diplomatic interlocutor for Washington—are perceived as if they were a zero-sum game.

The other, and even more fundamental, difficulty goes, beyond perceptions, to the heart of the matter: conflicting interests and goals. Any serious analysis of Soviet policies and statements reveals three things. One is a profound insecurity—a continuing sense of qualitative inferiority, a fear of being put in a position of diplomatic and military subordination by the United States and its allies. Second, there is the constant, driving ambition to be recognized as an equal superpower and accepted by the United States as a co-manager of world affairs, with equal rights and equal say. Third, there is a willingness to create enough difficulties and setbacks for the United States to oblige it to treat Moscow as an equal, if Washington does not do so voluntarily.

191

These factors explain, for instance, why the Soviets seem to have taken so seriously the declaration of principles adopted at the Moscow summit of 1972, with its vague statements about cooperation and its fatuous renunciation of unilateral advantages (only Kissinger seems to have taken this equally seriously). They explain why, while accusing the Americans of having, since 1973, destroyed one by one the links of détente, thus affecting the balance of considerations Moscow had to weigh *before* moving into Afghanistan, the Soviets also accuse the Americans of having destroyed détente *after* Afghanistan by imposing sanctions on the Soviet Union.

They explain above all why Moscow is so obdurate on the subject of the theater nuclear forces in Europe. For the Soviets divide the world into two slices: there is the Soviet-American relation, and there is the rest. Since their SS-20 missile doesn't threaten the United States, the NATO decision to deploy in Europe 572 missiles capable of hitting the Soviet Union, under American control, is felt by Moscow to be a violation of the spirit of SALT II, indeed of its key principle (an equal number of launchers capable of hitting each superpower). Thus the Soviets compare NATO's decision to their deployment of missiles in Cuba in 1962. But Moscow is quite unwilling to recognize the validity of the Western Europeans' fears, caused by the substitution of the mobile and precise SS-20 for the older Soviet missiles aimed at Europe, by the development of the Soviet Backfire bomber, and by the absence of comparable theater forces on the NATO side.

These three aspects of Soviet policy clash directly with American perceptions and conceptions. We have our own insecurity, fed by Soviet quantitative build-ups and qualitative advances. Defining military parity or "equal security" seems beyond human achievement. Moreover, Soviet niblings at and attacks on previously Western or pro-Western positions feed the American inclination to contain and repel, not the inclination to negotiate and share. If, as I believe is probable, Soviet moves in Africa and around the Persian Gulf since 1975 are in considerable part a response to our "exclusion" of the Soviets from the Middle Eastern peace process, first in 1973 and again after Sadat's visit to Jerusalem, the least one can say is that these moves have not made Americans more eager to reintroduce the Soviets into the process.

Finally, we remain deeply reluctant to grant them equal rights: our values and interests are too different to encourage us to take part in a condominium. Their regime violates our deepest beliefs, and its ambitions threaten our strategic, economic, and political positions. We may concede (unhappily) military parity, but we do not derive from it political parity, for we find the Soviets too lacking, and threatening, in the other dimensions of power to grant them such equality. Indeed, we see in their demand for it a way for them to gain a foothold in various regions, to inject themselves into issues (southern Africa, or the security of Persian Gulf sea channels, or international economic issues) where their claims are dubious and their credentials are shaky; in other words, we see in this demand a clever way of increasing their power and control at our expense.

And so we seem doomed to competition. Their attempts to reach parity (whether they are diplomatic or unilateral) are seen as a challenge by us; our attempts to deny them political parity and to restore military parity where we deem it threatened are seen by them as efforts at intimidation. When we act to preserve the "correlation of forces" they interpret our moves as hostile; but their definition of friendship seems to require of us a good-natured willingness to let that correlation shift in their favor without reacting.

All of this means that the U.S.-Soviet relationship is bound to remain a troubled one. We should have no illusions about the grimness of the Soviet regime or its policies. But an unrestrained competition would condemn us to unbearable insecurity, and we should deny neither the possibility of a slow evolution of the Soviet Union, nor our ability to affect it (for better or worse). No rational policy can fail to acknowledge their enormous military and economic resources—while they face internal tensions and failures, we can hardly pretend that all is well in our land. Our strategy will have to be complex, and to mix competition and restraints, containment and cooperation, deterrence and preventive diplomacy. The difficult search both for restraints and for areas of mutual benefit is essential, and will require constant communication and diplomacy. We cannot, as the Soviets sometimes seem to invite us to do, settle the world's problems jointly and override the interests of allies and third parties. But we can, as they also suggest, see to it jointly that third parties do not drag us into confrontations, and we must try to dampen their disputes when these threaten to get out of hand.

This in turn requires that each superpower be more willing to exert pressure on its clients than to score gains by supporting them. And this, in turn, requires a far broader range of cooperative links than exists at present. Indeed, without such links a pattern of restraint is hard to imagine, even though the moderation of Soviet behavior might sometimes result less from understandings than from Moscow's need to acknowledge the wishes of other nations (another reason for sound preventive diplomacy on our part). But only if we keep trying, despite all setbacks, to turn an adversary relationship into a mixed one and if we understand that what is at stake is not an untenable status quo but the management of inevitable change will the Soviet drive for status become less maniacal, more differentiated, and our resistance to it less fierce and more discriminating.[6]

A third American imperative is to provide our allies with no excuse for Finlandization or further estrangement. This entails far better consultations than in the recent past, and above all a willingness to consider a common strategy, one that recognizes that we cannot separate the Soviet-American issues from the various economic ones that confront us, or from the Middle Eastern ones. It also means that we ought to get out of the ruts into which we have fallen.

Concerning relations with Moscow, we face a contradiction between our interest in imposing costs on Moscow in order to deter a repetition of Afghanistan and our interest in the kind of policy I have sketched. Similarly, the Soviets face a contradiction between their stake in Afghanistan and their frequently stated interest in avoiding a return to the Cold War. If we remain locked in our attempt at punishment or expand our military cooperation with China, or if the Soviets keep seeking total victory in Afghanistan, chances for a better future will be destroyed. Therefore, we should explore the possibility of an explicit or (more likely) implicit bargain in which the Soviet Union would commit itself to a withdrawal from Afghanistan, begin to carry it out, and accept an enlargement of the Afghan regime (and not mere window dressing for Karmal).

For the reasons I have mentioned, time will be crucial. We would in exchange guarantee Afghanistan's neutrality, resume arms control negotiations on issues such as a comprehensive test ban, or chemical warfare, or antisatellite weapons, resubmit SALT II to the Senate, and move toward a speedy SALT III negotiation that would include theater nuclear weapons in Europe. Concerning the Arab-Israeli conflict, we should be ready to support initiatives aimed at linking the Camp David process, which has gone about as far as it can, to a renewed search for a comprehensive settlement, acknowledging the Palestinian right to self-determination (and thus going beyond the Camp David ambiguities).

For the Western Europeans there are imperatives as well. Some are negative. There should be no more indulging in the cheap pleasures of mere bitching, no attempt to pose—singly or collectively—as mediators between East and West, no displays of national or collective independence from Washington when the only effect would be to encourage Moscow's hope or belief that a wedge can be driven between the United States and its allies, or to demonstrate Western Europe's impotence. Another negative imperative is that there should be no Western European offers to Washington of the kind of division of labor that is likely to justify American suspicions about the allies—a division in which the United States would provide the armed defense of the oil supplies, while the Europeans do business as usual with Moscow and the Arab countries (and contribute some financial assistance only to Turkey or Pakistan).

But there are positive imperatives as well. Given the deadlock of current American policy, and the bleak choices offered in the presidential campaign, this could be the historical moment in which the Western Europeans

THE CRISIS IN THE WEST

overcome the habit of dependence and propose to their handicapped ally their own strategic conception. Precisely because they are not on the front lines, and because their domestic situations—even in the cases of West Germany and France, which are in a preelectoral period, but with much better prospects for the incumbents—allow them to think of the long range, their leaders could perform a major service for the alliance as a whole, as well as seize this crisis as the opportunity to lift European cooperation out of its own rut of petty concerns with fish, lamb, and pennies. They perform no service at all when they merely go along with measures they deem futile (such as sanctions against Iran), just in order, as one of them put it, to buy the right to say no the next time. This is doubly irresponsible.

In East-West relations, a European strategy for the alliance could have as its motto: neither cold war nostalgia (at a time when the dangers of superpower confrontation are much higher than in the 1950s or 1960s, and when both the absolute and relative levels of superpower might are so different from what they were then) nor incoherence à la Carter nor détente illusions à la Kissinger (that is, hoping to get the Soviets to self-contain themselves and to accept our notion of international stability). Such a European strategy would, in particular, continue to combine the modernization of NATO defenses and the pursuit of arms control; it would also reexamine the current discordant trade and credit policies toward Moscow and suggest a common allied policy that would preserve and enlarge existing links, yet avoid excessive dependence on Moscow over key resources, and state as clearly as possible in advance what kinds of Soviet moves would lead to a reduction or severance of these ties.

With respect to the Middle East, a European common strategy ought to aim at reducing more rapidly dependence on oil imported from the area, and at providing a successor to (but not a repudiation of) the Camp David process. It would *not* be wise to begin such a European initiative with an attempt at getting the UN Security Council to revise Resolution 242—for this would provoke an American veto; nor should one begin with an attempt to draft a new General Assembly resolution, since any prolonged debate there risks becoming a competition in extreme language and a further cause of superpower opposition. But a declaration of the Europeans which recognizes both Israel's right to exist in secure borders and the Palestinians' right to self-determination, acknowledges the necessity of including the PLO in the negotiations leading to it, and proposes a mutual renunciation of force on such a basis could do a great deal to prevent a new radicalization of those Arab states and forces which, after Camp David, had moved away from pure rejectionism, and which see in the present deadlock, and in Begin's policies, reasons to give up any hope for a negotiated settlement. Without ruling out a role for Jordan, such a declaration could also, if endorsed by the United

States, help convince the Israeli Labor party not to lose any more time in the fruitless quest for the kind of "Jordanian solution" that tries to leave out the PLO and the West Bank leaders altogether.

There are other problems (such as the world economic ones) about which the Europeans could propose a strategy, and there is another imperative for their own long-range future: a return to the subject—taboo since 1954—of a European defense organization, allied to the United States, in which France would be a key member, and the British and French would engage in nuclear cooperation. This would redress, in part, the imbalance between, on the one hand, Europe's military subordination to the United States (a subordination which, given the structure of NATO and France's separate role, far exceeds the actual unavoidable military dependence on Washington), and, on the other hand, the economic and political progress of the Nine.

In the meantime, Europeans have an overriding interest in overcoming their own rivalries and their tendency merely to react to Washington's policies. For only if they present their own plans do they have a chance either of helping a new Carter administration regain a sense of direction and of steadiness or of saving a Reagan administration from its delusions about European desires and expectations and from leading the alliance straight into what might be its biggest crisis ever.

Inversely, if they wait until Washington has defined its course, and it is one that is either too short-sighted or too dangerous for them to approve, they will be faced with highly unpleasant choices. One would be grudging consent; but it would strain the domestic politics of several European nations. Or else they could make an attempt at collective independence, but it would only lead to a disastrous showdown with the military protector in Washington, and to a demonstration of impotence and a real danger of Finlandization in relations with Moscow. Or else there could be a new division among the Europeans—with, as usual, London siding with Washington and Paris choosing autonomy, but with the major risk of having Bonn associated with Paris, unlike in the 1960s.

A European effort to redress the Atlantic diplomatic balance is not assured of success. Washington may well choose not to listen. But one more European abdication would be especially lamentable at a time when America's vision is either cloudy or absurd. Collective myopia and cumulative nonsense on the part of all the Allies might, despite the caution induced by nuclear weapons, bring about a repetition of 1914, especially at a time when military "experts" begin to seek ways of waging and winning nuclear wars.[7] And yet, anyone who in June 1980 would predict that the European leaders will indeed behave as responsible world statesmen and not as good local managers with a shopkeeper's cautiousness and a taste for

THE CRISIS IN THE WEST

rebelliousness, anyone who would announce a new European vision or the appearance of a sane and steady American one would have to be an optimist—or a dreamer.

NOTES

1. See the sober and powerful analysis by Seweryn Bialer in *Stalin's Successors* (Cambridge, England: Cambridge University Press), 1980).
2. Quoted by Karen Elliott House, *Wall Street Journal,* June 3, 1980.
3. Peter Jay, "Regionalism as Geopolitics," *Foreign Affairs, America and the World in 1979* (special issue, 1979):485-514.
4. Robert W. Tucker, "America in Decline," *Foreign Affairs, America and the World in 1979* (special issue, 1979):449-484; and "Reagan Without Tears," *The New Republic* (May 17, 1980):22-25.
5. Cyrus Vance, Harvard Commencement speech, June 5, 1981, *New York Times,* June 6, 1981.
6. See Chapters 6 and 7.
7. See for instance Colin S. Gray and Keith Payne, "Victory is Possible," *Foreign Policy 39,* (Summer 1980):14-27.

CHAPTER 10

DRIFT OR HARMONY?

I.

A NUMBER of factors have led, in the past couple of years, to an acute sense of crisis among the members of the Atlantic alliance and to heightened tensions within it.[1] Of those, the recent report of the Directors of the American, French, German and British Councils or Institutes of International Relations constitutes an excellent survey.[2] Clearly, the three fundamental considerations are: a new awareness of the fact that the world has become a single strategic stage, and that the security of the members of the alliance can be threatened by events occurring outside its geographic area, especially in the Middle East and Persian Gulf region; the unfavorable evolution of the military balance in Europe, because of the relentless modernization of Soviet conventional forces and of the development of new Soviet middle-range nuclear weapon systems that are both mobile and highly precise; and the collapse of the Soviet-American détente.

In this essay, I will concentrate on what I deem essential: the different reactions to these events within the alliance, and the causes of these divergences. I will then suggest certain ways to restore harmony.

It is important, in analyzing the current drift, to diagnose correctly the nature and the limits of transatlantic discord.

It is not a simple matter of disagreement between the United States and Western Europe. Western European opinion covers a whole range of attitudes, not only *within* each country (the same would be true of the United States) but *among* governments. Today, the official position of Britain is closer to that of the Reagan administration than is the position of the Bonn government; yet another gap exists between the major three Western European powers and some of the smaller European members of NATO (one of which has recently been accused of neutralism by a French President).

Disagreement centers *not* on the existence of a renewed Soviet threat to Western security interests; in this respect, the divergences over the response to the Soviet invasion of Afghanistan are actually less profound than the split in the alliance in October 1973, when many Europeans refused to view the October war between Israel, Egypt, and Syria as a confrontation between Washington and Moscow, as Kissinger saw and wanted them to see it. By contrast, in 1980, all the Allies deemed Soviet behavior in Kabul unacceptable.

There are, in academia and among public officials on both sides of the Atlantic, two different conceptions of Soviet behavior; both can be found in varying degrees in every country of the Western alliance. To simplify, I would call one the *essentialist* view; it stresses the radically *different* nature of the Soviet system (either because of its imperial essence, or, more usually, because of its revolutionary one.) In a manner comparable to George Kennan's in 1946-1947, the essentialist view describes the Soviet Union as an inextricable mix of power and ideology on the march, driven to paranoia because its whole rationale is the assumption of external hositility, and to expansion because its survival depends on the elimination of its enemies (within as well as abroad). Thus, it is a system with which no mutual gains or lasting cooperation are possible. The West is condemned either to endure inexpiable conflict with that system (the "harder" version of this conception), or to practice perpetual containment of it (Kennan's early notion, or Raymond Aron's formulation, "to survive is to win.")[3]

The other view of Soviet behavior describes it as relentlessly opportunistic. Ideology is important to Moscow as a world map (drawn around the "correlation of forces") and as a method of domestic legitimation, but not as a compass. This view puts greater emphasis on the similarity between Soviet behavior and the behavior of other great powers in history; on past experiences as the roots of paranoia and expansion; and on the cumulative effect of gradual changes within the Soviet Union and of transformations of the international system. It is, in short, a more empirical approach, paying greater attention to the context of decisions. Finally, it attaches greater importance to internal difficulties, as a way of placing external behavior in perspective. Accordingly, the second of these views prescribes a mix of containment and search for agreements as a means to induce Moscow to behave in a more "responsible" way.

Among policymakers, one finds agreement on a number of key factors. There is an increased Soviet threat because of the Soviet arms build-up, which gives the Soviet Union both dangerous new military options in Europe and the ability to project its power abroad. In response to these developments, France has taken measures of accelerated armament since 1976, and Chancellor Schmidt, in 1977, raised the issue of the Euro-strategic nuclear balance. That threat is made more dangerous still by a perceived Soviet determination to exploit opportunities in the Third World (hence the key issue of Third World "destabilization"). A third source of agreement focuses on the threat posed by Moscow's perceived unwillingness to interpret détente in a nonconflictual way. This consensus points to Moscow's insistence that détente means neither a reduction of ideological conflict nor an end to attempts at changing the "correlation of forces" by support of "national liberation" or "progressive" forces. Finally, all members agree that what is dangerous, and could become explosive, is the mix of Soviet domestic weaknesses and external reliance on military might as the main instrument of Soviet policy.

For their part, the Allies are in official agreement on the need to improve the military preparedness of NATO (as exemplified by the long-range defense program) and to meet the threat of new Soviet theater nuclear forces with, for instance, NATO's December 1979 decision, and comparable French policies.

There are, however, important *nuances and disagreements* that divide allied officials; they center on five issues.

The United States, since 1978-1979 and especially after Afghanistan, has moved away from that more complex worldview that sees the East-West conflict as only one corner of the tapestry, and the conflict itself as manageable through the pursuit of both containment and détente policies (arms control, economic agreements, occasional diplomatic cooperation). Gaining ground in American policy is a view of the world that is intensely bipolar and conflictual. That view either relegates to the back burner issues that are not reducible to the bipolar contest (as the New International Economic Order), or analyzes those issues (such as human rights, turbulence in Central American countries, Africa or the Middle East) in East-West terms. The Soviet Union is to be dealt with, according to this conception, from a position of strength and in the context of explicit linkages subordinating agreements to good behavior. Even in France and Britain—where a stern view of Soviet expansionism and a highly critical one of President Carter's vacillations have dominated public opinion during the past several years—there is considerable unease about so bipolar a view. For whenever bipolarity is most intense, the freedom of maneuver of European states is minimal. The newly conflictual approach of American policymakers is similarly discomforting, and has given rise to the current effort of diplomats in Western Europe to convince the new American administration to resume a dialogue with Moscow rapidly. Such a confrontational stance is seen as provocative, possibly dangerous, and there is considerable skepticism about the effectiveness of explicit linkages.

The new U.S. administration reflects far more than a newly militant public opinion: it reflects neonationalism; a desire to restore American pride and prestige; a will to put an end to humiliation; a determination to restore American leadership; and a conviction that Soviet daring and alliance drift can be explained by past American failures to lead. Many statesmen in Western Europe welcome the promise of a new American consistency and clarity of purpose; the same individuals nevertheless wonder whether the new American Administration is aware that a number of factors act to prevent a simple return to the days of American hegemony. Among those factors, several are particularly pronounced—changes in the respective economic power of the two sides of the Atlantic; the progress of the Nine (now Ten) in political cooperation; the rise of new middle powers in the developing world, and the desire of Third World countries for independence. More bluntly, at a time when Washington seems to see only the challenge of Moscow on the geopolitical map, Western Europe sees a multiplicity of problems: Moscow, to be sure; but also the various troubles and conflicts in the different parts of the Third World; the specific crisis of Poland (a case in which some Western Europeans believe that there is, or ought to be, a possibility of finding interests common to them, the Poles, *and* the Soviets); the difficulties that too aggressive an American policy could create; and the need to protect from internal tensions and external pressures the Western European enterprise itself, a delicate construction whose progress requires a stable environment.

The Reagan administration, although its domestic economic priorities are the curtailment of inflation and the increase in productive investment as a way of restoring American industrial supremacy, has given to the military budget a priority that may well detract from both goals. It could be highly inflationary; and by reinforcing the drive to cut the nonmilitary expenditures, thus reducing the savings capacity of many victims of such cuts, and by giving a clear priority to defense industries, it could divert from and delay the indispensable industrial "redeployment." Meanwhile, the countries of Western Europe are all giving priority to their own internal economic difficulties. Since they do not have the political ability to dismantle the social services of the postwar welfare state (or would provoke major social explosions if they tried), and since most of them have been hit by the second oil shock much harder than by the first (and harder than has the United States), their margin for maneuver is very narrow, and the limits within which they can increase their defense expenditures are very strict. They have to explain to Washington that such an increase at the expense of their economic health and social stability would be senseless—just when the Americans explain that economic recovery and military preparedness must go hand in hand.

There is also disagreement about the precise nature of the Soviet threat, and therefore about the desirable response. Washington emphasizes the Soviet military menace: Moscow's arms machine is doubly dangerous, insofar as it can "cover" Soviet nonmilitary expansion (by making a Western military response more risky) *as well as* encourage those in the Kremlin to use direct military action, as in Afghanistan; hence America's determination to reply in kind, to restore a "margin of safety" and to build a military presence in the Middle East. Western Europe deems the Soviet build-up dangerous *primarily* because it makes nonmilitary destabilization, or destabilization by proxy, safer for Moscow, whereas in the past the West often responded with the use of force (for example, Lebanon, Vietnam, etc.). The Soviets' emphasis is now on opportunities in the Third World rather than on direct aggression. Hence the Europeans' preference for a more nuanced response; on the one hand, the Allies endorse a restoration of global military balance, but with less emphasis on the need for specific military balances, and with a plea for prudence in deployments; some deployments, they argue, could actually be counterproductive and destablizing, as in the Middle East. Instead, they recommend a greater willingness and ability to play the *politics* of each area (which requires a certain decentralization of roles: France in Africa, West Germany in Turkey, a European role for the resolution of the Palestinian issue, and for a resumption of the North-South dialogue). In short, the foreign policy priorities and preferred methods of pursuing them are not identical on both sides of the Atlantic.

There is finally disagreement about the degree to which, and the way in which, the outside world can influence the explosive mix of Soviet power and weakness. In the United States there is a tendency to deem Soviet intentions irrelevant, to focus only on the effects (actual and potential) of Soviet moves, to dismiss détente as having been a failure since it placed no significant restraint on Soviet behavior, and to characterize détente as indivisible (and therefore dead).[4] Leaders in Western Europe believe that even if Soviet intentions are (inevitably) mixed and the effects of Soviet policies clearly bad, the West has the ability to affect Soviet calculations at the margin by a combination of clear advance warnings (for instance the Schmidt-Giscard communiqué of February 1980, and more recent NATO statements on Poland) *and* preserve the "dialogue" and those aspects of the Soviet-West European détente that have proven beneficial to all sides. This is the basis of the European tendency to declare détente divisible, and of warnings to the United States not to seek military superiority or confrontation.

II.

What are the reasons for these divergencies? Although they concern the key issue of coping with Soviet challenge, they actually do not have much to do with differences in evaluating Soviet behavior. They result from geography, history, domestic politics, and national character (or political culture). Geography remains the most fundamental factor of divergence, in two ways.

When the United States contemplates the security of Europe, it sees a choice between emphasizing deterrence (that is, extended deterrence, through a credible threat of nuclear retaliation) and emphasizing defense. Should a strategy resting on the threat of mutual assured destruction appear implausible, warfighting strategies (conventional *or* nuclear, concentrating on counterforce) are conceivable. Western Europeans have only the luxury of discomfort. Mutual assured destruction always seemed to them hardly compatible with extended deterrence: MAD stresses a counter-city strike, while extended deterrence requires the ability to strike Soviet military targets first if necessary; indeed, as General Gallois tirelessly reminds us, MAD was one of the incentives for the building of the French *force de frappe*. But at present, the credibility of extended deterrence is being undermined by Soviet advances and advantages in theater nuclear forces: the main function of the SS-20 and Backfire bomber may well be one of the counterdeterrence, making a Soviet conventional thrust possible, by placing NATO before the unholy dilemma of either fighting a defensive conventional battle or else taking a nuclear initiative that would expose NATO's conventional targets *and* nuclear installations to retaliatory destruction by the Soviet theater nuclear forces, or even expose America's vulnerable land-based missiles to a Soviet strike.[5] Moreover, as prestigious and knowledgeable an American as Henry Kissinger in September 1979 proclaimed that it would be a mistake for the Allies to believe that extended deterrence was still credible. But a purely conventional defense of Western Europe would mean devastation (given the certainty of a Soviet invasion: NATO does not aim at striking first). And scenarios of actual nuclear warfighting, whether in the form of James Schlesinger's limited nuclear options, in that of Carter's Presidential Directive-59's emphasis on counterforce targets, or in that of integrated warfighting strategies for NATO,[6] seem like extermination compounded. In this respect, the new Soviet ability to strike military targets in Western Europe with precision, that is, to resort to (geographically) limited nuclear war for actual fighting purposes, is coupled with this growing American tendency to doubt the credibility of deterrence (whether in its MAD or in its extended versions), and to emphasize the need for warfighting capabilities, if only in order to match Soviet strategic doctrines that appear to envisage fighting and winning nuclear wars. The two combine to provoke, in various European countries and parties, a new wave of quasi-pacifism.[7] Hence, a desire to get out of an insane world, a tendency to withdraw altogether: what is sometimes (wrongly) called Scandinavization and is most eloquently expressed in E.P. Thomson's recent "Letter to America."[8] This explains why many leaders in Western Europe insist so strongly on the need both to contain the risk of actual nuclear war through arms control (hence the linkage of theater nuclear deployments both to SALT II and to theater arms control), and to deal with Moscow not only by military containment and confrontation but by détente.

Geography also explains the different attitudes of the United States and of Western Europe toward Eastern Europe. As was already clear during World War II, the United States never had a truly distinct policy toward Eastern Europe (Brzezinski tried in 1966 and 1977, but words were not enough). To Western Europe, Eastern Europe is not a Soviet *glacis* but a wound—and this is especially true for West Germany vis-à-vis East Germany; this is another reason to try to save what the Western European-Soviet détente has achieved—providing the only breath of fresh air coming into the Eastern European cage, the only opportunity for wide contacts between the *frères séparés*.

History is another source of divergence, in three respects. In Western relations with Moscow, there have been two separate détentes, resting on two separate sets of wagers. The Western European-Soviet détente came first. DeGaulle was its initiator; then came the West German détente. On the basis of the recognition of the territorial status quo, Western Europeans made a bet on the dynamic transformation of the East, and on a possible decrease of their defense effort as a result; the Soviets bet on receiving benefits from economic links, and on a decrease of American influence in the political systems of Western Europe. The results, clearly, were mixed; but the Soviets did obtain economic benefits (as did the West), and changes were achieved in Eastern Europe—some, as in the case of the Berlin agreement, with Soviet consent, others, despite Soviet resistance, through the dynamics of greater openness (as in Poland). The Soviet-American détente of the early 1970s corresponded, on the American side, to Kissinger's complex theory of linkages and networks, and, on the Soviet side, to the hope of achieving thereby a formal recognition of military equality and political

DEAD ENDS

condominium, a consolidation of the Soviet system through American economic and technological aid, and a demobilization of America abroad, leading to advances for the "progressive" forces. By 1979, both sides, not so strangely, felt cheated; the United States, by Soviet moves in the Third World and by the Soviet arms drive; the Soviet Union, by the failure to receive the aid expected, by the American rejection of duopoly (especially in the Middle East), by evidence of new moves to strengthen NATO, and by America's and Japan's rapprochement with China. Today, leaders in Western Europe often tend to believe that the balance sheet in Europe is rather unfavorable to Moscow: the momentum of détente has "destabilized" Poland and, to some extent, East Germany. And the Berlin and Helsinki agreements, by keeping the Central Front quiet, facilitate the redeployment of American forces toward the Middle East. But Americans are skeptical; they believe that insofar as Eastern Europe is destabilized, the Soviets will as usual resort to brutal repression, and that détente in Europe has doubly served the Soviets. It has made, they believe, defense efforts politically more difficult for the Western European members of NATO, and above all, it has given the governments of Western Europe such a stake in preserving trade with the East that they become far too accommodating to Moscow in political and military affairs. Moscow pursues a two track policy—economic cooperation with Western Europe, and political and military expansion. Both tracks serve Soviet power. But Western Europe finds it difficult to object to and counter the second of these pursuits out of fear that too strong an anti-Soviet stand on the strategic-diplomatic chessboard could jeopardize the economic gains of that burgeoning relationship.

In relations with the Third World, the United States has a tendency to militarize issues, partly because of disillusionment with economic assistance, partly because of difficulties and even disasters encountered in the manipulation of domestic politics abroad. Western Europeans have had, on the whole, disastrous military experiences in the days of decolonization, but look at their economic deals with Third World countries (for example, the Lomé agreements) with some pride, and they have had some great successess in dealing with the politics of troubled countries (for example, the British in Zimbabwe).

History has also opened an important gap of experience between the United States, with its postwar quasi-monopoly of decision in the alliance, and the quasi-abdication of Western Europe. With the exception of France under the Fifth Republic, responsibility for security is seen as a NATO (that is, a largely American), more than a national or European responsibility (and the French semi-secession has served to keep the other Europeans glued to Washington). The proper function of the European entity is seen as the development of Europe as a civilian power: this reinforces the interest in trade relations (with the East in particular), and feeds the indifference, in the smaller countries, to military issues. And whereas the United States does not want to accept the Soviet Union as an equal superpower (except in the military realm), the Europeans have an old experience of dealing with the Soviets as a (difficult) partner in the game of nations.

Domestic politics also contribute to the breach. In the United States, the constituency for détente has always been limited (a small part of the business and intellectual communities). The majority of the public has been skeptical; most of the debate in the postwar era has only been over how best to resist Soviet expansion. In Western Europe, foreign policy has played a far more important and variable role in domestic political battles, and the Soviet Union has not been the only, or even the dominant factor. In Britain, the Labour left expresses a deep desire to concentrate on domestic reform, a resentment of the outside world of NATO, the United States, and Europe, and an old unilateralist and pacifist dream. In West Germany, some of the same feelings can be found in fragments of the Social Democratic and Free Democratic parties. The hope for more contacts with the *other* Germans in the East, if not for reunification, is an added element—one that is often exaggerated, but carefully watched, in France, where some always suspect, as did Pompidou and Jobert, *Ostpolitik* to be a nationalist prelude to a reunification strategy. In France, the left's dislike of power politics, its preference for arbitration and disarmament, and its distaste for U.S. "imperialism" have been a notable feature of the political landscape. The most recent shift in French opinion, culminating in the May 1981 election of Mitterrand, reflects the bitter split between the French Communists and Socialists, and a thorough disenchantment with Moscow's ways. Giscard d'Estaing's preelection shift in policy reflected that evolution, as well as the former President's apparent conviction that the biggest threat to his reelection, on foreign policy issues, would not be from left wing utopianism, or communism, but from the Gaullist demand for toughness, in which Mitterrand—sensing the public mood—concurred. There is also a perhaps temporary decline in the fear of American domination, and a hope of influencing Washington through friendliness, now that Bonn's privileged relation to the United States has soured, and that London's special relationship has atrophied. But both Giscard and his Socialist challenger kept stressing their desire for peace—Giscard's posters showed him "struggling for peace"—and a moderate world. And Mitterrand's stance is against *any* imperialism in the Third World; his party, government and entourage contain elements critical of American actions there. In Italy, foreign policy has always been a weapon in domestic political maneuvers, a movable symbol of internal alignments and realignments.

DEAD ENDS

Domestic differences thus aggravate the effects of an unfortunate geography and a humiliating history for the Europeans. America's native tendency is, perhaps not isolation, but self-concern: to redress the balance, and to jerk Americans away from their concentration on domestic issues, U.S. officials must often engage in overkill and sound a global alarm—in 1947 as in 1980. The political systems of Western Europe are the victims of a "tyranny from the outside": either because of the presence of powerful Communist parties, or because of a constant battle between domestic demands and foreign policy needs in countries with limited means. For the Nine, building the European Economic Community has been a partial answer to that competition. In turn, the European construction leads to tension with the United States: first, because it can best proceed when the outside world places no demands on the members of the Community (hence the resentment against Kissinger's pressure in 1973, just when the EEC was trying to "absorb" Britain); second, because, in an effort to compensate for its internal cleavages and multiple deadlocks with the *fuite en avant* of political (that is, foreign policy) cooperation, the European community finds compelling reasons to define stands different from Washington's. All of this, then, tends to give to American policies an arrowlike quality, and to the Europeans' the aspect of a highly complex piece of clockwork.

Finally, there are factors of political culture that should not be neglected in such an analysis; they result in three lines of cleavage within the Atlantic alliance. The first could be called simplicity versus complexity. Americans prefer simple policies to complex ones. When complications had to be introduced into the anticommunist policy of containment, it was mainly for pragmatic reasons: the costs of purely military approaches (as in China in 1948-1949), for instance, and the defection from Moscow of a communist country (Tito's Yugoslavia). Détente, as I have tried to show elsewhere, was partly "sunk" by widespread resistance toward a mixed policy of rewards and punishments; first, it had to be oversold, and when it appeared to have failed, a formidable reaction set in.[9] A complex policy toward China, in the 1970s, always threatened to "tilt," becoming an overly enthusiastic "China card" policy. The same craving for simplicity affects current American readings of the Central American situation, and explains the tendency to interpret Soviet behavior in terms of a coherent, deliberate Soviet plan. Statesmen of Western Europe have some skepticism toward simplicity. Their historical experience is both that of the balance of power, with its nuances, shifts, and switches, and that of the disasters caused by Europe's own "terrible simplifiers" in the twentieth century.

Second, attitudes toward conflict are not the same on both sides of the Atlantic. Many Americans still dream of ultimate harmony—a pleasant dream—but show a terrible rage against those who seem to block it (like the

208

Jacobins of the French Revolution, who also tended to believe that the obstacles to the dream were not the nature of things, but evil human beings). Recall, for instance, Truman's or Carter's reaction when they felt bullied and duped by Moscow. Against such human obstacles, force is a legitimate instrument; and Americans sometimes project on others the idea that force is a privileged tool on behalf of one's mission. Robert Legvold has shown how Soviet strategic literature looks at *America* as a creature of force, while Americans, of course, believe that the *Soviets* put force at the center of their policy; each side sees itself as merely reacting to the threat of the other.[10] In 1980, as in 1950, many in America saw in a local military aggression—by North Korea then, later by the Soviet Union in Afghanistan—a possible prelude to a generalized use of force. And American discussions of policy have been almost obsessively focused on the nightmare scenarios of Minuteman vulnerability, and on the threat of Soviet aggression in the Persian Gulf. Western Europe looks at international affairs less as a duel with swords, more as a game played with a whole range of cards, is more concerned with the overall correlation of forces than with the balance (or imbalance) of military force, and is more Clausewitzian, that is, more interested in the variety of ways in which force can serve political objectives.

The United States is still (or again) in the throes of "exceptionalism"— the belief in the unique mission of America. This tends to promote a peculiar kind of insecurity: the need to ask oneself at every moment if one still is number one, if one is up to the task, faithful to the mandate. It also makes it difficult for Americans to understand experiences different from their own—social revolutions for instance—and it makes them want to project abroad the experiences that have made America great—free enterprise, political democracy. A sense of mission makes sharing responsibility—not only with an evil power, but with allies—equally difficult. The politics of Western Europe are not those of exceptionalism but those of survival. When the Cold War intensifies, dangers for survival and for political autonomy increase, giving rise to the two tendencies of either wanting to opt out altogether (which often prevails among those far from power) or else of working to improve the atmosphere—pleading for summits and negotiations thus often exposing European statesmen to the charge of being naive and of playing right into Moscow's hands, of helping Moscow's attempt to lull Europeans to sleep, and to estrange them from Washington.[11]

These three lines of cleavage cumulatively amount to different conceptions of stability. In the United States, stability means preserving the status quo; it means a world in which the Soviets eschew subversion, the exploitation of revolutionary opportunities, the support of revolutionary forces—a world in which peaceful change becomes the norm. The Western Europeans assuredly hope for a moderation of Soviet behavior, a stabilization of the world when (as at present) things have gone out of kilter. But they have no real expectation of preserving the status quo all over: they expect less and they demand less—they would, on the whole, be happy if the inevitable (and, often, inevitably violent) changes occur in such a way that the vital interests and values of the West are not destroyed in the process.

III.

What is to be done? The recommendations of the four Council or Institute directors constitute an excellent set of proposals.[12] Rather than repeat them, I would like to concentrate on a few essential points. Most important is the need of a rapprochement between the United States and its allies (including Japan), aimed at devising an integrated policy on the "single strategic stage" mentioned above. That policy should take into account such factors as the following: first, the great advantage the alliance has, but does not always exploit, in being able to count on the diverse capabilities, experiences, interests, and skills of a number of major states; second, the advantage that lies in the wide spectrum of power at the disposal of these states, ranging from the most advanced forms of military power and technology, to economic resources that can be used for development, to financial institutions essential for the recycling of petrodollars, to diplomatic credit, and so forth; and third, the inseparability of security issues from other issues whose mismanagement could create serious dangers for Western security and opportunities for Soviet advances. Among these issues are race relations in South Africa, nuclear proliferation, energy, human rights, and so forth. Dispersion, or the lack of coordination of power resources and the tendency to fragment issues, can be tolerated when resources are abundant, and challenges reasonably separate; this is no longer the case in a world where both superpowers compete far from their borders, and regional conflicts risk escalation; in which domestic and foreign policy issues are interwoven; and in which economic and strategic problems are inseparable (as in the Middle East).

An integrated, worldwide policy requires that American leaders modify several of their current attitudes and beliefs, some of which will have to be discarded because they may turn out to be dangerously counterproductive. Among those are: the predisposition to project a bipolar grid on complex local and regional issues, for instance in the Middle East or South Africa; and the tendency to try to find predominantly military solutions to complex problems (for example, El Salvador) or to dismiss problems that seem to detract from the grand issue of competing with Moscow (such as

210

human rights violations in "friendly" countries, or North-South negotia tions). Others will have to be changed, because, whatever the justification for American skepticism or impatience, such attitudes or beliefs make fruitful cooperation with the Allies much more difficult: greater willingness to resume a dialogue with Moscow and to seek new paths toward arms control may well be a prerequisite for such coordination. Similarly, it may have to be made clear to the Europeans that the "margin of safety" sought by Washington is only a restoration of the military balance where it is in danger, and not a quest for superiority where it would be either futile or dangerous (as in the nuclear realm).

The leaders of Western Europe too would have to abandon certain practices of the past. They have tended to react—often negatively—to American proposals, and frequently failed to make coordinated and constructive suggestions of their own. In particular, they have let the major initiatives concerning the security of Western Europe come from Washington (the French are only a partial exception, insofar as their own initiatives have been purely national) so that when the final decision appeared to be left in the hands of the Europeans (as with the neutron bomb), the result was a fiasco. When the final decision resulted from an American determination to push ahead, as with TNF, some Europeans saw it as a move in the American rather than the European interest. And when the Western Europeans develop initiatives of their own, they must be more prepared than in the past to go beyond deploration and suggestion, to actual policy—that is, to provide the means for enforcing their recommendations (and, for instance, to guarantee the security of Israel once the pre-1967 borders are restored).

Achieving such a rapprochement raises troublesome issues of machinery for policy coordination. The present machinery is inadequate for a number of reasons: the NATO Council is not competent to deal with the area beyond the North Atlantic treaty's scope, and an amendment would meet formidable obstacles; the yearly economic summits are far too hectic and superficial to deal competently with all the other issues; and finally, both the NATO procedures and the absence of a satisfactory mechanism for extra-NATO affairs reinforce the vicious circle of an American inclination to unilateralism (or policy monopoly), and Western Europe's cringing and negative reactions. This circle engenders American exasperation with what seems to be European dilatoriness, pusillanimity, and impotence, and Western Europe's habit of reacting to American moves rather than to the issues themselves, as well as of vacillating between fears of being abandoned (or "decoupled") and fears of being unnecessarily exposed to danger.

The "principal nations" approach advocated in the document of the four Council or Institute heads is a sound pragmatic proposal aimed at coping, in coordinated form, with the problems of a given area or with a crisis.

However, a more general Directory is needed, in order to avoid the perils of fragmentation and ad hoc responses. The report suggests using to this effect the seven-nation summits, with a "permanent though small secretariat." Whether this would be the most effective organ is dubious however, since—to be entirely candid—neither Italy, nor Canada, nor the President of the Commission of the EEC (who has no authority in foreign policy and defense matters) are premier global strategists. But only the establishment of a regular organ for such strategy, involving key officials and a secretariat, will be able to cure the mutually reinforcing diseases of the alliance: America's instinct for unilateralism, disguised as leadership, Western Europe's inclination to abdicate, disguised as prudent criticism.

Overcoming this vicious circle will ultimately require a reform of NATO as well. Defense remains the most critical issue for Western Europe; its leaders can hardly be expected to behave as responsible actors on the world scene if they act as dependents on their home front. But to insulate NATO from the rest of the world stage would be impossible. There must, in short, be a role for the Europeans in extra-NATO affairs, as well as some vehicle through which to play that role.

The purpose of NATO's defense policy ought to be to make impossible the Soviet belief that the Soviet Union could win a conventional war in Europe, or that it could save its own territory from nuclear attack should it launch such a war or a first nuclear strike on Western Europe. This means:

—providing NATO with conventional forces sufficiently well-equipped and deployed to present a real challenge to an aggressor, and making a resort to a first nuclear strike by the defenders plausible;

—providing the alliance with theater nuclear forces that would both deter a Soviet first use of nuclear weapons, and give the allies the option of initiating a nuclear attack on the aggressor within the European context, thereby escaping the dilemma of either sticking to and perhaps losing a conventional war, or initiating strategic, intercontinental nuclear war; and finally,

—having theater nuclear forces that are invulnerable to conventional or nuclear Soviet attack and which are able to hit the territory of the Soviet Union after such an attack. If the Soviets made their own initial attack a nuclear one, they would thus expose themselves to nuclear retaliation from Europe; if they were hit by European TNF (either in such retaliation, or in a first strike by NATO after a Soviet conventional attack), the onus of turning the war into a strategic intercontinental conflict would then be on them.

Such a strategy requires specific measures: first, a greater NATO readiness for a war of maneuver, and better anti-tank equipment; second, a will-

DRIFT OR HARMONY?

ingness on the part of Western Europe to replace American forces, should some of these be moved to the Middle East; third, pursuit of the TNF program decided in December 1979. Fourth, as long as the ultimate decision to resort to TNF (whether in response to a Soviet conventional thrust, or in retaliation for a Soviet nuclear attack on Western Europe), thereby exposing the American "sanctuary" to a risk of Soviet retaliation, remains exclusively in American hands, Western Europeans will remain fearful of a possibility of "decoupling" *in extremis*; it is therefore important that the Western Europe's own nuclear forces—strategic and tactical—be included in the alliance's war plans.[13] What does not seem to be required is a resort to "mininukes" (such as the neutron bomb), for their effect would be decoupling; the nuclear threshold would be considerably lowered, but the deterrent effect resulting from the probability of escalation to a higher nuclear level and from the likelihood that nuclear war would devastate the aggressor's own territory would be diminished.

This kind of a strategy, pointing to a larger conventional role for Western Europe (primarily West Germany and Italy) and to greater integration of the nuclear forces of Britain and France, will require the gradual formation of a Western European Defense Organization. The French are not likely to accept a larger West German conventional contribution, or a more intense and planned coordination of their own nuclear arsenal (including the possible stationing of middle-range French missiles on West German soil) with that of their allies, unless all this takes place, not within NATO as it is presently constituted, but within a European Defense entity in which a certain division of labor takes place. At a time when the United States itself is likely to press for a bigger European contribution to the protection of Europe, past American objections to any reorganization of NATO, or past American failure to encourage a separate European defense entity (ever since the 1954 fiasco of EDC) would become irrelevant. And the fear often expressed in West Germany that such a transformation might encourage the United States to "decouple" from Western Europe, or serve as a pretext for American withdrawal, is certainly not justified under current circumstances. Indeed, it is the present NATO setup (France's absence, and recurrent U.S.-West German, or U.S.-Dutch, Belgian, Danish frictions) that is a factor of mutual exasperation. Moreover, the tendency of some of the smaller NATO members to drift toward nuclear pacifism—a tendency fostered by the larger countries' dominance of NATO, and one that could be worsened by the exclusion of these small nations from a Directory and from "principal nations" bodies—could best be stopped or reversed by the establishment of a purely Western European Defense Organization.

There is a role for nuclear arms control in European security. The objections to TNF arms control are strong. Technically, a negotiation limited

213

on the Soviet side to the SS-20 and the Backfire would leave out many other weapons systems capable of hitting Western Europe—including a sizable fraction of Soviet ICBMs and SLBMs. A negotiation including, on the NATO side, only the future long-range TNF would paradoxically be both insufficiently interesting to the Soviets (who have always wanted to include the American Forward-Based Systems [FBS] in arms control talks) and incapable of bringing forth the kinds of reductions in already deployed SS-20s and Backfires that would be of interest to the Europeans. But a negotiation that would include the FBS would run into formidable problems of delimitation since many of them are dual-capable.[14] Politically, a negotiation could become a way of delaying the deployment of NATO's future TNF, thus consolidating the Soviet advantage in middle-range nuclear weapons. However, as long as this political issue is squarely faced—as long as negotiation, and failure to conclude it satisfactorily, do not become pretexts for abandoning the 1979 decision, any more than the conference on Mutual Balanced Force Reductions became a pretext for scuttling conventional force modernization—it would be wise to stick with the December 1979 deal. A willingness to negotiate provides a necessary political basis, which thus strengthens the military rationale for TNF. And since the alliance's strategy rests on coupling American strategic forces with NATO, there is much to be said for a negotiation that would "merge discussions on theater systems with those on central systems,"[15] and aim at a SALT III (or SALT II½) agreement that would incorporate the main elements of SALT II, perhaps negotiating further reductions, and avoid the formidable difficulty of dealing with theater systems only.

Americans have expressed considerable unease over Western Europe's economic relations with the Soviet Union. They have pointed out that the West is, in effect, helping Moscow to keep its creaky economic and bureaucratic ship afloat (and thus saving the Soviets from the need to initiate deep reforms). It is, moreover, helping the Soviets divert more resources to the military sector, and turning the Western Europeans into dependents (as in the case of the recent multination gas deal). That, in any case, is the judgment of many Americans.

In reply, the West Germans claim that the Soviets cannot use this relationship for blackmail purposes, since any interruption in the promised supplies would end the transfers of machinery that the Soviets want from Western Europe. Americans, in turn, rejoin that the West is then at a double disadvantage: the fear of an interruption of supplies *and* of the loss of markets suffices to affect the *Weltanschauung* of Bonn, and, in particular, almost to rule out a West German resort to economic sanctions against Soviet acts of aggression. Moreover, since the purpose of Soviet acquisition of machinery and technology is to achieve self-sufficiency, a Soviet threat to interrupt supplies for political purposes is perfectly conceivable in the event of a crisis. Some Europeans' reply to this is that economic sanctions are in any case not an adequate response to acts of force, and that the present and, in all likelihood, lasting Soviet need to modernize equipment with outside help may explain in part the relatively restrained Soviet behavior in Europe, and apparent Soviet reluctance to crush the Polish dissidence.[16]

This dialogue of the deaf, which pits an American strategic view of the world against strong West European political and economic interests, should not go on much longer at its present level of abstraction. What is needed is a serious effort, first, to establish a criterion that will clearly distinguish unacceptable commercial transfers from the acceptable or merely dubious ones; second, at reaching an agreement on what constitutes dangerous and one-sided dependence; third, at agreeing on instances in which economic sanctions would be appropriate and effective; and fourth, at deciding what kinds of economic deals with the Soviets do indeed hold out the possibility of mutual gains. These points may well be the subject matter of one of the "principal nations" groups mentioned above.

Secretary of State Haig has spoken of the need to cope with the Soviet threat to the Middle East in tandem with efforts to resolve the Palestinian issue. But recent American policies and statements suggest that priority has been given to the military dimension of the issue, with the goal of establishing an American armed presence (not limited to naval and air forces) in the form of permanent bases. This clearly puts the cart before the horse, since no such bases are likely to be available as long as the road to a settlement of the Palestinian issue is blocked, and as long as there has been no adequate consideration either of the whole range of threats to Western interests in the area, or of the ways in which a large American military presence could either deter, defeat, or aggravate these threats. Nor is it likely that the Allies will increase their military efforts as long as these problems have not been faced.

Here again, there is a need for coordination—both in a general way, by a supreme Directory, and more concretely, by a "principal nations" group. It may turn out to be in the interest of the whole alliance to let Western Europeans pursue, perhaps in cooperation with whatever Israeli government emerges from the June 1981 elections, the so-called European initiative for the resolution of the Arab-Israeli conflict. They may similarly want to arrive at a formula that puts emphasis on strengtheing the defense capacity of the states in the region and on preparing outside forces for quick deployment in cases of extreme tension or crisis only, as an alternative to the early introduction and stationing of such forces.

In any case, it makes more sense to let the Western Europeans play a larger role in the defense of Western Europe, than to insist on their providing substantial forces for that of the Persian Gulf area: their resistance is likely to be great, their contribution limited, and the effort would divert energy from the necessary reorganization of alliance relationships in Europe.

IV.

The biggest threat to the alliance today is not the Soviet menace, however serious its military dimensions and global its scope may be. The gravest threat lies in the centrifugal potential of the present situation: an America that tries to reassert its leadership with a militantly and almost obsessively anti-Soviet worldview; a Germany increasingly unhappy about American trends and eager to preserve opportunities for agreement with Moscow; a France that, in the wake of the May 1981 elections, will be feeling its way in the realm of foreign policy, under the wait-and-see scrutiny of its European neighbors and the United States, and will most probably continue to try, somewhat acrobatically, both to maintain the Franco-German entente that is the motor of European cooperation, and to restore a Franco-American entente at a moment when the Soviet-French one appears sterile, and the Washington-Bonn one a bit frayed; a Britain that favors both a close American alliance and European political cooperation, yet suffers from serious internal weaknesses that affect its performance in Europe and on the world stage; an Italy absorbed in the morose contemplation of its stalemated politics; and the smaller European nations tempted to drift to neutralism.

Both the alliance *and* the European enterprise are threatened by these developments. And yet, we cannot return to the days when strong American leadership either succeeded in rallying most of Western Europe, or provoked a collective European resistance that was good for European unification without being dangerous for NATO. This is why a major effort at political compromise, strategic integration, and institutional innovation is needed. Nothing short of what will serve the purpose of further European cooperation, and preserve the trans-Atlantic alliance. But it will require a drastic turn away from American unilateralism, and a new European willingness not merely to claim but to play a world role—starting with defense at home.

NOTES

1. See Chapter 9; also Stanley Hoffmann, "Reflections on the Present Danger," *New York Review of Books* (March 6, 1980):18-24; and "Europe

and the New Orthodoxy," *Harvard International Review* (December 1980/January 1981):117-21.

2. Karl Kaiser, et al., *Western Security: What has Changed? What Should be Done?* (New York: Council on Foreign Relations, January 1981).

3. Raymond Aron, *Peace and War* (New York: Doubleday, 1966).

4. Robert W. Tucker, "The Purposes of American Power," *Foreign Affairs 59* (Winter 1980/1981):241-74.

5. Pierre Lellouche, "Introduction Générale," *La Sécurité de l'Europe dans les Années 80*, (Paris: Institut Français des Relations Internationales, 1980), pp. 15-81; Stanley Hoffmann, "New Variations on Old Themes," *International Security 4* (Summer 1979); and Pierre Lellouche, "Europe and her Defense," *Foreign Affairs 59* (Spring 1981):813-34.

6. Richard Burt, "L'Alliance Atlantique et la Crise Nucléaire Cachée," in Lellouche (ed.), *La Sécurité de l'Europe*.

7. Josef Joffe, "European-American Relations: The Enduring Crisis," *Foreign Affairs 59* (Spring 1981):835-51.

8. E.P. Thomson, "Letter to America," *The Nation* (January 24, 1981):1 ff.

9. *Primacy or World Order* (New York: McGraw Hill, 1979), Chapter 2. See also Chapter 4 of this volume.

10. Robert Legvold, "Military Power in International Politics: Soviet Doctrine on Its Centrality and Instrumentality," in Uwe Nerlich, ed., *The Soviet Asset: Military Power in the Competition over Europe*, Volume I of *Soviet Power and Western Negotiating Policies* (Cambridge, Mass.: Ballinger Publishing Company, 1983).

11. For a powerful argument along these lines, see Uwe Nerlich, "Change in Europe: A Secular Trend?" *Daedalus* (Winter 1981).

12. Kaiser, *et al, Western Security*.

13. Lellouche, "Introduction Générale," pp. 72-73.

14. These problems are discussed by Raymond L. Garthoff, "The TNF Tangle," *Foreign Policy 41* (Winter 1980-81); and by Lellouche, "Introduction Générale," pp. 15-81; and Burt, "L'Alliance Atlantique et sa Crise," pp. 255-74.

15. Lawrence Freedman, "The Dilemma of Theater Nuclear Arms Control," *Survival* (London: International Institute of Strategic Studies, January-February 1981), p. 7.

16. See, for further discussion, Otto Wolff von Amerongen, "Economic Sanctions as a Foreign Policy Tool" *International Security 5* (Fall 1980): 159-67; and J. Fred Bucy, "Technology Transfer and East-West Trade," *International Security 5* (Winter 1980/1981):132-51.

CHAPTER 11

NATO AND NUCLEAR WEAPONS: REASON AND UNREASON

I.

THE HISTORY of the Atlantic alliance is a history of crises. But we must distinguish between the routine difficulties engendered by Western Europe's dependence on the United States for its security, as well as by the economic interdependence of the Allies, and major breakdowns or misunderstandings that reveal not simply an inevitable divergence of interests but dramatically different views of the world and priorities. At the present time, complaints from Western European leaders about the effects of high American interest rates on their economies, or about President Reagan's skeptical approach to North-South economic issues, belong in the first category. The current controversy in Europe over nuclear weapons belongs in the second, and now confronts the alliance with one of its most dangerous tests.

On its face, that controversy revolves around NATO's double decision of December 1979 to deploy by 1983 new long-range nuclear forces in the European theater and to enter into arms control negotiations with the Soviets about such forces. It does not yet pit allied governments against our own. But in Western Europe, the widespread popular movement opposed to the new deployments indicates both the existence in several nations of a broad politically destabilizing gap between government and a sizable, mobilized section of the public, and a growing divorce of feelings and perceptions between the two sides of the Atlantic. Far more than technical questions of deterrence and strategy is at stake; these serve primarily as symptoms of fundamental issues.

DEAD ENDS

The present popular movement in Western Europe is not the first of its kind. A vigorous campaign for nuclear disarmament attracted many British followers in the early 1960s, and we should not forget the strong opposition in West Germany to the development of nuclear energy in recent years. Nor is the current agitation evenly strong: the demonstration that took place in Paris on October 25, 1981, was organized and dominated by the Communist Party and one of its front organizations; and while the Rome demonstration on that same day went beyond the orbit of the Italian Communist Party and labor union, it did not offer the same agglomeration of forces as in the northern part of the continent.

Nevertheless, the current movement is new and formidable in several respects. It is a mass movement of continental dimension, which mobilizes and moves people across borders—something quite exceptional even in the partly integrated Western Europe of today. It entails the active participation of women and of a large number of religious movements and churches—predominantly but not exclusively Protestant—in countries where they have rarely taken part in big rallies. It is particularly strong in the country that has been, until now, the most reliable partner of the United States on the continent and the linchpin of NATO strategy: the Federal Republic of Germany. While it brings together people from a variety of parties, particularly in the Netherlands and Scandinavia, and is often led by well-known priests, intellectuals or politicians, the movement is largely a gathering of young people, a generational protest—the first since 1968. Above all, like the May 1968 movement in France, it is, in de Gaulle's word, *"insaisissable"*—beyond grasp—for it represents a convergence of different concerns, fears and aspirations on a single issue, and offers more emotion and passion than hard-headed analysis. Hence the difficulty of finding an appropriate adjective that would define it.

Some—for instance those on the left wing of the British Labour Party—argue for the complete denuclearization of Europe and for unilateral action toward that goal; others want mutual arms reductions to be negotiated between Washington and Moscow. Some remain committed to NATO, minus the December 1979 decision; others dream of a neutral Europe. Many denounce both superpowers, described as brainless monsters, and attack the "policy of blocs" that keeps Europe divided and dependent; others concentrate their fire on the United States alone. Most seem to fear nuclear war above all; yet many are also moved by indignation about what they feel to be a mistaken emphasis on military approaches to international problems, and the excessive costs of defense at a time of high unemployment, cuts in social services, and sometimes—as in Britain—severe industrial depression. Some are members of political parties, highly politicized and expert at manipulation. But many are almost defiantly un- or anti-political, in quest of a "concrete utopia," or convinced that in a world in which traditional power politics has failed to bring lasting peace or to remove the threat of nuclear destruction, spectacular gestures of renunciation could prove contagious; they believe that examples of self-abnegation, even by small nations, could shame the superpowers into respect or imitation. In the German movement, many are inspired by a determination to repudiate any form of policy that smacks of Germany's past—hence any reliance on force as a key instrument—and seek an identity that would be pure and blameless; others seem moved by a more resentful or ambitious nationalism.

II.

Why has this complex movement arisen over the issue of long-range theater nuclear forces? Two questions are involved: why now? and why does it focus on this point?

There are profound differences between the mood of the late 1950s (when peace movements flourished in various places) and that of the present. Then, paradoxically, there was both general confidence in American nuclear superiority (hence relatively low fear of nuclear war) and general agreement that the Soviets were the bullies threatening to disrupt the peace in Europe. This was the era of the Berlin crises: what was feared in West Germany—and in West Berlin, whose mayor was Willy Brandt—was American softness. Now we find the opposite mix. There are serious doubts about the U.S. promise to preserve Western Europe's security through extended nuclear deterrence. In an age of nuclear parity, Washington seems unlikely to risk America's survival for the protection of Europe, despite ritual official reassurances. Given the new properties of nuclear weapons such as accuracy and mobility, nuclear strategy seems to point to war-fighting, as deterrence through the threat of massive city-busting is no longer wholly credible, and deterrence through the threat of a first strike against Soviet forces appears eroded by the loss of American superiority.

Western Europe's view of the Soviet Union has furthermore been transformed, mellowed by the experience of the détente years and affected by the spectacle of Soviet embarrassment in Eastern Europe. In particular, the Polish "example" has had an enormous effect. The spectacle of a nationwide grass roots movements restoring freedom, of workers rebelling against a stale bureaucracy and insisting on their rights and dignity, and of a relatively small and weak country resisting a superpower and—so far—deterring the Red Army, has instilled in many Continental young people a feeling of pride—as Europeans—and not a little envy.

To these general factors, one must add some that apply particularly to the Federal Republic. A new generation with no experience of European crises—the invasion of Czechoslovakia was thirteen years ago—has appeared, marked by deep revulsion against both Germany's past and Germany's present. In its view the older generation had been either too busy trying to build a new honorable society or too eager to forget about a dishonorable past—too sure of its own virtue, insofar as its members had been anti-Nazis, or too guilty to want to spend much time looking backward. Now, their sons and daughters ask questions about the bloody history of united Germany, reawaken the nagging issue of German identity and, rather romantically, seem tempted by the notion of a new mission for Germany as the harbinger of peace and emancipation for all of Europe.

Moreover, many of Germany's young people have been taught, in school or at the university, about the evils of postwar West German society—hucksterism, materialism, consumerism, conspicuous displays of wealth, and so forth; even those who were educated in areas where the Marxist or New Left does not dominate classrooms find the same themes on the screens of movie houses or television, and in the novels of the Republic's best-known writers.

Finally, many West Germans seem to have parted from, and even discarded, the American model. America-as-the-example, a notion that was still prevalent in the late 1950s and early 1960s, has been replaced, if not with America-the-menace (although there are clearly some elements of this), at least with a sorry picture of the United States, soiled by Vietnam and by domestic violence, by ethnic strife and widespread electoral abstentionism, and by a bizarre mix of militarism in policy and a complacent refusal to institute a draft.

Thus we encounter the first of many paradoxes. Instead of believing that the United States provides security and that the Soviet Union breeds insecurity, many young Europeans now feel the opposite. Insofar as they still understand that insecurity might come from the East, they react in a direction contrary to that of the United States. Here, the public mood, expressed by the election of President Reagan and by the new Congress, is one of restoring America's strength; in Western Europe, the public mood is one of fearing war, of believing that the accumulation of weapons can only lead to war, and of wanting the superpowers to deal with their differences in other ways, less dangerous to mankind. Hence the emphasis—by the governments themselves—on negotiations with the East, and the temptation—of the public—by various forms of escapism, from denuclearized zones to neutrality. The dramas of the 1970s have affected Americans and Europeans differently. Americans seem to want to "stop being pushed around" in the world and to turn to fundamentalist means for economic recovery:

private enterprise and a reduced role for the state. Western Europeans concentrate on their domestic troubles and, whatever their government's political orientation, rely on state initiatives and a mixed economy.

In recent years Americans and Western Europeans, even at the official level, have diverged on three essential issues. Americans, in their relations with Moscow, have reverted to a view and to a policy in which hostility predominates; Western Europeans have benefited from, and want to preserve, a mixed relationship. Americans, seeing a worldwide Soviet challenge, have nudged their allies toward a global alliance; the Western Europeans have insisted on the geographical limitations of the Atlantic alliance and resented Washington's attempts to present El Salvador as a test of alliance solidarity, or to look at North-South issues from a cold war angle, or to give, in the Middle East, precedence to weaponry over diplomacy. Americans are convinced that the central problem of the age is the containment of Soviet imperialism, and that the military dangers posed by the Soviet Union are in many ways compounded by the huge weaknesses of the Soviet polity; Western Europeans see these dangers, but think they are reduced, offset, or neutralized by those weaknesses, and by Soviet entanglements in Afghanistan and Poland.[1]

III.

Against this background it is not hard to see why the controversy has come to focus on the issue of long-range theater nuclear forces. The NATO decisions of December 1979 were "rolling" decisions, calling for future deployments and arms control negotiations. Although the intergovernmental consultations that led to the decisions were careful and prolonged, the public in the key countries of Western Europe was never truly engaged. There was no great debate in advance, and, in the atmosphere described above, it can now be seen as almost inevitable that controversy would come to focus on this issue. It is practically the first time that detailed strategic discussions go beyond the very narrow circles of Western Europe's experts, into the media and the rallies. There is indeed a democratization of the strategic debate, and it both reflects and increases an acute sense of danger; but one cannot help feeling that the level of sophistication in strategic analysis has not kept pace with the spread of concern, as is shown by a tendency, among members of the movement, to present as self-evident assertions that are either obviously false or highly debatable.

The opponents of the deployment of Pershing II and ground-launched cruise missiles in Western Europe combine a disbelief about Moscow and a belief about Washington. They do not believe that the Soviet Union has, in recent years, transformed the military situation in Europe to its advantage; and they believe and fear that the United States is preparing to fight a nuclear war limited to Europe. On the first point, American officials and most American experts emphasize that the SS-20s and the Backfire bomber provide the Soviets with new military options in Europe. The Soviets may want to make a purely conventional war possible—one in which they would enjoy many advantages—by neutralizing NATO's nuclear arsenal, and through the improvement of their own short-range nuclear weapons and above all their new longer-range forces, which NATO cannot match. Or else they may want to be able to begin with a devastating counterforce strike against NATO's existing nuclear installations and other military targets, believing that the United States would hesitate to retaliate with its central strategic system, and thereby risk provoking a Soviet attack on the United States. Protesters in Western Europe react with skepticism. On the one hand, they doubt that a conventional war, in a continent stuffed with nuclear weapons, would be containable, and that the Soviets could confidently believe that a nuclear war would remain limited. Why, they ask, would Moscow want to conquer a devastated Western Europe? On the other hand, they often accept the Soviet argument that the SS-20 is merely a modernized version of older Soviet missiles; to be sure, it is much more accurate, yet the dense geography of Western Europe still means that any nuclear strike on military objectives would kill millions of civilians, and (an argument also presented by McGeorge Bundy)[2] these objectives could, in the absence of the SS-20, be hit by Soviet long-range strategic missiles. Why, if they intend to deter a Soviet attack on Western European soil as if it were an attack on America itself, should the Americans treat differently, so to speak, a warhead on an SS-20 and a warhead on a Soviet ICBM; why would they want a new retaliatory system placed in Western Europe, unless they intend to spare their own territory?

The debate on the second point—the risk of a nuclear war limited to Europe—has an Alice in Wonderland quality. Protesters in Western Europe often seem to believe simultaneously that a Soviet attack would escalate (and is therefore unlikely) and that America's plans could keep destruction limited to the continent. Americans stress the recoupling effect of the new planned deployments; as Henry Kissinger formulated it at the September 1981 conference of the International Institute of Strategic Studies in Williamstown, the Soviets would not distinguish between an American missile hitting them from West Germany, and an American missile hitting them from the high seas or from the United States; it is the present situation, in which NATO cannot strike the western part of the Soviet Union from within Western Europe, that is decoupling, and it is the December

1979 decision which reenforces deterrence. Americans assert that it restores symmetry: since the Soviets can hit Western Europe without hitting the United States, NATO should be able to strike the Soviet Union without resorting to the central systems; otherwise the Soviets might believe that their territory could remain a sanctuary, while they devastate Europe. The Western Europeans who protest and march, however, place themselves in the perspective of the disasters that would follow from a failure of deterrence, not in the perspective of a strengthened deterrence. They quote American statements about the end, or decreasing plausibility, of extended deterrence—as in Kissinger's speech in Brussels in 1979—and they suspect Americans of moving toward a war-fighting rather than a deterrence strategy. In their eyes, Carter's Presidential Directive-59, with its emphasis on counterforce targets, Reagan's recent decision to proceed with the production of neutron bombs, the decision to build a formidable but vulnerable MX, and a flurry of statements about "horizontal escalation" or the readiness to hit Soviet weak points should Moscow go on the move, all form an alarming pattern. The protesters also point out the radical difference between NATO's existing nuclear arsenal, with its limited range, and the planned Pershing II, which could reach the Soviet Union in less than five minutes (the fact that there would be too few Pershings to cripple the Soviet's own first-strike force is rarely mentioned; but it could be aimed at Soviet command, control, and intelligence centers). It is thus both a first-strike weapon, and, given its vulnerability, an invitation to a Soviet first strike. The protesters, who often discount the difference between the SS-20 and the SS-4 or -5, and reject the argument according to which the former, and the Backfire, have created a new asymmetry at NATO's expense, believe that the Pershing II gives the United States an asymmetrical advantage at the Soviet Union's expense.

Even when they acknowledge the existence of a "theater nuclear forces gap" in the long-range weapons category, they are reluctant to close it with first-strike weapons aimed at the Soviets, rather than—as in the past—relying for extended deterrence on second-strike forces such as the Poseidon submarines assigned to NATO. They argue that if—as many American officials keep saying—extended deterrence remains plausible in an age of parity, there is no need for new systems in Western Europe. But should deterrence fail, three possibilities would occur. If long-range theater nuclear forces are indeed "recoupling," they are likely—being under American control—not to be used at all, since their use would expose America to Soviet retaliation; and, with these weapons remaining useless, Europe would be devastated either by a conventional war or by a war that entailed the use of short-range and battlefield nuclear weapons. Or else, if the United States resorts to Pershing II and ground-launched cruise missiles and the Soviets use their SS-20s and Backfires, the two superpowers might still remain sanctuaries while Europe is destroyed, providing the United States restricts the use of its own long-range nuclear forces to targets in Eastern Europe. Finally, even if the United States does not, it is still possible that only territory in Europe and western Soviet Union would be hit, while the territory of the United States would be spared. Thus the stationing of the new NATO long-range forces in Western Europe is either superfluous, or dangerous.[3]

Behind these arguments and counterarguments, there is a long history of interallied disagreements on strategy, especially with respect to nuclear weapons in NATO.[4]

In the first place, there never has been any agreement on the military function of theater nuclear forces in NATO's strategy. Throughout the 1960s, Americans wanted NATO to increase its conventional forces as the best way of deterring a Soviet attack, or rather as the best way of giving plausibility to the strategic nuclear guarantee of the United States. They argued for a firebreak between a conventional and a theater nuclear conflict, and looked at NATO's theater nuclear weapons mainly as a deterrent against a Soviet use of theater nuclear forces, as well as a last resort should conventional defense falter. But the Europeans would have preferred the threat of an early first use of NATO's theater nuclear forces, in order to make it impossible for the Soviets ever to believe that they could start and fight a purely conventional war in Europe. The "flexible response" strategy formally adopted in 1967 was a compromise that resolved nothing.

Second, there never has been any agreement on the kinds and amounts of theater nuclear forces required. If their function is primarily to demonstrate America's commitment and to contribute to the deterrence of Soviet aggression, there is no need to match the Soviet capabilities in kind. Indeed, Soviet theater capabilities—the new SS-20 medium-range missile and the Backfire bomber—can be offset by U.S. strategic forces. Western Europe has always tended to believe that "escalation matching"—the ability to confront the Soviets at every level with weapons as capable as their own, so as to deter them from escalating to a level at which they have an advantage—deters less than strategies that threaten the early initiation and uncontrollable escalation of nuclear war.

Third, the NATO decision of December 1979—calling for new medium-range missile deployments inferior in numbers to those of the Soviets—seemed to lack any operational rationale. Was it, as some American officials have imprudently suggested, aimed at replying to (although not matching) the SS-20, and at saving the United States from having to resort to its central strategic forces in case of a Soviet use of the SS-20? This is a view heatedly rejected by Western European supporters of the December

1979 decision, both because it feeds the protesters' suspicions about America's willingness to risk its own territory on behalf of Europe, and because they fear that any attempt to establish a kind of tit-for-tat balance on the continent would indeed have the effect of "decoupling" U.S. strategic forces from the European theater. Is, then, the rationale the reestablishment of the link between European security and the central systems, a link weakened by recent Soviet deployments? But if this is the purpose—a restoration of deterrence—are vulnerable Pershing II missiles and less vulnerable but difficult to disperse ground-launched cruise missiles the best instruments? Or is the rationale primarily to provide NATO with a bargaining chip for negotiations?

Finally, there is no agreement among the Allies on the arms control aspects of the decision. While the decision does not subordinate the deployments to a failure of the negotiations, one must expect resistance to the deployments to increase if there appears to be some hope left for a deal that would allow for more limited deployments, or even for none at all, on the Western side.

Unlike the Multilateral Force (MLF) project, which attempted in the early 1960s to create a nuclear force manned on an integrated basis by several NATO nations, the December 1979 decision was not an attempt to give a military answer to a political problem; it tried to give a military *and* a political answer to a military problem. But given the uncertainties of nuclear strategy and the various theologies about it, there was no agreement either on the true significance and dimension of the problem created by the Soviets, or on the right answer. Given the sensitive nature of the issue, it was absurd to believe that the decision would put an end to anguish.

Clearly, the present debate is but the latest manifestation of the permanent West European fear of becoming a war zone. If the United States, by refusing to risk its homeland in the event of a Soviet attack on Western Europe, "decouples" because of its loss of nuclear superiority or for any other reason, such as NATO's present inability to strike the western part of the Soviet Union, Western Europe could be left to the mercy of the Soviets, or destroyed in a conventional or limited nuclear war. Yet if the United States takes measures that are seen to be recoupling, and assumes, for instance, that the Soviets would not distinguish between an American missile striking them from Western Europe and an American missile hitting them from the high seas or from U.S. territoy, Western Europe still cannot be sure that Washington will actually use its nuclear weapons, since Americans retain final control over their use. Moreover, if the superpowers are heading toward a global war, would recoupling make much difference anyway?

It is awareness—dim or blinding—of these points which explains the psychological contradictions and contortions of the European protest movement. People who are in an impossible position, or in a position in which the only good outcome—peace—seems increasingly unlikely, tend to react with a mix of illusions, resentments, and inconsistencies, because the grammar of emotions has nothing to do with the logic of the mind. Remember the ways in which Frenchmen, eager for peace and convinced that another war would destroy their country, reacted to the Nazi threat in the 1930s (a comparison made here because of the psychological, not political, parallels). There are Europeans who refuse to believe that the SS-20 is more than just a modernized version of older Soviet missiles, or to accept the notion of possible Soviet military superiority, or to admit that the Soviets could militarily exploit any superiority they have, yet who are quite willing to believe that the United States can no longer deter a Soviet attack because it has lost *its* superiority. We Americans have done too good a job, in recent years, of stressing our relative decline, and—as Henry Kissinger did in Brussels in 1979—our inability to provide extended deterrence any longer. In the United States, the perception of decline has led to a renewed and often indiscriminate will to arm, but in Europe it has encouraged doubts about America and wishful thinking about the potential Soviet threat.

One finds also, among the protesters, a desire for plausible deterrence (since only successful deterrence makes any sense), yet simultaneously the fear that no form of deterrence is fully plausible anymore. One finds suspicion of American strategic moves and a new determination to resist them, insofar as they seem to indicate a shift from a deterrence to a war-fighting strategy. The protesters see an alarming pattern in Carter's Presidential Directive-59, with its emphasis on targeting Soviet offensive forces, and President Reagan's decisions to proceed with production of the neutron bomb and to deploy the new MX intercontinental ballistic missile and the Pershing II medium-range missile, both of which are formidable first-strike weapons and, given their vulnerability, an invitation to Soviet preemptive attack.

Yet one also finds the conviction that the defense of Europe and the neutralization of any Soviet threat against it will always remain an essential American interest, whatever the Allies might do and however hard they may kick their protector. One finds a conviction that even if the Soviets are stronger in some areas, they cannot transform military superiority into political advantages (Tito's Yugoslavia, Ceauşescu's Romania, a free Finland have survived), but little understanding of why. In fact, the reason for the limits on Soviet influence has been Western European-American solidarity, and a break between the two sides of the Atlantic would leave Western Europe dangerously exposed. One finds, most dangerously, a tendency to blame the protector as the real source of trouble (conversely, in the summer' of 1938, many Frenchmen blamed their protégé, Beneš'

Czechoslovakia, for creating difficulties with Hitler) and to seek an escape hatch by putting excessive hopes in arms control or even in unilateral restraint. Just because peace is the only sane and sensible goal, must a form of pacifism be the only reaction of young Europeans to the shifts in the nuclear balance and in the international political climate?

IV.

We have seen, in the history of the alliance, several examples of crises created by Europe's defense problems. In two cases, the United States retreated: Lyndon Johnson over the MLF and Jimmy Carter over the neutron bomb. In another case, the pursuit of an increasingly hopeless course led to a crash, fortunately followed by a rescue operation: the collapse of the European Defense Community in 1954 followed by the decision to rearm West Germany within NATO. These are not happy precedents.

There can be, in the near future, no retreat from NATO's decision. Unlike earlier procurement decisions, this one was collective, and even if the Belgian and Dutch governments find themselves unwilling or unable to enforce it, Britain (except in the improbable case of a return of the Labour Party to power), Italy, and West Germany will try to stick to it. Although the present West German government risks collapse should the Social Democratic Party (SPD) repudiate its ministers, or should domestic issues become divisive, a successor government formed by the Christian Democrats would be even more committed to the NATO decision. Also, any retreat now would pull the rug from under the arms control negotiations.

The real threat, then, lies below the official level, in the relations between governments and their publics. Governments may find themselves unable to confirm a tentative commitment (as in the cases of Belgium and Holland), or to carry out the very commitments they maintain (in West Germany's case). For the gap between the governments and the protesters to be closed, one would have to imagine several events occurring, none of which is likely. One is a successful arms control negotiation. Even if one believes that the bargaining should be limited to theater nuclear forces in Europe (and thus leave out Soviet ICBMs aimed at Western Europe, or Poseidon and Trident submarines assigned to NATO, or the new submarine-launched cruise missiles [SLCMs] which will be built by the United States and could serve as a coupling link between the central systems and Europe), there are formidable technical and political obstacles.

On the technical side, which weapons are to be included? What is it that should be counted (missiles, launchers, warheads)? What level of limitation would make sense—and is there any level that would "save" the Europeans from new deployments, unless one believes, to quote a recent NATO communiqué, in the "ideal circumstances" of a zero option whereby Russia dismantles its SS-20s and America need not deploy its own theater nuclear weapons? Is not the absence of a clear military rationale on the Western side likely to make an agreement—even, first, among the Allies—more difficult? What price, if any, will the Soviets require in order to consent to a dismantling, and not a mere displacement, on the SS-20s? How would this be verifiable?[5]

On the political side, whereas NATO's December 1979 decision was aimed at providing Western negotiators with the added bargaining power that flows from firm deployment commitments, what was intended to be a decisive chip has turned out to be a source of division and weakness. The Soviets have little incentive to conclude an agreement rapidly. All they have to do—all they keep doing—is to make reasonable-sounding proposals, wait for the fallout from public opinion in Western Europe, and sharpen the conflict between "negative" Western governments and eager protesters.

Another event capable of closing the gap would be some Soviet move that would convince the protesters that the Soviets are indeed still a formidable threat. A Soviet invasion of Poland—shown all over Western Europe's TV screens—might demoralize the peace movement. But it would at the same time doom the chances for arms control, thus largely offsetting whatever boost it might have given to Western cohesiveness. In any case, one should neither always count on being rescued by the Soviets nor hope for such a tragedy.

What if, by the time the deployments are supposed to begin, there has been no breakthrough on arms control, and the superpowers' contest remains what it is today? Skillful maneuvering within the German SPD might postpone a showdown from its April 1982 Congress until 1983, so as to give to the arms control side of the December 1979 decision a chance to progress before going ahead with actual deployment of the weapons involved. But can a settlement of accounts be delayed forever? A showdown over internal or external matters could lead to a rift that might doom the SPD-liberal coalition, and bring a coalition of the Christian Democratic Union (CDU) and liberals to power even before the election of 1984. Such a return to power of the CDU could theoretically put an end to the crisis. But there is a major difference between the period when Chancellor Konrad Adenauer succeeded, through perseverance, in converting the SPD to his foreign policy priorities—integration into Western Europe and NATO—and the present period, in which the CDU itself is not entirely immune to the antinuclear epidemic and shows itself eager to reassure the public about its commitment to negotiations as well as to strength.

NATO AND NUCLEAR WEAPONS

It certainly is not in America's interest to have the NATO decision, and by implication the strategy and policy of the United States, be either the decisive issue in a battle for control within the SPD or the central issue in German politics—something that would happen should the ruling coalition fall over it and the SPD be captured by its left wing. The Federal Republic, for all its economic strength and political stability, remains a fragile plant.

The solidity of the alliance in Western Europe has always rested on the existence of a broad foreign policy consensus among noncommunist parties. It might therefore be wise for the United States to start thinking about an alternative, should the December 1979 decision become politically unenforceable. The worst that could happen would be an American insistence that enforcement is the test of loyalty to NATO, coupled with mutterings about Finlandization and threats of American troop withdrawals. It is not in our interest to hold European governments hostage and to force them to choose between NATO and their domestic support. After all, the NATO decision to counter Soviet deployments with land-based missiles in Western Europe was aimed at reassuring the West Europeans. There are other ways, militarily, of coping with the threat; it is in our interest to find one that satisfies the governments *and* the publics, and to avoid the perils of polarization. To be sure, with time the protesters might lose heart, grow tired, give up. But the opposite might happen, and it is not in our interest to risk the further growth of the mix of dark fears and rosy fantasies that marks the current movement.

This is where the lesson of the ill-fated European Defense Community and 1954-1955 should be remembered. As long as there was a chance to get the European Defense Community through the French Parliament, the U.S. government probably had to insist that there was no good alternative. But it was foolish for Washington to threaten an "agonizing reappraisal" and not to prepare for an alternative; moreover, it was lucky that British Prime Minister Anthony Eden and French Premier Pierre Mendès-France came up with one. This time, it makes sense to think of one immediately. The aim would be to reach the sensible objectives set by NATO in December 1979, but in ways that would be politically less costly. Insofar as we are dealing at least as much with the psychology of perceptions as with military certainties (which do not exist in the absence of any experience of nuclear war, as the cacophony of the experts confirms), we should not be tied to a single approach.

An alternative should be based on the following considerations. One, the reason for the December 1979 decision remains valid—preventing the Soviets from believing that their new theater arsenal could allow them to strike without risking American retaliation on their own territory. Two, such a strengthening of deterrence is more plausible if it does not rely exclu-

231

sively on the central systems: the "certainty of uncertainty" about an American reply, which is, as McGeorge Bundy puts it, what deters a major Soviet attack, is greater if the United States is not faced with a choice between limited, tactical nuclear retaliation and a strategic first strike against the Soviet Union. Three, the credibility of the deterrent, and the defensive, second-strike character of the weapon systems are reinforced by their invulnerability.

While the concerns of coupling and invulnerability are partly at odds, there are ways of reconciling them: one would be to preserve a limited land-based capability in the form of a small number of cruise missiles (which are preferable to the Pershing II because they are slower and less vulnerable and thus less of an incentive to a Soviet preemptive attack), and to complement it with offshore, sea-based cruise missiles such as those whose construction was approved by President Reagan. A sea-based cruise missile force was rejected by NATO in 1979 because the key concern was visible coupling, which only land-based systems provide. But if a sea-based force might be deemed a less effective deterrent because of its migratory nature, one could also argue that it would be a *more* effective deterrent due to its reduced vulnerability. In any case, a deterrent whose domestic acceptability is low is less effective than one that does not raise such divisive controversy or drive people into absolutist and absurd positions.

One could conceive of an arms control agreement limited to long-range theater forces, in which the Soviets would agree to end their deployments and even to cut them down, in exchange for Western consent to limit NATO deployments to the new kind proposed here.

On the other hand, a failure to reach agreement on theater arms control on the basis of the December 1979 decision might serve as the occasion for replacing that decision with a new one. The alternative could include the deployment of a mix of long-range theater forces more acceptable to the public, and a reduction of NATO's stockpile of short-range nuclear weapons, which is currently too large for deterrence, too vulnerable to a pre-emptive strike, too close to the battlefied for crisis stability, and which, if used for fighting purposes, would destroy Europe without at all guaranteeing a successful defense.

One last option, of course, would be the abandonment of any long-run theater nuclear reinforcement. Two plans of this sort have been suggested; both are questionable. One is the reliance on U.S.-based air-launched cruise missiles (ALCMs), on the basis of that theory of deterrence which counts on the "certainty of uncertainty" rather than on exact matching or on a "seamless web" of deterrence.[6] While it is true that our deterrent posture should be based on our own assessment of NATO needs, not on an obsession with matching every Soviet capability, one of the needs is to provide the *plausibility of coupling.* The problem is not that U.S. strategic forces cannot adequately deter the new Soviet forces, but that their location matters from the Europeans' viewpoint; the solution, less difficult than squaring the circle, is to make the location more reassuring than threatening to them.

The other plan would put all of NATO's efforts into conventional reinforcement.[7] An improvement of the conventional balance is indispensable, but it is not a panacea. Politically, it would be very difficult to get our allies to agree on a policy that puts the bulk of the financial burden on them (unlike the December 1979 decision); moreover, it would be resisted as decoupling, as has always been the case in the past. And militarily, it may not be a valid option at all—unless all nuclear weapons were removed from Western Europe (something which many of the same protesters who today call for denuclearization would brand as proof of abandonment by the United States).

V.

From the story of the December 1979 decision, there are three main lessons to be learned.[8]

One concerns NATO's major military decisions. They tend to be shaped too much by the circumstances that prevail at the time—and by short-term considerations—and to be too dependent on the political climate of the moment. Once again, the parallel with the European Defense Community is worth stressing. West German rearmament was a long-term necessity; but the haste and manner in which it was undertaken could only be explained by the shock of the Korean War. And a treaty drafted in the somber period of late Stalinism looked quite different after the tyrant's death, in what seemed a possible prelude to a thaw.

In the current instance there was, again, a legitimate long-term concern, resulting from the Soviet build-up in Europe. But the way in which the decision was taken reflected two short-term considerations. One was to reassure Western Europe that SALT II would not create, or rather leave, a "Eurostrategic imbalance"—even though it was already clear in the late 1970s that the evolution of American nuclear programs, and particularly the development of cruise missiles, was likely to transform the balance of nuclear forces to America's advantage by the late 1980s, as well as to blur the distinction between central and regional systems. The other consideration was to show firm U.S. leadership so as to avoid repeating the neutron bomb fiasco, in which the Carter administration reversed its decision to produce and deploy enhanced radiation weapons, embarrassing European governments that were going to endorse the plan.

Above all, the context of the decision evaporated almost as soon as the decision was reached. Insofar as it was an instrument for a post-SALT negotiation, it assumed both the ratification of SALT II and a continuation of what was left of the Soviet-American détente (which was the exploration of arms control areas). But when the German Chancellor came to the United States in June 1979 in order to help get SALT II ratified, he may well have sensed here the mounting hostility to the treaty, and his enthusiasm for the emerging NATO decision may have cooled a bit. The train was, however, on its tracks and became an infernal machine. Paradoxically, a resolution aimed at countering Soviet moves became less rather than more acceptable to much of the public after the aggression in Afghanistan; a military program aimed at redressing the balance in a climate of détente appeared as one more step toward Armageddon in a climate of renewed Cold War.

The second lesson concerns the United States. America's style, its tone, matter as much as its actual policy; we may not like the mood abroad, but we can't afford to tune out. Our leaders must learn the difference between restoring America's strength and appearing bellicose; between extending their protection to our friends and taking over; between shedding illusions about arms control and seemingly shedding arms control altogether; between helping allied governments to overcome domestic oppposition by avoiding anythying that would feed the suspicions and prejudices of the demonstrators, and exacerbating U.S.-European strains by sternly repeating ad infinitum the rationale of the 1979 decisions, and directly denouncing the protesters (something which should be left to their own governments).

Two things are particularly needed in this regard. One is greater sensitivity to Europe's fear of war. It is not, and should not be equated with, sympathy for Moscow: among the protesters, Moscow's admirers are a minority. But an America that sees the world in terms of the bipolar contest finds it hard to understand that, paradoxically, the disenchantment of Europe's young people and intellectuals with Moscow makes them more, not less, exacting toward the United States. (They feel neither responsible for, nor surprised by, the attack on Afghanistan, but as allies of the United States they felt implicated in the fate of Vietnam and were both revolted and self-righteous.)

Similarly, the European fear of war is not, and should not be equated with, a desire for appeasement and a cowardly rejection of defense. It ex-

234

presses a perfectly understandable determination to stay on the only sensible side of the great, perhaps fading divide that separates deterrence from war: the side of deterrence and arms control. It is of course true that in history some things have been worse than war. But the United States was not any more immune to appeasement in the 1930s than Britain or France; and it is easier to remind others of the merits of war, or to spin scenarios of nuclear war with cool pseudorationality, when one has never been occupied or devastated, or when one has a good conscience about never having inflicted wanton destruction on others in an evil cause, as many West Germans feel Germany did in the not-so-distant past.

There is, on this side of the ocean, a frequent lack of imagination and empathy. The subtle, subterranean solidarity in war-related traumas that links Western Europe, Eastern Europe and the Soviet Union is a fact that the Soviets exploit with skill. We must be aware of it, and walk softly. In this country, a flowing rhetoric may be the only way to make new policies possible, and the gap is often wide between the verbiage (invented anew by each administration) and the realities (where continuity prevails). But others tend to judge us on our verbiage, and to interpret harmless deeds or ambiguous statements in light of our rhetorical designs. To many in Europe, the President's decision to produce the neutron bomb and his off-the-cuff remark on the possibility of limiting a nuclear exchange to Europe appear as parts of a pattern. Americans may find this absurd. But they must make an effort to understand, or else they will be badly surprised again; in 1979, a distinguished journalist, now a high official in charge of relations with Europe, flatly stated that "you don't have people debating in little coffee shops at night about the Pershing II!"[9] Steadiness is essential. When many of those who once trumpeted the news of America's vulnerability and weakness start flexing muscles and anticipating "High Noon," a Western European public that needs both reliable American protection and a promise of peace inevitably gets confused and anxious.

What is also needed is a long-term policy toward the Soviet Union. Even those Europeans who were most impatient with the Carter administration's inability to define a coherent strategy toward Moscow, and who approve of the new administration's decision to strengthen America's defenses, worry about new inconsistencies and questionable new trends. They see an American government that presses them to take risks and disapproves of their hesitations as well as of their economic deals with Moscow, yet rejects the draft, lifts the grain embargo, and finds it politically expedient to put the MX into existing silos, however vulnerable.

Europeans often sympathize with Washington's determination to raise the costs of Soviet, or Soviet-supported, meddling in the internal affairs of countries in Latin America or Africa, and to protect the oil fields of the Middle East. But they worry about the U.S. tendency to give everywhere priority to the Soviet threat and to want others to give it the same priority, even over pressing local threats or internal concerns. They worry about the administration's apparent belief that no dialogue with Moscow is possible unless the Soviets accept American notions of restraint or (in strategic matters) of deep reductions. They worry about what they see as an American nostalgia for the 1950s, for the era of American nuclear superiority, a relatively quiescent Third World, and unquestioned American leadership of an alliance of unequals. Leaders in Western Europe need to provide their people with a perspective brighter than unlimited containment and recurrent clashes. They fear that the combination of a deep distrust of Soviet actions and intentions, the expectation of trouble, and the lack of any policy beyond the realm of the military may bring prophecies of confrontation to perilous self-fulfillment.

The third lesson concerns Western Europe. The reactions of the protesters reflect more than a legitimate fear of war, more than an idealistic demand for a future that leaves room for hope and progress. They also incorporate the heavy price of thirty-five years of dependence. Western Europe is a frying pan on a stove whose controls are in the hands of others. Irresponsibility and resentment are the inevitable outcomes. Nations that must rely on others for their defense, and consequently for much of their foreign policy, often tend to turn inward, leaving to those others the responsibility—and the blame—for difficult decisions. For many years now the architects of the European Community, trying to make a virtue of necessity, have argued that their new entity would be "civilian" in nature, repudiating power politics and behaving as a model for others. Defense matters have been left to NATO, where key decisions are made unilaterally by the United States, or collectively at American initiative. As a result, Western Europe has had the worst of both worlds—the trials of a collective new political entity, without control over the one issue that stands at the heart of sovereignty and authority.

It is not by coincidence that the only country in which the protest movement is marginal is France, where most of the opponents of civilian nuclear power, for instance, do not seem to object to the French nuclear strike force, and where since de Gaulle the government has been responsible for France's defense, nuclear weapons included. In France, over the past twenty years, optimists and utopians—for instance in the Socialist Party—have moved from opposition to French defense policy to acceptance and responsibility. France is not a model for other NATO countries; either they are too weak or—in the case of West Germany—the political costs of a quest for autonomy are too high, both at home and abroad. But their lack of national autonomy encourages a drift toward wishful thinking and romantic resistance.

For too many years, Western European abdication has fed American tendencies to unilateral action, and the latter has engendered Western European anger. Already, many Americans have accused their allies of trying to force them into a hopeless arms control charade; some angry but not unrepresentative American voices draw parallels between the spirit of Munich and the new protests, or the failure of several governments to support the original decision, and threaten to leave Western Europe to its own resources. And angry but not unrepresentative European voices, such as those of pastor Heinrich Albertz in Berlin and of SPD leader Erhard Eppler, call for an end to a situation that leaves Germany as target practice for the superpowers, and makes Western Europe a pawn on the superpowers' chessboard. A.W. de Porte, writing from the perspective of the great powers, was not wrong in seeing in the division of Europe a radical solution to the old German problem and a guarantee of stability.[10] But, as Pierre Hassner has so often pointed out, stability can be threatened not only by the external moves of the great—a threat reduced by the division of Europe—but also by the internal turmoil of the dependents—a threat which their impatience with dependence exacerbates. For even dependents can cause trouble, when—as in the case of Poland—they want to regain their domestic autonomy, or when—as in several countries in Western Europe—large groups long for some spectacular (and not necessarily wise) demonstration of foreign policy autonomy.

The dependence of America's NATO allies is not only bad for U.S.-European relations, it is a further factor of intra-European division. Yesterday, the Federal Republic resented Gaullist France's decision to leave NATO and to pursue a strategy that treated West Germany mainly as a glacis for French protection on which French nuclear artillery would fall, but not as a partner in forward defense. Today, it is the turn of the French, not only to describe with some condescension the protests in Germany as the direct effect of dependence, but also to suspect once again that the protesters might be moved by a desire for reunification in neutrality that would play into Soviet hands and undermine the alliance—a suspicion French President Georges Pompidou seems to have had already about the *Ostpolitik* of Willy Brandt.

To be sure, dependence on the presence of American conventional forces and on the American nuclear guarantee is a permanent fact of Western European life: the U.S. troops make the guarantee plausible, and the guarantee is the ultimate deterrent. Yet ways must be found to minimize the political effects of the West's inevitable geographical and military inferiority—a weakness which the present structure of the alliance exaggerates. This means, on the one hand, three policy shifts within NATO itself.

First, despite the Western Europeans' own reluctance, it is necessary that they share more fully and far more equally the important military decisions—decisions not only on deployments, but on doctrine and on the actual use of nuclear weapons. The December 1979 decision, it has been said, shows America's willingness to share the risks incurred by her allies. But as long as the ultimate decision to use or not to use the systems is America's alone, the allies will suspect that at the moment of truth the risk may be left to them alone. Second, even the most central military decisions are only part of an overall policy toward the Soviet Union: the alliance's defense posture serves as a platform on which the broader policy can stand, and military doctrine aims at coping with worst-case hypotheses. The overall policy, which must aim at making the worst case unlikely by political as well as by military means, can no longer be decided in Washington alone. The very divergence in conceptions mentioned above makes an attempt at reconciliation the only sane alternative to either a widening gap or a series of ad hoc fixes and compromises that leave the misunderstandings intact. Third, arms control negotiations dealing with the European theater should, like talks on mutual and balanced force reductions, be conducted on the Western side not by the United States alone, but by the United Sates *and* its military partners.

On the other hand, since within NATO the preponderant weight of the United States is likely to remain a source of tension, it is time for Western Europe to examine whether there is not room at last for the gradual development of a European defense organization. Such an organization would include the French and, in a first phase, would improve cooperation on upgrading conventional defense, as well as foster Franco-British nuclear coordination. The prospects of an increasing diversion of American resources from Western Europe to other parts of the world—which the Europeans do not consider NATO's responsibility—as well as of American impatience with the allies' apparent foot-dragging within NATO, and the need to buttress European political cooperation with cooperation on defense, suffice to justify the enterprise. If it should develop and grow and lead to a satisfactory process of collective decision-making, one could even envisage a joint effort, by all or by certain of the participants, to build European theater nuclear weapons (the French are already planning middle-range systems and have the means to produce neutron bombs) and a possible joint acquisition of American theater nuclear forces, to be transferred from American or NATO control to a European command. This would, of course, require the establishment of a European defense directorate, functioning in such a way that West Germany alone could neither initiate a resort to nuclear weapons nor produce and own such weapons, but could participate in decisions on the use of nuclear weapons and in the joint production and ownership of European theater nuclear forces.

Obviously, we are very far from such a prospect. Until now, Western Europe has preferred to leave the biggest decisions to the United States, and to criticize the United States for its errors or confusion. A specific defense effort in Western Europe also raises three formidable issues which have been insurmountable in the past—the risk of providing Washington with a pretext for reducing the American commitment to Western Europe (for instance, by withdrawing troops), the problems of West German participation in a European nuclear force, and the disjunction between a common defense and the very loose integration of foreign and domestic policies within the European Community.

The first issue may look very different in the future—mutual exasperation within the present NATO framework may itself pose the greatest peril for a continuing American commitment. But the other two problems remain. The German question ought to be faced squarely: Is not a Federal Republic with increased military responsibilities, exercised and contained within a European organization, preferable to a Federal Republic tempted by neutralism and nationalism? Would such a development, in the last part of this century, really be considered by the Soviet Union as a genuine threat, given the absence of any West German revanchism and the restrictions that would continue to limit Bonn's military sovereignty? As for the discrepancy between functions, must all sectors progress with the same rhythm?

The reasons for moving in this new direction are compelling, given the alternatives. And yet, it is not very likely that it will be chosen—partly because of each European country's preoccupation with domestic economic and social problems, partly because of the absence of any great European ambition, combined with the persistence of separate external interests and national perspectives, and partly because of the formidable weight of existing patterns and habits—both within NATO's military organization and within France, which is complacently used to the benefits derived from a combination of autonomy and cooperation with NATO. Simple, untroubled dependency is no longer a possibility (was it ever untroubled, anyway?). Turbulent dependency with a growing appeal of some mix of neutralism and pacifism—unless the United States shows far more finesse than it has in recent years—is the most probable outcome. But it is not a happy one.

Clearly, these considerations far exceed the theater nuclear forces tangle. But the reactions in Western Europe to this issue, and the failure, so far, to understand them on this side of the Atlantic, show that a resolution of the issue itself will either depend on progress in the areas just discussed or (should, miraculously, the December 1979 decision be enforced in a way that pleases all the Allies) leave the more fundamental problems unaddressed, and therefore bound to provoke new crisis later.[12]

DEAD ENDS

ADDENDUM TO CHAPTER 11

Shortly after this essay was published, and for several months now, the discussion of NATO's strategy, initiated by the article written by McGeorge Bundy, George Kennan, Robert McNamara, and Gerard Smith (see note 7 in this chapter), has focused not on the planned deployments of new intermediate nuclear forces, but on the first use of any nuclear weapons—tactical or strategic—by NATO in case of a Soviet conventional attack. A no-first-use posture would, according to the four authors, make new deployments—especially of counterforce weapons—unnecessary, while requiring new efforts in conventional defense. The four American writers correctly point out that, if nuclear deterrence fails and NATO initiates the use of nuclear weapons, it is unlikely that such a war could remain limited. But, as four West German writers have made it clear in their reply (see note 7), such a shift in strategy could make war more probable by liberating Moscow from the "nuclear risk." A no-first-strike strategy in a Europe stuffed with nuclear weapons might not appear very plausible to Moscow in any case—and so, why weaken the deterrent potential of these weapons by a statement that would create dangerous confusion and ambiguity? A no-first-use strategy accompanied by the removal of nuclear weapons from Western Europe would appear to most people in Western Europe as a fatal "decoupling," making Europe safe for conventional war and probably fatally wounding the alliance. As the four West German writers say, a reduction of dependence on an early use of nuclear weapons, by a combination of efforts in the conventional realm and of arms control, is a sound goal. But in the meantime, "the Europeans. . . . cannot give up the ultimate threat of nuclear retaliation to prevent both nuclear and conventional wars in Europe."[11]

It is true that in an age of nuclear parity, the initiation of nuclear war entails a reckless risk of mutual destruction that mortgages its plausibility. But it does not make the threat incredible, given the importance of the stakes: after all, it is up to the state that would initiate war in the first place—the Soviet Union—to decide whether the risk has vanished; and as Khrushchev once put it, no state wants to run even a small risk of total destruction. It is precisely this consideration that, on the one hand, vindicates NATO's decision to deploy new nuclear weapons aimed at shoring up its traditional strategy (whatever reservations one may have about the actual weapons selected), and, on the other hand, makes it unnecessary to try to match Soviet deployments weapon for weapon.

As for a West European defense system, it remains an idea, or an ideal, and nothing else. There is still no Franco-British nuclear cooperation. And while the president of France seems eager to discuss French nuclear strategy

240

with West Germany, cuts in the French defense budget affect mainly the forces in which Bonn is most interested—French conventional forces. French defense policy is more nuclear, and therefore more difficult to "integrate," than ever.

NOTES

1. For further elaboration see Chapter 10.

2. McGeorge Bundy, "Common Sense and Missiles in Europe," *Washington Post* (October 20, 1981):A23.

3. Some of these arguments are made by Hans Goebel in "The Wrong Force for the Right Mission," National Security Series, no. 4 (Kingston, Ontario: Center for International Relations, Queens College, 1981), pp. 60 ff.

4. The analysis of noncentral nuclear forces that follows is largely drawn from the third report, "Challenges for U.S. National Security," by the staff of the Carnegie Panel on U.S. Security and the Future of Arms Control (1982).

5. On these points, see William Hyland, "Soviet Theatre Forces and Arms Control Policy," *Survival* (September-October 1981):194-99.

6. McGeorge Bundy, "Instead of Missiles," *The New York Times*, May 21, 1981.

7. See the article by McGeorge Bundy, George F. Kennan, Robert S. McNamara and Gerard Smith, "Nuclear weapons and the Western alliance," *Foreign Affairs* (Spring 1982):753-68; and the reply by Karl Kaiser and three other German writers, "Nuclear weapons and the preservation of peace" and the correspondence in *Foreign Affairs* (Summer 1982):1157-1180.

8. See also Christoph Bertram, "Political implications of the theater nuclear balance," in Barry M. Bleichman, ed., *Rethinking the U.S. Strategic Posture* (Cambridge, Mass.: Ballinger, 1982), ch. 5, pp. 101-28.

9. Richard Burt, in W. Scott Thompson, ed., *National Security in the 1980s: From Weakness to Strength* (New Brunswick: Transaction Books, 1980), p. 235.

10. A.W. DePorte, *Europe Between the Superpowers* (New Haven: Yale University Press, 1979).

11. Theodore Draper, "How Not to Think about Nuclear War," *New York Review of Books* (September 23, 1982):60.

12. For further discussion see: Stanley Hoffmann, "American Liberals and Europe's antinuclear movement", *Dissent*, Spring 1982, pp. 148-151.

PART IV

A STRATEGY FOR THE
LONG TERM

THE TWO essays in this section present in more systematic form most of the themes developed in the previous sections. They are, above all, arguments for a strategy that would move away from a doubly simplistic view of the world—one which looks almost exclusively at the bipolar contest and one which, because of this, focuses principally on military power.

The two superpowers are what they are because of their overwhelming military might, which no third power can match. However, the difficulties both experience in controlling other states as well as outcomes are due, on the one hand, to the risks entailed by the uninhibited use of military power in the nuclear age (in these days of indignation against nuclear weapons, one should not forget that they have helped avoid military confrontations between Washington and Moscow). In other words, what distinguishes the superpowers most from all other states is precisely that power which they have to be most careful about using. On the other hand, military power is of very little use in a diplomacy that has to cover an increasingly varied agenda.

Abandoning simplistic views does not mean abandoning the search for a coherent policy. Indeed, both essays argue that the need for coherence is made only greater and more urgent by the complexities of the international system and the diversity of threats the United States and its allies will have to face in the last part of this century. But, some have argued, oversimplification (particularly one kind, often deplored in this volume, as well as in the writings of George Kennan: the focus on the military as the most important tool of policy) is necessary, because it allows the president to obtain the support of the public (a great part of which is almost inherently ill disposed toward entanglement in world affairs), to rally Congress (otherwise inclined to give priority to parochial concerns), and to keep both the legislative branch and the public alerted to outside perils. This is a dangerous argument, because simplification leads inevitably to frustrations, when the voters and the members of Congress realize that the world resists simple grids, or to disappointments, when ideas or programs are oversold, or to disbelief, when the president cries wolf too often. It leads to failures abroad, which boomerang at home. To be sure, the broad, deep, and lasting postwar consensus formed around a rather simple view—containment. But it corresponded to the situation of the late 1940s, and disintegrated only over Vietnam—a war that resulted from the misapplication of the original concept to a situation it did not fit. The simplistic ideology of President Reagan has been neither effective abroad, nor capable of creating solid and broad consensus at home.

Moreover, to argue that only simplistic views are capable of providing the president with the support he needs to carry out foreign policy suggests that this country has no chance of having a policy that can be effective both at home and abroad. This is a counsel of despair. The United States cannot give up playing a role on the world stage and therefore—although its domestic institutional, psychological, and social peculiarities will continue to affect both the definition and the performance of the role—the task of obtaining and preserving internal support for a policy that is appropriate to the world of the 1980s and 1990s cannot be declared hopeless at the outset. Indeed, perhaps even more than the task of devising an adequate strategy in world affairs, this may well be the greatest challenge that lies ahead for the American political system.

CHAPTER 12

SECURITY IN THE AGE OF TURBULENCE

I.

INTERNATIONAL SECURITY is both a relative and an uneven notion. In an "anarchic society" of nations that live in a condition of troubled peace or in a "state of war"—depending on whether one takes a more Lockean or a more Hobbesian view of world affairs—there will always be a modicum of insecurity. Not all the actors can be simultaneously secure as long as we have not reached the unlikely stage of living in a world without threats and enmities, or the distant stage of inhabiting a world so well organized that its members are both deprived of, and saved from, self-help. Moreover, the scope of insecurity is not fixed; the security of the world as a whole is threatened only by some perils, whereas certain regions, or individual members, can be endangered also by threats that do not affect the security of others.

For the purposes of this essay, I will define international insecurity as the sum of all the factors that can lead to serious confrontations between the major powers (those whose resources and policies are such as to shape the fate of a large number of other actors), to increases in the threat or in the reality of contagious or uncontrollable violence and to such a deterioration of, or such an increase in the unpredictability of, international economic transactions as to threaten the economic lives of large numbers of countries. I will argue here that there is a likelihood of considerable international insecurity in the 1980s, for reasons described below. I will then examine the general problem of how to cope with it and will finally discuss specific means of response.

The major factors that contribute to insecurity in the 1980s are not new. For many years now the international system has been characterized by three contradictions that breed turbulence. The first is the contradiction between the universal Cold War and the growing complexity of the system. It creates a serious dilemma for the superpowers. How far should they go in injecting their rivalry into a region? Noninvolvement spares one the risks of confrontation and the costs of economic or military presence. Involvement, however, yields opportunities for influence. The dilemma creates uncertainty, especially as local circumstances or domestic factors may, at times, facilitate or invite the involvement of one superpower and inhibit that of the other. The American attempt, in the 1970s, to find a middle way by relying on regionally influential states has been disappointing—their leaders turned out to have clay feet, like the shah, or pursued their own interests.

The second is the contradiction between what Raymond Aron once called the "unity of the diplomatic field"—the existence of a single international system—and the multiple heterogeneities of the field. These relate to:

—the types of actors: they range from peoples in search of a nation-state (Palestinians, Kurds), to states in quest of a nation (Africa), to nation-states, to empires; hence there are innumerable opportunities for conflict;

—the regimes and ideologies, despite universal lip service to the two principles of self-government and self-determination, which turn out both to have mutliple interpretations and to create insoluble problems;

—the economic and social systems and levels of economic development (here, heterogeneity has been and will keep growing);

—the nature of power: one observes a functional fragmentation of international politics, in which different games are played not only in different regions but over different "issue areas" (to borrow the language of Nye and Keohane).

As a result, we live in a world marked by two features. One is considerable asymmetry between the actors. Very few can be considered "full powers", endowed with a complete panoply of power; many actors have only one dimension of power—for example, economic but not military (Saudi Arabia), or military but not economic (Vietnam), or no power other than a good geographical location or a potentially usable vote in an international or regional organization. Even the two superpowers are asymmetrical, given, on the one hand, both the weaknesses of the Soviet economy (despite huge resources) and the Soviet Union's absence (on the whole) from the

246

open international economy and, on the other hand, the Soviet Union's willingness, in recent years to resort to self-help and ability to use proxies on a considerable scale. Second, there is a double transformation of the international hierarchy. It is being subverted, insofar as the superpowers are often inhibited in the full use of their power by a variety of factors (the risks of collision, their inability to achieve collusion, the inadequacy of their forms of power to deal with local circumstances and the ability of their clients to manipulate them), and insofar as states with limited power (such as Saudi Arabia or even West Germany) can achieve considerable influence in certain issue areas. The international hierarchy is also being fragmented, since the pecking order varies from one issue area to another.

A contradiction exists between the principle of sovereignty, which remains the basis of international law and international order, and the restraints which weigh on all the actors and provide the only safety nets in a very dangerous system devoid of common values: the concern for survival and the quest for development and welfare. In the realm of security this contradiction takes the form of another paradox: the coexistence of stable deterrence at the global level (despite the difference in military arsenals and strategic doctrines between the United States and the Soviet Union) and the search for usable nuclear strategies (that is, for war-fighting rather than for pure deterrence), as well as a continuing drift towards nuclear proliferation. In the realm of development and welfare the contradiction creates two acute problems: the problem of inequality, or the revolt against the international economic system largely created by the leading capitalist powers, and particularly by the United States; and the problem of monopoly, or the attempt by developing states endowed with key resources to exploit their advantages. In other words, the international system is characterized by the constant manipulation of the two restraints: it is a permanent and multiple game of chicken.

Unitl now, international insecurity has been kept at tolerable levels by different factors that have had the same result: they have prevented causes of turbulence from joining, or trouble in one region or issue area from spreading to the others. Fragmentation or dissociation has prevailed. First, in the superpowers' competition this has taken the form of a sort of division of the world into relatively autonomous subsystems, each one with its own "rules of the game", which depend on the configuration of local forces and of the superpowers' forces in the region. The limits of Soviet power, both in the economic realm and, until recent years, in the military domain, and the stability of the "balance of terror" provided by the chief rivals' strategic nuclear weapons have contributed to this fragmentation.

A second kind of dissociation has always been more fragile. The distinction between domestic politics and foreign policy has never been rigid in practice, and throughout the 1950s, 1960s, and 1970s we have witnessed inter-state conflicts over a regime, or over the application of self-determination, or over the combination of the two—this is what the wars in Korea and Vietnam were about—as well as domestic revolutions with international repercussions (as in Cuba and China). But again these explosions have been kept separate, and a great deal of domestic turbulence has not provoked international involvement or conflict.

A third dissociation, which lasted through the 1960s, was that between the open international economy and the strategic-diplomatic chessboard: the two-track system analyzed by Richard Cooper.[1] To be sure, that dissociation itself resulted from a political design—the United States' conception of a global order—and from the kinds of political bargains that Robert Gilpin has described.[2] And it was never total: the Marshall plan had strategic-diplomatic goals, and the West used economic warfare against the East. Nevertheless, within these limits it allowed for the reasonably successful management of the world economy—brilliantly, indeed, in relations between advanced capitalist states, less brilliantly in North-South relations. Deterioration, whose causes began to operate in the late 1960s, set in in the 1970s. However, despite inflation, recession and the multiple ramifications of the oil crises of the 1970s, a major disaster comparable with the Great Depression of the 1930s has been avoided.

The problem of the 1980s is the risk of an end of dissociation or fragmentation, for reasons that can be found within each of three realms just mentioned. In the first place, the factors of regional fragmentation of the superpowers' contest are weakening. The key development here is the Soviet ability to project military power abroad, and the Soviet determination to exploit Western weaknesses in the Third World in ways different from, and more effective than, the earlier Soviet methods that led to serious reversals not only in the Congo in 1960 but later in the Sudan, in Egypt and in Somalia—not to mention China. The Soviet Union, while continuing to support forces more promising than subservient Communist parties in places where these are insignificant, now prefers to help movements whose social goals and methods fit within Marxist-Leninist orthodoxy; and the Soviet Union sees to it, when its client gets to power, that his dependence is great enough, and the Soviet presence weighty enough, to prevent a repetition of what happened in Egypt in July 1972. Moreover, for reasons best analyzed by Seweryn Bailer,[3] the Soviet Union may, in the 1980s, be increasingly tempted to compensate abroad for domestic weaknesses and tensions: declining growth, serious economic inefficiencies, one or two succession periods, a growing need for oil from the outside, changes in the demographic composition of the Soviet Union—all may lead to a quest for external triumphs. There is an interesting asymmetry here:

turbulence in Eastern Europe would obviously affect the Soviet Union more profoundly than the West, but the desire to avoid Soviet repression (as well as another burst of tension and another display of Western helplessness) incites the members of NATO to prudence and counsels of moderation for the malcontents. Turbulence in Third World areas affects the United States and its allies far more than Moscow, and Moscow shows little reluctance to exploit it whenever the circumstances seem favorable.

Another development dangerous for regional disconnection is the activity of Soviet client states with important military means and ambitions of their own: Cuba in Africa, and Vietnam in Southeast Asia. A third development is the new American determination to contain more vigorously than in recent years such advances by Soviet proxies and by the Soviet Union. The final threat comes from strategic considerations. Regional fragmentation presupposes either a military balance (as in Europe), or such an imbalance that (as in Latin America) one superpower actually has the field to itself, or a willingness on the part of the rivals to compete primarily by means other than military (or merely by providing arms to local clients). But when both superpowers—or one superpower and the close allies of the other—decide to compete more vigorously and with armed forces, and when, in addition, there is a regional imbalance in conventional forces, the temptation for the loser to compensate either by exploiting its superiority elsewhere or by exploiting whatever advantages it may have (or believes it has) in the strategic nuclear realm will be considerable. In this respect, the gradual shift from the stability of mutual assured destruction, plus some arms control, to the instability of counterforce, war-fighting strategies—likely to be detrimental both to deterrence and to crisis stability—minus arms control is a last nail in the coffin of regional fragmentation.

In the second place, the collapse of the distinction between domestic and foreign affairs is likely to become universal: domestic affairs are likely to become the stake of international politics and intervention the empirical norm. We have almost reached the end of the protracted period of decolonization (only southern Africa is left). What we now find is a scene marked by the following features.

Many countries are endowed with artificial borders and are racked by destructive internal communal conflicts between tribes, ethnic groups, religious sects, and cultural factions, or by violent clashes between ideological opponents or rival army cliques, or a combination of all these. Recently Iran, India, Burma, Zimbabwe, El Salvador, Bolivia, Lebanon, and South Korea have been in the news for such reasons. A state with a badly or only partially integrated society or a tyrannical regime is likely to be a target for meddling, by a great power or by a neighbor intent on ensuring security or on expanding influence by removing a hostile regime or by exploiting

DEAD ENDS

internal dissensions next door. In recent years, Vietnam's move into Cambodia, Tanzania's overthrow of Idi Amin, Somalia's war in Ethiopia, Iraq's intrigues against Iran and Syria and her war with Iran, Israel's invasion of Lebanon, and Libya's probes in Chad all give us a taste of things to come. Finally, revolutions are likely in many places—it is through force that governments and regimes tend to change in the Third World—and many of these carry a risk either of realignment in the global Cold War or of withdrawal from a pro-Western alignment, as in the case of Iran in 1979.

Why should the threat of greater internal fragmentation in Third World countries, and of more inter-state conflicts resulting from it, lead to international rather than to mere regional insecurity? Partly because some of the countries that could be in trouble occupy important strategic positions (Egypt) or provide vital resources (Saudi Arabia); partly because internal factions or external meddlers seek and obtain outside support (think of the Polisario case: the guerrillas have Algerian and Libyan help; Morocco has American assistance); partly because of the way generalized turbulence affects the great powers' definition of their security. They always tend to oscillate between two poles. The narrow definition practically equates security with survival: national security means the protection of the nation (and of nationals abroad) against physical attack and the safeguarding of its economic activities from devastating outside blows. The broad definition tends to equate national security and foreign policy or national interests. This is excessive (and dangerous, either when such interests vastly outrun the nation's power or when they lead to so formidable an expansion of that power—in order to match the interests—as to frighten or threaten other states). And yet an expansive definition of security is inevitable, for two reasons. The first reason is valid for all states, major or not. Since the state is represented in world affairs by its regime, the latter will consider its own self-preservation as a matter of national security, a fact that tends to be neglected by authors who write in countries with legitimate and stable governments. Second, major actors, almost by definition, project their power abroad in order to provide their physical and economic security with a kind of *glacis*, and they do so in the two modes distinguished by Arnold Wolfers, when he wrote about possession and milieu goals.[4] They tend to equate their own national security with that of close allies—of states whose physical and economic survival is deemed indispensable to their own. And they define as essential to their national security the preservation either of a clientele of states (without whose physical and economic survival they could most probably live), or of international rules and regimes whose loss would markedly affect their influence and their status.

In a sense, the scope of a major actor's definition of its national security depends on two factors. One is power—the greater it is, the more interests

250

SECURITY IN AN AGE OF TURBULENCE

will be equated with security and national security with foreign policy. This happened in the United States in the late 1940s and 1950s; it is happening now in the Soviet Union. The other factor is external threats: when they multiply or become sharper, and even if national power is limited, the notion of national security tends to become more expansive; it expands to meet the threat, rather than the other way round. For the United States, the first half of the 1970s was a kind of golden period in which the definition of the scope of national security seemed somewhat relaxed (not all *that* much, as Allende found out). Earlier the scope was huge because of American power. Now it grows again, because of the rise of threats and also because of the recent dynamics of the superpowers' contest. Many Americans believe that the turbulence in the Third World and the rise of radical movements hostile to the West there are due partly to a perception of declining American power or will, and they are determined to reverse the trend. But in the meantime the Soviet Union has deepened its own involvement and has to protect its own investment or act in such a way as to become a necessary factor in most important disputes and an unavoidable counterpart for the United States.

The third dissociation that is vanishing is that between the economic and the political "tracks". Here again there are several reasons. The most obvious is the international economic crisis. International insecurity is increased by the persistence of inflation and recession in major industrial countries; by the brutal politics of oil, which, through the complicated bargains of OPEC, result in higher prices (partly as a reply to the industrial powers' inflation) as well as in uncertainty about levels of production (an uncertainty compounded by revolutions and wars in the Middle East); and by the enormous threat that the rising debt of the oil importing developing countries creates for the international financial system. The outcome is both an intensified contest among nations for resources (particularly those of the seas and oceans) and domestic tension everywhere: a weakening of the ability of governments to meet the demands and needs of citizens, the rise of protectionist pressures and the necessity for many governments in poor countries to cut back on social expenditures and development plans. Another factor is the contribution made by economic development itself to internal disruption, social dislocations, and political turbulence in many Third World countries—particularly in the oil-producing countries, where sudden wealth has spread corruption and has heightened the tensions between a crumbling traditional order on one side and its two very different kinds of foes—modernizers who often turn to socialist or communist models, and traditionalists intent on restoring threatened values.

If there ever was a line separating economic from political affairs, it has now been crossed at all points. Economics has become a political weapon:

for those oil-producing "radical regimes" that want to use higher prices and cuts in production as weapons against the United States or Israel because of the Palestinian issue; for the United States, which has resorted to economic warfare against Idi Amin, against Iran after the seizure of American hostages and, after the invasion of Afghanistan, against the Soviet Union; and for the international community as a whole, which used economic sanctions against Ian Smith's Rhodesia and may do so again against South Africa. Economic frustration can also have political consequences. We have seen that, on a small scale, in Britain's recurrent ultimata to the European Economic Community; a much more disturbing case was the Havana Conference of the nonaligned nations and the success of Castro's speech, centered on North-South issues, at the UN General Assembly in 1979.

If we combine these different features, we obtain the image of a world that is becoming much more dangerous and unmanageable because of the interaction of two contradictory trends. One is the renewed commitment of the superpowers to global competition. There are serious disagreements about the nature of Soviet ambitions, but there can be little doubt about Moscow's determination to be a world power, about its accumulation of military means (whether for actual use or, like money in the bank, as a guarantee of influence), about its determination to exploit—albeit at low risk—promising opportunities, and about the decline of the inhibitions that the hope for détente's benefits had temporarily induced. In the Third World, the Soviet Union now has important assets: it can turn against the West the very strong antiracist and anti-imperialist resentments there and can provide liberation movements, or national leaders, or both, with material help and with a kind of (adaptable) model of political control. As for the United States, not only does it still have vast assets of its own—in the realm of public and, above all, private economic assistance to states, most of which cannot afford self-reliance and find the Soviet economic model unattractive—but the cumulative effect of a string of Soviet successes (almost none of which has affected by itself the hard core, or the narrow definition, of American national security) has led to a return to the more expansive definition and to the new militancy mentioned above.

The other trend is both a kind of diffusion and a pulverization of power. Many countries, including those in the Third World, are becoming important economic actors; they produce and export their own weapons, and in some cases they seem to be moving toward the production of nuclear weapons. Yet they suffer from the internal weaknesses already discussed, and may indeed make them worse through external adventures of their own. The collision of the two trends gives a major reason for pessimism (in addition to the reason provided by mutual misperceptions and internal developments in the two superpowers): the ability now of clients or proxies to manipulate the superpowers or to provoke confrontations. The biggest peril lies in "gray areas," in which uncertainty exists about the extent of a superpower's commitment to an ally or friend and about the other's likely response. There the diversity of the vital national interests of the local players and the existence of the Cold War can combine to produce serious miscalculations and "misescalations." The superpowers, concerned with their credibility, have not developed adequate means of avoiding these through consultation and crisis management. Three parts of the world are candidates for such dangers: the Middle East (where the effects of a protracted political crisis in Iran, of a long and costly war between Iraq and Iran, and of an indecisive war in Afghanistan have now been added to all the other ferments), southern Africa, and East Asia. The combination of antagonistic nationalisms, rival ideologies, imperatives of "face" (or alliance preservation, or balance of power) and domestic instabilities is frightening in all three areas.

To be sure, the danger of reconnection is not of the same order all over the world. A more detailed analysis would have to make distinctions between different areas. There will still be a number of subsystems, each one with its own dyanmics—in Europe, North and South America, Africa, the Middle East, East Asia. But all the signs point to greater turbulence in all of them except Europe (which does not mean that there will not be serious instability within both Eastern and Western Europe) and to a greater risk of the spread of insecurity from one area to others.

II.

There is another disturbing element. We have little to learn from past periods of turbulence. I have, at some length, tried to explain elsewhere why previous methods of coping with international insecurity are of little use now, and shall not repeat the arguments here.[5] But it may be worth looking briefly at two specific periods.

The first one is the period of 1870-1914, when the great powers indulged in the scramble for colonies and frequently clashed in what is now called the Third World. Despite Lenin's biased analysis of imperialism, it was not because of those expeditions and conflicts that World War I broke out. France had frequently opposed Britain and Italy, and Britain had opposed Russia, yet they ended up allies. It was not Franco-German conflicts over Morocco that led to the War. The causes began at the very core of the European state system, because of the fatal weakness of Austria-Hungary and of her vulnerability to Slav nationalism. But the precedent of that period does not suggest that turbulence in the Third World today can be treated lightly. With the exception of a few areas (that were not immediately threatened by the great powers' rivalry in Europe), the economic and strategic importance of the colonial empires was limited (of course, Tirpitz's naval policy worried Britain, but *that* race was over several years before the war began). Today, several parts of the Third World are very closely tied to the national security (even narrowly defined) of one or the other superpower or of both: obviously, the Middle East and Persian Gulf regions are areas that, in hostile hands, could threaten the vital interests of the West (and Japan) and that the Soviet Union has a vital interest in keeping from being entirely controlled by, or friendly to, her chief rivals. There are major American interests in Central America (raw materials, communications, and the containment of Cuban influence) and very similar ones in mineral-rich parts of Africa. While Southeast Asia may not be intrinsically more important to the superpowers than the Balkans to Germany or Britain in 1914, neither one can afford to see its own regional ally or friend—Vietnam or China— defeated or humiliated. In 1914 each camp's leaders were dissatisfied with the results of past restraints, afraid that new compromise or concessions would undermine their domestic or diplomatic position, convinced that time was working to the other side's advantage, confident that the other side would find it easier to back down. Whether or not one agrees with those who, rather glibly, equate Soviet policy with Imperial Germany's, the comparison between the pre-1914 period and the present is far more frightening than reassuring, as Miles Kahler has brilliantly shown (particularly when he refers to "the complications introduced by great-power rivalry superimposed upon local conflicts" and to foreign policy as a means of escape from domestic insecurity).[6] It is absurd to misapply the Munich analogy to recent Western or American behavior: Soviet advances have not been the result of appeasement; Washington and its allies have launched countermoves; no ally of the United States has defected out of fear of Moscow; and the reluctance of various states to align themselves with the United States results from local factors and from the strength of nationalism. But the 1914 analogy cannot be easily dismissed.

The other comparison would be with the post-1945 period—a period of great instability in the Third World, since it was the era of decolonization, marked by major wars and the involvement of both superpowers. However, one of the very sources of turbulence in the 1980s is the decline or disappearance of the reasons why the crisis of decolonization, and other crises in the Third World, were handled reasonably well. The first is, of course, the change in Soviet capabilities: we are no longer in 1946, when Truman could force Stalin to give up his claims to Turkey and his attempt to remain in Northern Iran. The contrast between the Soviet fiasco in the Congo and the operation in Angola, too, is stark. The second factor is a certain decline in American power—a complex notion, about which one must be careful. In the 1940s and 1950s American military and economic power was greatly superior, and there is no doubt that it provided a stabilizing backdrop to turbulence. There has been a relative decline due to the rising power of other nations, often helped by American policies. There has also been, since the Vietnam experience, less willingness to use overt or covert force by comparison with the days of Guatemala, Lebanon, the Congo, or Santo Domingo. This, of course, is reversible. But what is not reversible is the inadequacy of military power to counter some of the threats—what Robert Art recently called the inherent limits of military power to achieve economic objectives.[7] And there has been a decline in the ability to use another instrument that had figured prominently in the American arsenal of the postwar era—economic assistance—for reasons that are largely internal to the United States and could be reversed (see below), but not easily.

However, the most important factor is the third: the diffusion of power to Third World countries. Many, as noted above, now produce their own weapons (or can diversify their sources of supply). They increasingly strive for control over their natural resources and over the operations of foreign enterprises. The oil producing countries have domesticated the international oil companies.[8] In other words, these countries are both more capable of creating difficulties by their own actions and more capable of depriving of their efficacy the instruments of power that the United States used to police world affairs in the postwar era. Some believe that the effrontery of the "pygmies" is a direct result of the decline of the power of the United States; they do not understand that the fall is a direct result of the rise of the lesser powers. To describe the passing of a (much idealized) Pax Americana as the cause of our troubles is myopic. Pax Americana emerged not merely because of the will and vision of the United States but also in circumstances that have vanished, and it declined not primarily because of political decadence in Washington but because of changes in world affairs with which Washington finds it hard to cope. The limits on the usability, or usefulness, of the power of the United States are far more serious than the alleged decline of will or the relative decline in the amount of power. One of the biggest evolutions since 1945 has been a transformation in the nature of power, which in part affects its ingredients in the sense that there is an increase both in offensive and in defensive capabilities, which in turn creates new opportunities for conflict (think of oil, or the spread of nuclear technologies). Mainly, however, it affects the conditions of the use of power. It is increasingly delicate, because in a complex world of multiple and diverse actors it depends so largely on external opportunities that the would-be user of power can try to exploit but may be unable to create—that is, his own success is at the mercy of chances povided by others—as well as on his own domestic processes and priorities that may be crippling or may, on the contrary, dictate unwise exertions of power. External and internal political preconditions for the successful deployment or uses of force by the United States existed when the areas concerned were Western Europe and Japan. Now that they are in the Third World there is (after Vietnam and Iran) far greater doubt in the United States and a far bumpier road abroad. Also the uses of power are increasingly asymmetrical; states that are above all military machines (the Soviet Union or Vietnam) are not likely to look at the scene in the same way as states whose deep involvement in the "economics of interdependence" causes a host of constraints: advanced industrial societies find themselves cosseted and corseted between inflation and recession, trade expansion and protection, and have narrow margins of maneuver, while developing countries with limited resources and huge needs are often obliged to accept the drastic dictates of the International Monetary Fund. From the viewpoint of the United States, it all amounts, in the words of one official, to having both less to offer and less to threaten with.

III.

This means that we have to face the future without much comfort from the past. The key question is: in a world of multiple instability and insecurity how can we distinguish between threats and conflicts that are of vital importance and the others? Here we find two extreme positions, both of which I find unacceptable. The first argues that the only way to fill the gap between proliferating Western or American interests and available power is to redefine the former more stringently and to return to a strategy aimed exclusively at containing the expansion of the Soviet Union and of her close allies.

There are three problems with this proposition. First, it fails to address itself to a multitude of issues that can provoke serious insecurity even in the absence of Soviet intervention (for instance, in international economic affairs) and which, if we ignore them, could provide the Soviet Union with fine opportunities for exploitation. We would have no other resort than opposition, too late, with military means; whereas we might otherwise have blocked its efforts by earlier and much less dangerous action. In other words, if we neglect such issues as the economic well-being of Third World countries, or the poor treatment of citizens by many of their governments, or festering regional conflicts, we both allow our chief opponent to get on the right side of the issues and condemn ourselves to an excessive militarization of our policy (about which more later). Second, the position assumes that any expansion of Soviet (or Cuban, or Vietnamese) influence is necessarily bad for us and should be checked. Despite the intention of narrowing our notion of security, this would end up by extending it to areas or issues of questionable importance and would in fact give the Soviet Union the ability to determine where and when we shall be engaged—and it is unlikely that the Soviets would choose places and times favorable to us. It is the indiscriminateness of what might be called "reflex containment" and the arbitrary separation between the superpowers' contest and all the issues that form the vortex into which they are drawn, as well as the absence of any ultimate vision of world affairs or world order, that makes this approach unsatisfactory. Third, it is unrewarding because Soviet influence and presence may take so many forms that the somewhat simple-minded imagery of erecting barriers or the goal of excluding Soviet penetration turns out to be far too blunt and inappropriate. In a sense, containment is a necessary overall objective for the West, but it does not define a strategy.

A second approach suffers not from a selective but from an all-inclusive Manichaeism. It is a conception that has gained popularity with the American right (old and new), the blessings of Richard Nixon, and letters of nobility from Henry Kissinger.[9] It amounts to a kind of universal linkage. The world is seen as divided between those who represent international stability and the values of moderation (and who, in Kissinger's latest version, include both traditional regimes and their "aberration," the authoritarian ones) and the radicals who assault the present international structure and whose rule would spread totalitarianism (described as an aberration of democracy). Our duty is to resist not only Soviet onslaughts but radical attempts as well, since there are objective and subjective convergences between the two kinds of threat. Where the first approach suggests that we ignore the domestic character of countries and watch only for the Soviet Union and her allies, this approach tells us to look closely at the nature and methods of domestic forces, since these will shape their external behavior, and to oppose the bad ones uncompromisingly—by force if there is civil turmoil, or by timely reforms that will keep our friends safely in control either before any turbulence begins or after it has been crushed, or by foreign policies designed to prove that pressure on us does not pay. It is a neo-Metternichian vision, with the advantage of putting us at least verbally into the position of defenders of freedom (since, by contrast with totalitarian ones, traditional regimes are deemed to be restrained, and authoritarian ones are deemed to be capable of leading to democracy).

The strength of this view is that it points quite accurately to the weakness of the opposite approach: the latter implies that only Soviet power threatens our core values; this view states that a world dominated by hostile forces, Soviet or other, would strangle our ability to pursue our interests and to promote our values. But there are formidable flaws here, too. It turns a distinction which is often one of degree or of opportunity—moderates versus radicals—into a fundamental division and thus relinquishes the opportunities to affect positively the views and behaviors of the radicals in favor of fighting them. Thus, it is a recipe for extraordinary overextension, since it amounts to underwriting "friendly" regimes everywhere and would commit our forces not only to the defense of borders against aggression, but also to the destabilization of hostile regimes (or regimes assumed to be hostile), as well as to the preservation of governments from revolution. (Had this view been followed, the civil war would go on in Zimbabwe, and Somoza and the shah would have been kept in place by force—at what cost?) It is also a poor guide for policy whenever the United States is caught between the contradictory demands of conflicting "moderate" friends—for instance, between those of Israel and Egypt, or of Israel and Jordan or Saudi Arabia, or of Greece and Turkey. It is, finally, a self-destructive view. By judging every internal or regional conflict not on its merits but according to the state of play between moderates and radicals, or between us and the Soviet Union, it would provide splendid opportunities for the latter, could provoke a major crisis in the United States' alliances, and could undermine Western influence in much of the Third World. It would, for instance, make us treat South Africa as an ally. Despite the attempt to show that such a policy is compatible with our values, it ignores the fact that many "moderate" regimes refuse to reform in time and, since it wants us to desist from undermining them by pressure, it condones the kind of repression and mismanagement that breed radicalism, Soviet influence, and distrust for Western double-talk or double standards.

Moreover, it is a view based on some ignorance of recent history. Not only should we be careful about embracing all "moderates," but we should also remember that not all "moderates" want to be too closely embraced by us, and that nothing is more capable of radicalizing a regime than a clumsy attempt at forcing it to choose sides. In the Middle East in the 1950s "containment failed, not because the remedies used were necessarily inappropriate, but because the diagnosis of the disease was faulty. . . . Soviet victories were largely achieved, not in spite of Western regional defensive efforts, but because of them."[10]

A proper approach must not begin from the top—the superpowers' contest—nor try to fit a complex world into a maddening intellectual straitjacket. (It is fashionable, in the circles that wish for a more "muscular" United States, to deride the dreary preachers of complexity, but history shows that the real threats are the terrible simplifiers.) We have to start from the bottom. This entails three imperatives. The first is to distinguish between those areas that are not of vital interest—either because they are not of major strategic importance or because they contain no important resources—and the others. It is, of course, a relative distinction: no area is totally without significance, and even from a poor and devastated country (Angola) an enemy can move into friendly territory (Shaba). But the attempt to let the stakes be determined by the simple fact of a foe's presence or influence, or escalated by the mere possibility that his victory might have unpleasant side effects (which might actually be handled or neutralized at low cost) is a recipe for overextension.

The second imperative is to distinguish, in the vital areas especially, between the different kinds of threat. The key issue is to decide what is unacceptable, what is tolerable and what, in between, is dangerous or unpleasant but bearable under certain conditions. My own list of unacceptables would include outright aggression—a blatant crossing of internationally recognized borders—except in the rare cases where it is a humanitarian intervention (India in Bangladesh, Tanzania in Uganda). My list would also include the military occupation of a country following such an intervention (Vietnam in Cambodia), or accompanying or following a coup that put a friendly leader in power (as in Afghanistan in December 1979). It would also include the cutting of vital economic resources by foreign powers or by terrorists. Such acts are unacceptable whether they are undertaken by the Soviet Union and her allies or by others. Dangerous but not unbearable is the coming to power of local radical forces that are not simply the agents or puppets of Moscow, Havana, or Hanoi, yet have received or called for the support of the Soviet Union or of her allies. We are much too dependent on our own network of clients to be able to apply double standards. And yet Moscow-oriented nationalists are obviously troublesome, especially when the country in question controls resources essential to us. Also dangerous would be the coming to power—through revolution or even mere evolution, such as ordinary succession—of nationalists whose economic policies, based on their assessment of their nations' interests, would mean higher prices and less oil for the rest of the world. Many in the West would regard such decisions as unacceptable.

But this is where the third imperative comes in. While we cannot always align ourselves with forces that have history on their side, to use Peter Jay's formula[11]—many Third World conflicts occur among factions that do not have a safe claim on history—and while we should not appease radicals or condone terror because of some debatable theory of political or economic development, or in the vain hope of co-opting our adversary into our own designs, we must start from a clear understanding of the aspirations, ambitions, and problems of the local forces, and we ourselves must understand

DEAD ENDS

that their main concern is not the superpowers' contest but their own struggles and objectives, their own survival, or their own triumph. We need, in other words, to begin by fully accepting one of the long-term effects of decolonization—the desire of nations to be treated as independent forces, not as tools. On the other hand, we have our interests, which often transcend a given country or region. This is why we must combine respect for the will-to-autonomy and for the force of nationalism with the need to avoid what I have described as unbearable outcomes, and to make those outcomes I have described as dangerous more rather than less bearable (to prevent more Cubas, for instance, or to prevent the radicalization of friends or neutrals that a violent intervention aimed at forcing a sovereign state to meet our estimated oil needs would provoke). This requires a willingness both to influence friends whose policies are suicidal, and to deal with adversaries whose hostility can still be disarmed.

Soviet policies in the Third World have been successful. They have, for instance, resulted in the granting of military facilities to the Soviet Union, whenever and as long as Moscow appeared to identify its interests with the concerns of local leaders: in Vietnam, in Mengistu's Ethiopia, in South Yemen, and currently in Syria. When Moscow failed to serve its clients' interests the Soviet Union lost: in Egypt in 1972 and in Somalia in 1976-77. The United States has been successful when it has been able to meet the needs of a foreign leader (as in the case of Sadat since 1973) and when that leader has avoided undermining his domestic position, as the shah undermined his own in the 1970s. But in the Middle East, Black Africa, and Latin America, Washington has often failed to avert two dangers: quasi-colonial behavior (expecting local leaders and peoples to conform to American concerns and priorities) and association with highly repressive and reactionary regimes—equating stability with the status quo.

A great power must behave in world affairs as a chameleon, not as a vampire. The United States and its allies are not without assets. There is much they can provide both to the governments and to the peoples in the Third World. Moreover, for the first time the Soviet Union has indulged in blatantly colonial behavior in the Third World by invading Afghanistan (Vietnam has done the same in Cambodia). This provides opportunities to the West as long as it addresses itself to the fears and needs of the new nations. This is precisely why the best way to contain the Soviet Union is neither to throw the radicals into its arms nor to neglect the issues of security, economic development, or human rights that are the concerns of the Third World, but to address these issues directly. And the best way to deal with the dangerous demise of the dissociations of the past is not to try to return to them, but to devise the right mix of restrained globalism and careful regionalism.

IV.

I have neither the space nor the competence to describe here how this mix should look in each area. Instead I will offer some remarks on specific means.

A most important issue is that of the framework for action. The approach I have suggested implicitly rejects two theoretical ones. One is a return to Dullesian pactomania. The experience of the "Northern Tier," of the Central Treaty Organization (CENTO) and of the Southeast Asia Treaty Organization (SEATO) should not be repeated. Incidentally, Soviet experiences with comparable treaties have also been mixed: treaties have worked when they strengthened or signalled ties with close allies (Cuba, Vietnam); they have not worked when the ally proved too independent (Egypt, Iraq, and even Afghanistan). It is instead in our interest to support existing regional organizations such as the Association of Southeast Asian Nations (ASEAN) or the Organization of African Unity (OAU). Military agreements are worth concluding with those who ask for them—unless they also ask for a political price that we have no interest in paying (as with Somalia's war in the Ogaden or Pakistan's request for guarantees against India). In any case, we should not beg others to let themselves be protected by us.

The other unwelcome framework is that which Chinese rhetoric (but not Chinese deeds) often suggests: a holy anti-Soviet alliance of the United States, Western Europe, Japan and China (plus assorted anti-Soviet Third World countries). The reasons why a policy of balance is preferable to a united front strategy have been indicated by Robert Scalapino, Allen Whiting, and others.[12] The latter strategy would risk producing unrestrained globalism by feeding Soviet paranoia (and some legitimate fears as well) and making Soviet cooperation with the West more difficult. It would impose heavy military obligations on the United States without commensurate gains in collective strength. Neither Japan nor Western Europe shares the enthusiasm of some Americans for the "China card," and China's military growth may serve interests that are not those of the West. It may also frighten some of the West's friends in Asia.

The problem of the framework is the problem of the Western Alliance—NATO—and of the United States-Japan security treaty. It is highly unlikely that Japan, even if it plays a more important role in preserving the military balance in the western Pacific and in providing economic assistance to Third World countries, will want to formalize this role, unless a kind of Western Directorate is set up, of the sort General de Gaulle proposed to the United States in September 1958 (but with a different membership). The obstacles to such a formula remain large. The United States is reluctant to endorse it, since it would acknowledge the promotion to a world role of powers that Washington has frequently annoyed by describing their interests as merely regional—and to a world role, moreover, as equals, whereas Washington has periodically exhorted them to transcend their parochialism only so that they could play their part in a global enterprise defined by the United States alone. The problem of membership would remain vexing. Another obstacle is the desire of several likely candidates (Paris, Bonn, Tokyo) to preserve a margin of distinction, or at least a nuance, between Washington's Soviet policy and their own, and to exploit (not necessarily for selfish purposes) the fact that they are sometimes seen and treated more favorably by Third World countries than is the United States.

Yet at least an informal Directorate is indispensable—a political and strategic equivalent of the economic summits. (The attempt to pile vital diplomatic and strategic issues on top of the vexing economic ones practically sank that of 1980, appropriately held in Venice.) A great deal of cooperation can take place through bilateral diplomatic exchanges and within the increasingly more coordinated procedures of the Europeans' political cooperation. But the impulse and general directives will have to come from the top if one wants to avoid mutual recriminations and, in the United States, a dangerous (albeit partly unjustified) sense that her allies prefer a division of labor that leaves all the heavy risks and burdens (the military ones) to Washington. NATO suffers from four handicaps: the partial absence of France, the total absence of Japan, more than enough work within its own orbit, and the geographical limitation of the Treaty (an attempt at revising it might open a can of worms). This is why an institution other than the NATO Council must be established. The days are gone when the United States could try to provide both the strategy and the means by herself; now it needs the resources of her allies, as well as their own expertise in these matters. Indeed, Western pluralism is one of our main assets. But this is another reason for the approach I have suggested: neither the fixation on the Soviet-American contest nor the global Manichaean view has much of a chance of being adopted outside Washington.

If we turn from the framework to the means, we find at once a heated controversy concerning the role of military force. The first necessity is to discard theological cobwebs. The debate, especially in the United States, has been described by the champions of a greater emphasis on force as the pitting of those who believe that international politics remains what it has always been—a contest of power—against those who believe in the growing irrelevance of force. This is, of course, absurd. Most of those who have stressed the limits of force or the difference between available power and useful power have been very careful to point out, for instance, the enormous importance of nuclear deterrence or of regional balance in Europe. And those who write as if they believed that force is a panacea have been equally careful to keep to themselves their ideas, if any, about the specific (rather than the generalized) uses and benefits of military power or about the precise composition, missions and purposes of the forces they endorse. They have been so busy reminding their intellectual adversaries of something few people ignore—the fact that politics is about power—that they themselves appear to have forgotten that power is about politics. And never more so than when the world is a single, turbulent, strategic stage.

A few points are not in doubt. The presence of American or Allied forces in various parts of the world can act as a tripwire against a Soviet invasion in areas that are both close enough to the Soviet Union to make it difficult for the West to achieve a conventional balance, and important enough to the West to suggest to the attacker that such an invasion, if it succeeded in defeating the available Western forces, might trigger nuclear escalation or the geographical extension of the conflict to an area where the West enjoys conventional superiority. It could also deter or defeat an invasion by a Soviet client. Moreover, a military presence can have a generally quieting effect by creating among radicals or revolutionaries a fear of Western intervention, or by giving Western powers the means to help a friendly regime to defend itself against an attempted coup, or by preventing a local war from escalating and from affecting access to Persian Gulf oil (as in the Iraq-Iran war so far). Showing the flag also has the undoubted virtue of affecting the balance of perceptions and thereby possibly the balance of influence.

However, there are serious limitations to force as an instrument of policy. Not only is it of debatable use if the main threat is not a Soviet invasion or an attack by a Soviet proxy but internal instability or a domestic change of policy, but its presence in an unstable area could aggravate internal turbulence, turn the opposition to an anti-American or anti-Western direction, and tempt the Western powers into using the available force to control events, which might be a fatal mistake. When domestic strife is the issue, or when the issue is a regime's threat to deny the West a vital resource, intervention can be both dangerous—if the use of force should, for instance, lead to the destruction of tankers and oil fields—and insufficient because prolonged occupation may become necessary. American or Western bases tend to commit us to the support of the regime that has granted them and thus to deprive us of means of influence. Rather, bases give it the means of blackmail while compromising the regime further in the eyes of its internal or external opposition. As we learned in Vietnam, and as Samuel Huntington once put it, our leverage decreases with our commitment. Ultimately, there is no substitute for sound political, economic, and social conditions in the area to be defended; othewise military bases are built on sand.[13]

This is not a condemnation of the American Rapid Deployment Force. A greater air- and sealift capacity and a greater ability to patrol the seas (without depleting existing fleets) are necessary. But the main threats to Western security in the Gulf area are *not* likely to be direct Soviet or Soviet-sponsored attacks. They will probably result from internal instability, corruption or repression, from traditional interstate conflicts and from the Palestinian issue (all of which may provide opportunities to the Soviet Union). To the reduction of these dangers, external military forces can make only a meagre contribution, and they risk aggravating them. It is, of course, true that the West has a vital interest in the free flow of oil, but there are two major differences between, say, the American commitment to Western Europe and its recent commitment to the Persian Gulf area. In Western Europe it is a pledge to the defence of people against aggression, and it was given at the request of their governments. In the Middle East it is a commitment to keep oil flowing to the West; it has serious divisive effects in the area; and it does not resolve the issue of how to react, for instance, in Saudi Arabia not to a bungled coup such as that of November 1979, but either to a surgically successful one or to a revolution (or another kind of leadership change), followed, as in Iran, by a decision to reduce oil production, which would make perfect sense from a purely Saudi viewpoint. Also, access to oil is inseparable from the very underlying political conditions in that part of the world—conditions in the oil-producing countries and the Palestinian issue—which no military pledge can cope with. All these considerations plead for a light rather than a heavy force (with respect to composition, numbers, and deployment: the emphasis ought to be on facilities, not permanent bases, on air and naval more than ground forces). The purpose is to increase risks for the Soviet Union, not to balance its might. Too heavy a Western force could easily become a distraction (from the most likely threats) and a provocation (for instance, to local terrorism).

Those limits on the usefulness of force suggest, to some, the wisdom of what the French call a *politique de Gribouille*. If conventional defense fails, we must have credible means of nuclear escalation. But, on the one hand, failure in that area risks taking the form not of a fiasco against an advancing army, but of an inability to prevent the coming to power of forces that might, for their own protection, turn to Moscow if they find us hostile, or of an inability to prevent internal turmoil in friendly countries such as Pakistan. To threaten Moscow with nuclear escalation in such cases would not be very credible. And the logic of the argument leads to an increasingly dangerous arms race: the spread of tactical nuclear capabilities and a major effort on the part of the United States to give itself a counterforce ability against Soviet missiles and military targets (many of which are close to cities). Should this lead the Soviet Union to protect and increase its own warfighting ability, and should the United States react by discarding the ABM Treaty and by providing its own land-based missiles with hard-point defenses (if this becomes technically feasible), the posture of the United States (MX plus such defenses, plus perhaps a new bomber and a program to hasten the increase in the accuracy of sea-launched ballistic missiles) could appear dangerously provocative to Moscow. The United States' advantage could be negated by a Soviet ABM effort, as well as by a Soviet effort to build mobile land-based missiles and to multiply launchers and warheads. This is a recipe for spiralling madness.

There is no perfect solution, no sure way of closing the gap between military possibilities in the Third World and possible threats. This suggests that such threats must be addressed by different methods, all of which could be called "preventive diplomacy." Let us return to the notion of a mix of regionalism and globalism. Insofar as the former is concerned, there are three directions to follow. First, there is, of course, the familiar method of security assistance—arms transfers to friendly governments or to governments that request them.[14] It can be most useful to restore a regional balance or to help a country against subversion supported from abroad or internal guerrillas. But it has its own serious dangers. Feeding an escalating arms race in a region may make a diplomatic solution more rather than less difficult, may help a regime to become more repressive, or may encourage it to develop excessive ambitions. Those who see in arms transfers a panacea should remember the U.S. experience in Iran. Those who believe that arms sales do not increase the probability of war should ponder the case of Iraq and Iran, or that of Israel in Lebanon.

Second, with respect to interstate conflicts that can be dangerous sources of international insecurity, a variety of diplomatic instruments have to be used, depending on the issue. Wherever possible, the Western powers should encourage regional security arrangements, limited to states in the area and aimed at preserving the members from aggression by external actors, be it the Soviet Union, or Vietnam, or even South Africa, the "cornered wildcat" described by Robert Jaster.[15] But the initiative should come from within the area. Bilateral links such as those that now exist between France and several of her former African colonies ought to be replaced gradually by such regional schemes. The most dangerous interstate conflict involving Third World countries remains the Arab-Israeli one. It is, of course, true that even after the Palestinian issue is disposed there will remain multiple sources of intra-Arab conflict. But the Palestinian issue is both a major factor of anti-Western-Arab (and Islamic) solidarity and a factor of internal turbulence within Arab countries as well as in Lebanon.

Creeping Israeli annexionism only further strengthens the anti-American bent of the PLO while increasing the pro-PLO fervor of the occupied Palestinians, thus reducing the chances for a moderate Jordanian solution. The Camp David process has gone about as far as it can. The dilemma here is that for a European or a new UN initiative to succeed it needs a green light from Washington. Yet as long as the deadlock is not broken in a way that guarantees, at the end of a transitional period, both Palestinian self-determination and mutual recognition between an eventual Palestinian state and Israel, it is absurd for American politicians to expect that Arab states will place themselves under Washington's protection, that the Palestinian issue will not weigh on the politics of oil, or that the Soviet Union can be expelled from the area.

Third, with respect to internal turbulence in the Third World, it is not enough to ask that the West be associated with neither repression nor revolution.[16] Only if we clearly dissociate ourselves from repressive regimes and keep the pressure on them to reform before they explode is there a chance that the forces in opposition, if they come to power, will remain pro-Western or reasonably moderate. It was not American harassment that provoked the shah's downfall or the overthrow of Somoza, but one of the reasons for the different consequences of the two falls is active American dissociation in Somoza's case. To be sure, the degree of possible dissociation varies from place to place. In Saudi Arabia it may well be very low. But this is where the other imperative comes in—willingness to deal even with a hostile opposition (both before and after its seizure of power), and not to take its initial hostility as final. We must take its own goals and priorities seriously. For the United States, which can expect a number of unpleasant changes and challenges in Central and South America, this would entail giving up the attempt to find third forces or moderate progressives (as in Nicaragua before the Sandinista victory) where they do not exist (any more than they did in China in 1946 or in Vietnam) and when the quest only increases polarization and violence. It would also mean formally recognizing the regime in Angola (with which a great deal of cooperation has been possible). For the West as a whole the strategy suggested here entails continuing pressure on South Africa (both for a solution of the conflict over Namibia and for internal change) and contacts with the Black opposition there, even that part of it that has turned East for armed support. It also means that where American relations with a new regime are bad (as in Iran) it is in the interest of the West that other Western nations try their influence.

I mentioned earlier restrained globalism. In this respect, three directions are essential. The first is the consolidation and preservation of a strong international antiproliferation regime, intended, through the cooperation of the suppliers, to slow down the rate and limit the degree of nuclear proliferation.[17]

Accelerated proliferation, especially among "enemy pairs" of states (India/ Pakistan, Israel/Iraq, Argentina/Brazil, and so forth), could not fail to increase both local insecurity (given mutual vulnerabilities and underlying political tensions) and to affect adversely the superpowers' contest, since the acquisition of nuclear weapons by the enemy of a great power's client is more likely to incite that great power to shore up the client than to promote mutual dissociation by the superpowers, at least in areas of vital importance to them.[18] It will also be essential to devise the antiproliferation regime in such a way as to protect the legitimate energy needs of the developing countries and their interest in the peaceful uses of nuclear power. A strengthening of the role of the International Atomic Energy Agency, where both suppliers and clients meet, is likely to result from the need to balance these concerns.

The second direction is that of the international economic system. Not only has the rate of growth slowed down in the advanced countries, but the combination of inflation and unemployment has adversely affected their economic policies toward the developing nations. While accelerated economic growth can produce dangerous upheavals in traditional societies, stagnation or actual impoverishment are both sources of internal tension and of anti-Western resentment. The problems discussed in the recent Brandt Report are urgent.[19] They have been postponed by the West, partly because of its own internal economic difficulties, partly because the measures recommended by practically all the specialists of North-South affairs would require painful internal readjustments. Three kinds of measures are needed. The first would be aimed at transferring resources from Northern to Southern countries (especially the poorer ones) so as to promote aggregate growth and industrialization among the latter—for instance, through increased development assistance, mechanisms (such as STABEX and MINEX in the Lomé Conventions) to stabilize export earnings and, above all, greater access of developing countries' exports to the markets of the advanced countries, a requirement both for development and for reducing the burden of debt. A second series would be aimed at dealing with the poverty within developing countries in order to ensure the basic needs of the population, particularly in food production. A third series would enlarge the role of the developing countries in the management of international economic regimes—for instance, in a new global trade organization or through the reform of the International Monetary Fund and the World Bank. For reasons excellently analyzed by Roger Hansen, mere cooperation of a handful of developing countries would not work.[20]

The effect of these measures would be to remove or to reduce one of the chief sources of collective anti-Western acrimony in the Third World. They would also give developing countries a stake in the operations of a reformed world economy and would link their economic growth—particularly through increased trade—with the open international economy (that is, with the West). The weakening of official economic ties between the nations of the West and the Third World, at least as much as the occasional high-handedness of private Western enterprises in the developing countries, facilitates Soviet influence there.

The third direction is that of U.S.-Soviet relations, which are an indispensable component of any attempt to improve international security. In the past, nuclear deterrence has not prevented Soviet attempts to exploit opportunities in the Third World at levels well below any risk of direct military conflict with the United States. In the future it is likely not only that such Soviet involvements will continue, but also that increased Soviet military capabilities will tempt Moscow to export its forces more often—as long, again, as the risk of direct military confrontation with Washington remains low, either because the area is not of vital importance to the West or because Moscow would have carefully avoided putting itself in the position of an aggressor and made it as difficult as possible for Washington to retaliate in kind (a fortiori, to escalate to the nuclear level—a threat that is credible only when the most vital interests of the West are threatened by an aggressive Soviet move). It is futile to expect Moscow to endorse Western notions of stability. The best that can be hoped for is not an end to competition but the acceptance by Moscow of certain restraints in the intensity and means of competition.[21] Our notions are often exceedingly static. Moscow expects the "correlation of forces" to change (at the expense of the West), sees nothing wrong in helping this happen, and deems destabilizing Western reactions against such change. It is equally vain to expect either that the Soviet union will accept restraints voluntarily or be forced to do so by containment alone. Preventive diplomacy may go a long way toward obliging the Soviets to restrict their scope of endeavors, but if it is Soviet intensity and Soviet methods that we may try to affect, we shall have to make efforts to find areas of cooperation.

One of them must be arms control, even if more fragmentary or more modest than in the past. The relevance of the strategic balance to the contest in the Third World may only be oblique, but it is not unimportant. First, instability, or a perception of instability, in the central balance may tempt the side that believes it has an advantage either to take more risks at a regional level (where it also has an edge) for purposes of intimidation, or to try to compensate for a regional disadvantage by threatening to escalate. To be sure, stability at the central level risks decoupling a region from it, but coupling would be neither credible nor sensible in case of secondary interests, and remains credible only when the interest at stake is vital, in the sense used in 1980 by McGeorge Bundy à propos Europe: "no one knows that a major engagement in Europe would escalate to the strategic nuclear level. But the essential point is the opposite: no one can possibly know it would not."[22] Second, the more the superpowers indulge their apparent appetite for war-fighting scenarios, the more attractive they make the possession of nuclear weapons to others. Third, the continuing nuclear arms race between them weakens the legitimacy and the authority of their stand against proliferation. Insofar as strategic arms control contributes to stability and predictability, it remains important. The scuttling of SALT II was a mistake, even if new discussions should begin soon and in earnest. But to postpone a serious negotiation of strategic arms limitations or reductions until after the United States has restored a "margin of safety" and given itself some leverage over the Soviet Union, would be at best prodigiously wasteful and at worst a dangerous gamble.

Conventional arms control will undoubtedly have to wait until local sources of instability and the opportunities for competitive influence that local requests for arms provide have dried out sufficiently, or until enough states produce what they need (by which time such arms control would come too late). However, even the conventional arms race of the superpowers could be submitted to restraints resulting from informal understandings aimed at greater superpower control over the purposes for which the arms can be used, and at limiting damage and casualties if they are used. Even these understandings presuppose a greater Western willingness either to deal directly (as was finally done in Zimbabwe) with forces or countries that have turned to Moscow for support, so as to give them an incentive to favor moderation, or to accept the Soviet Union as a partner in the search for the solution of regional disputes in which the latter has a vital interest (and not merely an interest in expanding her own influence or in dislodging that of the West). This would obviously not be the case in Central and South America or in southern Africa, but it would be in the areas that lie close to the Soviet borders.

One of the weaknesses of the two confrontational approaches described earlier is that they provide only for an interminable series of tests—as in the old Achesonian conception—conducted in the vague hope that the adversary, having been checkmated, will throw in the towel and behave according to our wishes. Neither the trends in the world nor internal difficulties are likely to force any foe to do so. The best chance for a gradual change in behavior lies in a combination of containment and cooperation. Even the cooperation is likely to be competitive. In a world of states each one, whether through conflict, self-reliance or cooperation, seeks its own advantage. But even the confrontation ought to leave the door open for political solutions, as was achieved in the Cuban missile crisis and as should be the aim of Western policies in Afghanistan and Cambodia. These may not be popular views today. But nothing is more important for a long-term policy than a sense of perspective, a refusal to accept intellectual fashions uncritically, and to yield to sudden bursts of opinion.

The new U.S. administration, if only in order to react against the strategic incoherence of its predecessor, is likely to seek a comprehensive policy, especially in the Persian Gulf area, and to want to enlist the support of its allies for it after months of mutual complaints, innuendoes, and stalemates. As long as the allies cringe at discussions about the role of force, try to convince themselves that regional fragmentation can still prevail, and refuse to hear American complaints about unevenly shared burdens, there will be little progress. But nor will there by any if the United States once more takes refuge in oversimplification, prefers military planning to political analysis or short-term fixes to a long-range integrated strategy, attributes Western European desires to safeguard whatever is left of détente in Europe to crass material interests or to fear alone, or generally behaves as if leadership could be exerted exactly as it was in the 1950s. There is little reason for optimism.

The methods sketchily suggested here would encounter not only the resistance of all those whose view of the world is different, but also two formidable obstacles within the West. The first one is economic. Unless Western economies in general and the U.S. economy in particular take strong domestic measures to reduce their dependence on Middle East oil, to fight inflation, but also to return to steady economic growth, they will face, in the case of quite probable turbulence in the arabian peninsula, an unsavory choice between economic disaster (should the flow of oil be interrupted or production levels be drastically reduced) and the formidable risks and costs of military expedition and occupation. And they will not have the resources needed to provide an economic underpinning for Western policies in the Third World. A willingness not to be outspent in military hardware nor outclassed in military deployments by the Soviet Union is fine as long as the effort required does not become a pretext for neglecting the long-term duty to "increase the resources needed to support our diplomacy, a diplomacy designed to reduce the chance our military forces may be needed," in Cyrus Vance's words.[23]

The other obstacle is internal as well. What is necessary is nothing less than a mental revolution—a willingness to discard nostalgia for past golden ages (that seemed not so golden at the time), to stop wavering, in attitudes toward Moscow, between total hostility and excessive hopes, and to abandon condescension toward the Third World. It is a particularly difficult reconversion for the American people, impatient with complexity, oscillating between two equally irrelevant archetypes of the United States— the sheriff at "High Noon" and the world missionary[24]—, troubled by mixed strategies, more eager for intervention against a foe than capable of steering toward reform or accommodation with partial or temporary adversaries, and more inclined, under the guidance of the familiar but tricky liberal principle of nonintervention, toward endorsing the status quo and thus becoming the victims of its clients and the unwilling artisans of its own defeats. But we can neither withdraw from the field, only to reenter when the Soviet Union and her allies approach, nor turn the whole world into that artificial division between good and evil which produces in crusading spirits such emotional satisfaction, a happy end to all cognitive dissonance and a formidable release of energy. It is a global contest—a complex one, but not a war. Coping with international insecurity is not a matter of winning against a single foe or against a deadly brotherhood of evils. It is a Sisyphean task of bringing more restraint, more order, *and* more justice into a world of turbulence and violence.

NOTES

1. Richard N. Cooper, *Economics of Interdependence* (New York: McGraw-Hill, 1968).

2. Robert Gilpin, "The Politics of Trans-national Economic Relations," in Robert O. Keohane and Joseph S. Nye, (eds.) *Trans-national Relations and World Politics*, a special issue of *International Organization XXV* (Summer 1971):398-419.

3. Seweryn Bialer, *Stalin's Successors* (Cambridge: Cambridge University Press, 1980).

4. Arnold Wolfers, *Discord and Collaboration* (Baltimore: Johns Hopkins University Press, 1962).

5. Stanley Hoffmann, *Primacy and World Order* (New York: McGraw-Hill, 1978), Part 2.

6. Miles Kahler, "Rumors of War: The 1914 Analogy," *Foreign Affairs 58* (Winter 1979):374-96.

7. Robert J. Art, "To What Ends Military Power?" *International Security 4* (Spring 1980):3-35.

8. Walter J. Levy, "Oil and the Decline of the West," *Foreign Affairs 58* (Summer 1980):999-1015.

9. Kissinger's view, which can be found in his *White House Years*, has been laid out even more starkly in his "statement on the geopolitics of oil" before the Committee on Energy and Natural Resources of the United States Senate, July 31, 1980.

10. Paul Jabber, "US Interests and Regional Security in the Middle East," *Daedalus* (Fall 1980):75-76.

11. Peter Jay, "Regionalism as Geopolitics," *Foreign Affairs, America and the World in 1979, 58* (January 1980):487.

12. Robert Scalapino, "Asia at the End of the 1970s," *Foreign Affairs, America and the World in 1979, 58* (January 1980):693-737; and Allan S. Whiting, "China and the Superpowers: Toward the Year 2000," *Daedalus* (Fall 1980):97-113.

13. See the remarks by Zalmay Khalilzad, "Afghanistan and the Crisis in American Foreign Policy," *Survival XII* (July/August 1980):151-60.

14. Richard Betts, "The Tragicomedy of Arms Trade Control," *International Security V* (Summer 1980):80-110.

15. Robert Jaster, "South Africa's Narrowing Security Options," *Adelphi Paper 159* (London: IISS, 1980).

16. The Atlantic Council, *After Afghanistan: the Long Haul.* Policy Paper (Washington, D.C.: The Atlantic Council, March 1980).

17. Joseph S. Nye, "Maintaining a Non-Proliferation Regime," *International Organization 35* (Winter 1980-81):15-38.

18. I disagree with Kenneth Waltz's complacent view in his "The Spread of Nuclear Weapons: More Could be Better," *Adelphi Paper 171* (London: IISS, 1981).

19. Brandt Commission Report, *North-South* (Cambridge, Mass.: MIT Press, 1980).

20. Roger Hansen, "North-South Policy—What is the Problem?" *Foreign Affairs 58* (Summer 1980):1104-28.

21. For further elaboration, see Chapter 6.

22. McGeorge Bundy, "The Future of Strategic Deterrence," *Survival XXI* (November/December 1979):271.

23. Cyrus Vance, Harvard Commencement Speech, *New York Times,* June 6, 1980.

24. See Chapter 5.

CHAPTER 13

FOREIGN POLICY PRIORITIES OF THE UNITED STATES

I.

WHILE INTERNATIONAL politics resemble a fever chart, with sudden lows around moments of crisis (many of which remain impossible to predict), the chart's trend is clear. Looking ahead at the rest of the century, we have no reason to be optimistic. Four main points stand out.

1. There is no escape from, and no end in sight for, the Soviet-American contest. The Soviet Union has accumulated great military power; and, while its leaders insist that their purposes are defensive, the security needs of a great power tend to be expansive, and a country that finds itself surrounded by hostile nations is always tempted to assure its safety by intervening abroad to remove threats and surround itself with clients or friends. Moreover, Soviet leaders cling to their ambition to make Moscow, if not master of the world (a difficult task indeed), then at least the co-ruler of international affairs. Insofar as Marxism-Leninism still plays a role, both to legitimize Soviet rule and to provide rudimentary guidance for action, it will continue to incite Moscow to weaken Western positions around the world and to support forces that proclaim themselves (or are seen by Moscow as being) progressive and revolutionary.

This does not mean that American foreign policy is nothing more than the management of the U.S.-Soviet contest. Nor does it mean that every trouble and conflict in the world results from Soviet machinations.

But it does mean that a premise of the Carter foreign policy simply will not work—namely, the possibility of separating the management of the U.S.-Soviet contest from the rest of international affairs. (This premise was shared by all the leading policy-makers of the Carter administration; the disagreements concerned the ways of managing the competition rather than the idea of insulating it.) It will not work because the Soviet Union can affect and exploit third party disputes and internal turmoil in many parts of the world.

2. The most probable development for the rest of the century is indeed internal turmoil. In a very large number of countries, we can expect strife, rebellions, attempted coups, civil wars, and revolutions, either because of political oppression, patterns of inequality and exploitation, the gap between expectations of material progress and bleak realities, or the disruptive and corrupting effects of sudden wealth. These developments may well affect the East as well as the West. For example, internal problems of the Soviet Union could reach a point where minimal reform from the top would no longer suffice (indeed, the central Soviet bureaucracy is part of the problem). And aspirations for freedom in Eastern Europe are unlikely to stay crushed. The ability of the Red Army, directly or indirectly, to suppress demands for reform may remain very great, but the costs of successful repression could rise and would thus add to internal strains. In the non-Soviet world, meanwhile, revolutionaries and rebels may take any one of several directions, ranging from Marxism to fundamentalist anti-Western reaction, such as the one which has swept Iran.

What is certain is the potential for violence in different countries. Often, there is a latent state of war between the population and a state machinery that is either inefficient or attempts to push masses of people toward activities, structures, and values they resist. Often, even in countries that have been nations for a long time, the state is too narrow and too isolated, and will be increasingly incapable of coping with demands for participation and for a radical redistribution of political as well as economic power. Often, there is, as of now, no nation at all. Ethnic, religious, tribal, economic, and factional disputes constantly test the ability of governments to function. For the United States, the danger lies in the following facts: that many countries that are in trouble are friends, allies, or clients of Washington; that many of them possess resources essential to the West; and that demands for change are often likely to be couched either in anti-Western or in specifically anti-American terms.

3. Proliferating internal turmoil creates dangers for international politics because of the possibilities for generalized intervention. We can expect

not only Soviet attempts to take advantage of the opportunities described above, but also attempts by regional troublemakers (who may be quite independent of Moscow) to exploit events in order to expand their influence (if not Qaddafi of Libya, then some other leader and state). There will be great temptation to seek diversions abroad from insoluble problems and frustrations at home. And the development of weaponry is particularly disturbing. Indeed, the management of crises may well become a Sisyphean task, and the ability to prevent internal explosions from triggering international crises may disappear altogether, because of four factors: more countries producing their own weapons; several industrial nations eager to supply clients with weapons (sometimes for purely commercial reasons); the prospect that a number of countries in the developing world will acquire the capacity to produce nuclear weapons; and the likely spread of a relatively cheap weapon capable of receiving either conventional or nuclear warheads—namely, the cruise missile accumulated by the superpowers, with its increasing capabilities for long-range intervention.

4. The United States will find itself in a particularly difficult position. Outside trends will challenge some of the most deeply ingrained American expectations, beliefs, and hopes that have managed to survive thirty-five years of contrary experience, such as the hope for a consensus around a kind of universal rule of law—the Wilsonian dream, or the hope for gradual moderation in the international system, or the hope for evolution ("peaceful change") prevailing over revolution in the internal affairs of others, or the belief that a modicum of order and democracy will result from economic development and foreign assistance.

The goal of American foreign policy has remained the achievement of stability, understood partly as a process of orderly change, and partly in substantive terms (not *any* order is acceptable); and yet stability is likely to be more elusive than ever. It is always difficult for the United States to sympathize with revolutionary movements that either espouse values profoundly different from those of American liberalism and capitalism or which seem to attack American interests and positions. The tendency remains very strong to explain such movements away as either unrepresentative or as products of machinations by the Soviets or their clients.

Above all, American unilateralist reflexes will be sorely tested by, and will be entirely inadequate to, the developments described here. The ability to control events—an ability provided in world affairs only by military preponderance and the disposition to use it—will vanish and indeed has already done so, because of three factors: nuclear parity; the American public's misgivings about the uses of force in internal conflicts abroad; and the difficulty of succeeding through force in such conflicts (the first and third of these considerations apply to the Soviet Union as well, outside its domain of absolute preponderance in Eastern Europe). Even the ability to influence events in directions deemed useful by the United States will increasingly depend on our talent at getting other countries—allies and regional influentials—to share our objectives and to endorse our methods. Such approval will require willingness on our part not merely to consult, but also to define overall strategy in common with others. The days are gone when we could expect to be the sole policy-makers, and then to discuss with others only the sharing of the burdens we have set.

II.

Management of the Soviet-American contest will remain the most important objective of American foreign policy. It will be especially difficult because of the difference between this competition and other bipolar contests in history. The latter tended to develop around clear lines of commitment. The danger points were either attempts by one great power to intimidate an ally of the other, to detach and attract a client state of the other, or to destroy a delicate balance of power by "acquiring" a previously neutral player. The two alliances in Europe after the Second World War correspond to the logic of this form of contest. But in the future, a great deal of U.S.-Soviet competition will be for the temporary and conditional allegiance of countries to which the superpowers themselves are only partly, vaguely, or uncertainly committed. It will be a much more fluid game, lacking clear lines—partly because fuzziness is a way of avoiding nuclear showdowns and partly because we are in a world in which, for many reasons, there is a disjunction between military might and the distribution of other forms of power.

Of course, in the contest with Moscow, Washington will have to continue to preserve a military balance. At the strategic level, we must worry not so much about the Soviets' ability to destroy our land-based missiles (the so-called "window of vulnerability" was always a fraudulent concept, and the reality of the late 1980s will be the vulnerability of all fixed land-based missiles). Rather, we must worry about a situation in which there could exist, in a given area like Europe, such a preponderance of Soviet nuclear weaponry that the likelihood of an American nuclear response, either to a Soviet nuclear attack limited within this area or to a massive Soviet conventional attack, would be in doubt. In the conventional realm, the United States most needs the ability to move large quantities of forces by air and sea to areas that may be close to Soviet borders. Every military equilibrium is a "balance of imbalances." We cannot hope to erase the ground force advantages the Soviets enjoy all around their borders; but we need to retain a margin of air and naval superiority to compensate for them.

It is the case, however, that our ability to rely on the threat of a nuclear first strike, as the ultimate deterrent and as the decisive "equalizer" in areas of Soviet conventional superiority, will continue to decrease. The risk of uncontrollable escalation may continue to operate in this way in those places either where there is a large assemblage of Western conventional and nuclear forces (as in Europe), or where there is a vital American and Western interest (as in the Persian Gulf). But most situations will be far less definite, and the United States could find itself caught between a locally bad military situation (because of conventional superiority on the part of the Soviets or their clients) and a highly implausible threat of nuclear escalation. Indeed, this threat would be equally implausible in cases where Soviet gains at the expense of important Western interests resulted not from the use of coercive force, but rather from either a political windfall (as, for example, in the Cuban and Ethiopian revolutions), or from an appeal for Soviet assistance by a friendly government or friendly forces in a civil war (for example, Angola today, and possibly Iran tomorrow).

Therefore, while military strength is indispensable as a precondition for a sound diplomacy, as a way of signalling to Moscow the importance of certain areas, resources and interests, and as a means for containing and repelling armed attacks on these states, it is no substitute for a policy. Neither nuclear nor conventional strength can always deter damaging domestic developments or prevent regional disputes from endangering American positions. The deployment of American forces may have a dampening effect on radicals or troublemakers; but it may have exactly the opposite effect as well, and often requires the consent of others who exact their own price.

As in the past, management of the U.S.-Soviet contest will continue to entail a large element of containment or confrontation. But even in areas where military containment is essential to our interests, we should pay more attention to two other considerations. First, what is the hierarchy of threats? Is a threat to invade militarily the most likely peril in the area? Or, if it is not, shouldn't we give to our military presence a less central role in our policy (although our military presence may remain indispensable wherever, in the absence of American and allied strength, a Soviet military threat might indeed develop)? These questions apply particularly to the Middle East, where since 1978 we have allowed a deadly but unlikely menace to dictate and misshape America's response.

Second, even in areas like Europe that seem stable militarily, and *a fortiori* in other areas, internal sources of turbulence (including those produced by bad economic conditions) may provide the Soviets with opportunities to undermine the barriers of containment. Both because of the loss of our earlier military preponderance, and because of the complexity of the relationship between domestic developments and foreign affairs, a wise containment policy becomes indistinguishable from the search, in every area, for policies adapted to the circumstances of the region and country, and capable of providing the most reliable deterrents of Soviet intervention and influence. In this sense, the famous debate between regionalists and globalists is a one-sided affair: the best globalists are those who take the realities of each region strictly into account and, instead of concentrating on mischief making capabilities or activities on the part of the Soviets and their clients, try to deal instead with the issues and disputes our adversaries could exploit.

A view of the future that offers nothing more cheerful than either endless confrontations, or the stark and elusive necessities of containment, would provide little inspiration for our allies or even for the American people. In our relations with Moscow, there must be a mix of hostility and cooperation. But we must be careful not to repeat some of the mistakes of the détente period. It is not wise to expect that a subtle manipulation of rewards and punishments would lead the Soviets, out of self-interest, to accept our notion of stability. Specifically, the Soviets will continue to seek opportunities for political and strategic gain, even at possible cost in the realm of economics. By contrast, we must define a policy which indicates clearly to the Soviets what kind of behavior we deem intolerable. Such kinds of behavior should not, as happened with both Afghanistan and Poland, be limited to outright invasion. In the former case, invasion was a direct consequence of the coup of April 1978, to which we did not react; in the latter, our concentration on the possibility of a Soviet invasion left us unprepared for the Polish army crackdown. For the policy described here to be effective, two conditions must be met. First, it cannot deem unacceptable every attempt by the Soviets to restore or expand their influence or to affect the "correlation of forces" in the world—that is, it must try to affect the level, methods, and instruments of the contest, rather than try to eliminate the contest itself. Second, effective U.S. policy must provide the Soviets both with clear incentives to behave in an acceptable way, and (when their behavior is intolerable) with sanctions clearly defined in advance.

Of course, these points raise the vexing problems of linkage and of economic relations with the Soviets. Henry Kissinger quite correctly argues that linkage is at the heart of all international politics, but this point does not dispose of the issue. Some forms of linkage are obviously inefficient (the grain embargo did not get the Soviets out of Afghanistan), and some are not in our interest. There can be no general answer in the abstract. The fact is that our leverage on the Soviets is limited; this is why economic relations are important—in the form of selling goods, transferring technology, or providing credits. On the one hand, East-West economic relations constitute an element of mutual interest. On the other hand, they are both a political weapon and a political liability: a *weapon*, insofar as the United States and its allies, by withholding certain kinds of supplies or credits, have the capacity to delay Soviet economic development and to make more difficult the shift of Soviet resources to the military sector; a *liability*, insofar as (1) trade creates Western dependence on certain Soviet products (for example, natural gas), (2) technology transfers and credits may help the expansion of the Soviet military sector, and (3) it is easier for the Soviets than for the West to exploit for political purposes the mutual dependence created by economic links. Both these links and the weapons build-up serve the cause of Soviet power; whereas, in the West, economic ties can become an incentive to acquiesce in the expansion or consolidation of Soviet might.

There is no perfect solution. An answer can be found only in concerted allied policy. Otherwise, every crisis in U.S.-Soviet relations risks becoming an alliance crisis; in addition, the uneven development of American, European, and Japanese trade relations with the Soviets risks becoming a source of strain among allies. Even in an area of mutual allied interests, we must be willing to accept certain sacrifices as a way of forcing the Soviets to pay a price for serious transgressions. But our allies are not likely to accept this point of view, unless economic sanctions are put at the service of an overall policy which they endorse, and unless economic relations are first accepted by us as a reasonable (if problematic) way of creating a sphere of mutual interests capable of leading in the long run to some Soviet restraint, instead of always being treated with suspicion as though we derived no benefits at all from East-West economic relations.

Even more difficult is the recognition of common interests in the political realm. Given the intensity of the U.S.-Soviet contest, it is difficult for the American public and its leaders to accept the idea of mutuality. Yet two kinds of developments are needed. One belongs in the category of crisis management: We need to talk to the Soviets about existing crises and about potential troubles (if only to indicate what we deem to be dangerous or intolerable). These talks should not be reduced to an exchange of warnings; they should aim at informal understandings that would set limits within which each side can pursue its goals without risks of collision. The other development would entail actual Soviet participation in negotiating and enforcing regional settlements. The obvious case is the Middle East—an area of vital importance to us, but also both sufficiently volatile and close to the

Soviet borders to be of great concern to them, and an area in which the Soviets retain sufficient influence on some of the regional actors to make their exclusion both impossible and dangerous.

Arms control is another area of mutual Soviet-American interests—again, one about which we should avoid excessive hopes. Just as weapons are no substitute for policy, so is arms control no substitute for diplomacy and no guarantee of improved political relations. But as we have seen in the last few years, the *absence* of arms control increases fears of war, worsens the East-West political climate, and strains inter-allied relations in the West. It is an absurd waste of resources to accumulate weapons that are either unusable or, if used, suicidal. In addition, the evolution of technology is likely to make the nightmare more oppressive. Fixed land-based missiles are becoming vulnerable (and could thereby provide incentives for preemption); mobile, heavy land-based missiles are formidably expensive and agreements controlling them may be unverifiable; and the cruise missile (another unverifiable weapon) will soon blur the old weapons' distinctions as between nuclear and conventional, and as between strategic and tactical. For all of its flaws (for example, high ceilings on weapons numbers, new weapons allowed, theater forces left unconstrained), SALT II had the great merit of putting comprehensive limits—both quantitative and qualitative—on the superpowers' forces.

The arms control imperatives for the coming decade are clear: (1) a comprehensive nuclear test ban (CTB), which would make future technological "breakthroughs" far more difficult; (2) an agreement that would entail limits on intermediate-range as well as on strategic nuclear forces; (3) a beginning of drastic reductions in the superpowers' nuclear arsenals, once strategic and intermediate-range ceilings have been agreed upon (reductions are unlikely to be negotiable before ceilings are set); and (4) a gradual elimination of land-based ICBMs (which the Soviets would probably accept only if there were corresponding reductions in American bombers and submarines, since the Soviet nuclear arsenal consists primarily of ICBMs). Arms control negotiations ought to be immune from linkage manipulations, since both superpowers have an overriding interest in taking measures to prevent nuclear war, to provide for crisis stability, and to make the Soviet-American contest both more predictable and less wasteful. Moreover, the importance of its military establishment prevents the Soviet regime from paying enough attention to its economic problems at home, and keeps Soviet rule at home and in Eastern Europe both rigid and dangerous (given Moscow's tendency to seek in external successes a compensation for internal strains). Arms control thus may be the only effective way—rough, oblique, and gradual—to redirect Soviet priorities.

III.

Managing America's alliances will be as difficult and important as managing the competition with Moscow. The reasons for the existence of those alliances will not disappear—the Soviet threat above all, plus the economic interdependence of the advanced capitalist economies. But the remarkable resilience of both NATO and the Japanese-American security relationship cannot be expected to endure forever.

The Japanese-American alliance is being affected by two irritants: American resentment of the continuing protection of the Japanese domestic market; and Japanese resistance to American pressure for better "burden sharing"—that is, for a greater Japanese rearmament effort. Yet this pressure is likely to be counterproductive. It will be unwelcome in Southeast Asia, where there is fear of all the potential regional mastodons; and it will be divisive in Japan, where it may indeed stimulate some demands for the atomic armament of Japan as the only course capable of giving Japan greater independence at smaller cost.

NATO's woes are deeper. Increasingly, Western Europe suffers from three discrepancies. The first is between the stalled internal development of the European Community and the recent, more successful effort to define a common foreign policy. In a sense, the more deadlocked are members of the EEC on matters such as agriculture and the yearly budget, the more tempted they are to compensate on the world stage, and the greater their incentive to distinguish their offerings from those of the United States. The second discrepancy is between the "civil" powers of the EEC and the defense function, which is entrusted to NATO. The third discrepancy is between the strategically exposed position of Western Europe—which is a half-continent where successful deterrence (an elusive notion) is the only sensible strategy—and the fact that the fate of the area remains ultimately in American hands.

It is most likely that, despite the horrors of Soviet-style "normalization" in Eastern Europe and the steady increase in Soviet nuclear and conventional weaponry facing Western Europe, the desperate aspiration in Western Europe for some sort of normality in East-West relations will persist, as will the desire to affect the superpowers' behavior by all means available. These means include both conversations with the potential enemy, in order that the dialogue with Moscow not be left to the vagaries of American diplomacy alone, and resistance to American pressures that could make the Cold War hotter, whether in Europe or abroad. It is in the long-term U.S. interest to set up the kind of alliance directorate recommended in 1981 by the heads of four allied Councils on Foreign Relations, in order to arrive at a common, global alliance strategy and to cover issues that fall outside the geographical boundaries of NATO.[1] It is also in the long-term U.S. interest to encourage a gradual transformation of NATO itself.

NATO's present structure fosters a kind of irresponsibility in Western Europe. Western Europe's members of NATO resent their dependence on the United States, but find a powerful incentive in NATO's institutions against undertaking the effort to build a distinctive European defense system, whether conventional or nuclear. Revolts in Western Europe against these conditions thus take the form both of protests against the United States and of flings of wishful thinking. France is an exception, insofar as it has its own defense policy, and has shown willingness to increase its military effort. But the underlying French postulate is unrealistic—that is, the postulate of defense independent from that of the rest of Western Europe and concerned above all with protecting France's integrity. Reorganizing NATO—transforming it into an alliance between the United States (represented in Europe by troops and nuclear forces) and a European defense entity (with conventional *and* nuclear forces of its own)—is indispensable to preserving the most impressive achievement of postwar American diplomacy.

In recent years, we have prodded our allies in Western Europe to obtain greater military support from them outside NATO, and we have discouraged them from taking diplomatic stands of their own, for instance in the Middle East. We should do the opposite: we should encourage them to play a constructive diplomatic role in parts of the world where we suffer special handicaps; and we should encourage them in matters of defense to increase their efforts in Europe, rather than to prolong a situation in which many Europeans denounce as dangerous the moves we take there in their own interest (as we see it!), and in which they resist the moves we want them to take abroad as being contrary to Europe's interests.

IV.

It is impossible to present a complete picture of all the issues the United States will face during the next ten or twenty years. For example, what follows will not describe in detail what is necessary in the areas of human rights and nuclear proliferation—not because these issues are not of extreme importance, but rather because there is little of great use that can be said at a high level of generality. However, three remarks concerning these areas must be made.

First, as President Carter understood well, whatever may be said about actual policy-making in his administration, these issues deserve not merely a declaratory policy but also a strategy for action. In the case of proliferation, this course is essential because of the obvious dangers for the international system if the rhythm of proliferation greatly increases, and if countries engaged in particularly implacable and unresolved disputes acquire nuclear weapons in circumstances where the peculiar restraints operating among the existing nuclear powers do not exist. In the case of human rights, meanwhile, we can act neither as though the reach of our values stopped at the water's edge (or at the borders of our alliances), nor as though international politics were a jungle in which only power matters. Nor should we distort a latent (and often manifest) universal aspiration into a cold war propaganda tool, on the basis of shabby intellectual distinctions such as those popularized by the neoconservatives.

Second, if nonproliferation and human rights are important, then we should be reluctant to give priority to other considerations, or at least to let them prevail so thoroughly that we drop any conditions relating to such basic interests ("other considerations" include both support to "friendly" governments under pressure from the Soviets or their clients, and the Western need for resources from friendly governments who either are repressive or have nuclear ambitions). In particular, the tendency must be fought to let cold war calculations turn the United States into an unconditional supporter (that is, a dependent) of those who need us.

Third, a successful strategy for nonproliferation and human rights requires American ability to enlist the support of allies and other states.

Five kinds of U.S. foreign policy priorities will emerge with regard to the rest of the world. First, we will need to respond in a far less grudging way to reasonble aspects of the demand for a "New International Economic Order." Much of the concept is demagogic and inflationary. Some of the most flamboyant rhetoric emanates from almost ostentatiously corrupt leaders. But there are also desires for a greater transfer of resources from the right to the poor, for greater stability in export earnings, for the means to develop those economic sectors which private investors find unprofitable, for technology transfers able to benefit the masses rather than just the few, and for broader access to the markets of advanced nations. These desires are justified and correspond to the long-term interests of the advanced nations, even though satisfying these wishes may entail short-term sacrifices and disruptions on our part.

We are faced, of course, not only with demands for greater justice but also with demands for greater power. But the only way to get the makers of these demands to behave with a greater sense of responsibility for the system as a whole is to grant them more power. (This certainly does not mean entrusting a body such as the General Assembly of the UN—which is irresponsible by definition—with powers of decision and control in these matters.) America's reluctance to negotiate, plus our blanket endorsement of capitalism, only consolidate the common front of our critics and perpetuate a paradox: despite all our contributions to the development of Third World countries, we are far more often the target of their anger than is the Soviet Union, which contributes far less.

Our second priority concerns the settlement of regional disputes that could endanger world peace. The two most important and lasting cases of such disputes are found in the Middle East and in the Far East. Moving toward a comprehensive resolution of the Arab-Israeli dispute will certainly not bring stability to that part of the world—since there are too many other sources of trouble—but that dispute does remain the most formidable issue in the area. Through the Palestinian diaspora and the way in which the competition for leadership in the Arab world interacts with the Palestinian problem, this issue not only creates a permanent risk of war between Israel and its neighbors, but also deeply affects the survival of Lebanon and the internal security of all Arab states. The set of proposals outlined several years ago in a report by the Brookings Institution remains the most sensible.[2]

The fundamental obstacles to peace are Israel's refusal to move in the direction of a settlement of the Palestinian problem entailing self-determination for the Palestinians (indeed, the policies followed by Israeli Prime Minister Menachim Begin make impossible a settlement of the Palestinian issue acceptable to *any* Arab state), and America's failure to confront Israel except on marginal issues. If Israel showed a willingness to put an end to the creeping annexation of the West Bank, and to accept the principle of self-determination for the Palestinians, then Arab intransigence, which has already been dented since Sadat's breakthrough, would probably recede further or be limited to eccentric states. In coming years, the United States will have to choose between a course that, if continued, will undermine the positions of moderate Arab governments with which Washington has been cooperating; and a more energetic course that will severely strain the special U.S. relationship with Israel and the body politic in America. Only the second course offers any positive prospect for fulfilling the strategic and economic interests of the United States in the Arab world, as well as for ensuring Israel's long-term ability to live in peace and to play a role as a member of the (troubled) family of Middle Eastern nations.

In the Far East, meanwhile, Soviet hostility to China, China's toward Vietnam, Vietnam's ties to Moscow, and Beijing's support of anti-Vietnamese forces in Cambodia place the United States in a particularly difficult position. Our interest is to preserve our new relationship with China and to deter any Soviet action against it. But it is also in our interest to loosen the bonds between Hanoi and Moscow; and it is *not* in our interest to encourage

China against Vietnam, to make our China policy hostage to or dependent upon our relations with Moscow, or to arm China (not only the Soviets but also other Asian countries would deem such a policy provocative), except for providing certain clearly defensive weapons. Thus we will need extraordinary balancing skill, plus firm guidelines that give each country in the area a definite idea of our objectives and positions. The magnitude of China's internal problems is such that the likelihood is small of Beijing's becoming a major actor in world affairs in the near future. Our aim ought to be to provide whatever economic assistance China's leaders may need and want, and to discourage China from external adventures, but without becoming too deeply engaged with any Chinese leadership, or too enamored of the idea that China's interests and ours are identical, even with respect to the Soviet Union, or too worried about a Chinese-Soviet rapprochement.

Our third priority is to manage the external effects of internal change in areas of particular turbulence: for example, the Middle East, Central America, and southern Africa. It will be impossible for the United States either to prevent radical changes, to ensure that they will be nonviolent and gradual, or to stop other powers (in or outside the regions) from meddling. The rules of policy, which are easy to formulate but admittedly hard to apply, are simple. Whenever we have been tightly associated with a regime that appears to be digging its own grave (through repression, corruption, or petrification), we should do all we can to encourage not only economic reform but also political reform. As the shah's fate shows, the worst possible combinations are economic progress with political immobility, and urbanization and industrialization without political outlets. If we find ourselves without influence, or if reform comes too late, we ought to try dissociating ourselves from a doomed regime, in order to avoid giving the opposition a needlessly anti-American thrust and to preserve chances of cooperation with a successor government. Only in this way can we eventually hope to play a role in mediating between those in power and the opposition, and in trying to help resolve violent internal conflict through negotiation. Committing ourselves to the survival of weak regimes—that is, to protecting them against their own people—is both beyond our means and ultimately suicidal. It is not enough for us to engage in progressive rhetoric, while actually hesitating to disengage from repressive or corrupt governments (especially when we find the Soviets or the Cubans helping the other side). Nor is the fact that successor regimes are often equally or even more repressive a reason for us to cling to regimes whose position is clearly untenable, and whose very excesses or mistakes contribute to the extremism of their opponents. Unconditional support, economic or military, to repressive regimes—almost a tradition in postwar American foreign policy—puts us at the mercy of our clients, and condemns us to impotence, to complicity, and to sinking along with them.

DEAD ENDS

Our fourth priority has been much neglected in recent years: namely, the need to strengthen the executive and enforcement powers of international and regional organizations. One great power or a handful of self-selected states cannot undertake management of international regimes, the administration of economic bargains negotiated between the "North" and the "South," the providing of peacekeeping forces in regional disputes, and the mediation even of internal conflicts. There is one common requirement for successful resolution of issues involved in the Law of the Seas negotiation (especially the exploitation of seabed resources), in commodity agreements and agreements on technology transfers that could result from discussions on a New International Economic Order, and in strengthening global antiproliferation policy. All require international regimes—that is, sets of rules, restraints, procedures, and institutions—for collective management, for resolution of disputes, and for the introduction and preservation of greater predictability in international affairs. Groupings such as the Association of Southeast Asian Nations (ASEAN), the Organization of African Unity (OAU), and the Organization of American States (OAS) will need to be strengthened to meet both the need to resolve regional disputes without outside interference and the needs of cooperation for regional economic development (including the advantages of increased "collective self-reliance" as a way of decreasing reliance on a wildly fluctuating world market or dependence on great powers). Rather than trying to prevent international regimes that might put limits on unbridled free enterprise and collect embryonic world taxes, and rather than trying to break cartels such as OPEC, the United States ought to recognize that a global economy requires bargaining groups and institutions for collective management. Finally, if U.S. relations with the Soviet Union move from the pole of hostility to the middle of the spectrum that runs from enmity to cooperation, and if several of the major regional disputes move toward a settlement, then prospects for regional arms control entailing sharp limits on arms transfers would become possible. Here again, international agencies would be necessary.

Fifth, the United States must be more concerned than in the past eighteen years about the effects of its own domestic economic policies on the international economic system, and about the domestic imperatives that result from our global economic interests. On the one hand, we must avoid the kinds of economic policies that export inflation and undermine the world's monetary regimes (as we did in the late 1960s), or else export recession and thereby increase protectionist pressures all around (as is currently the case). In other words, given the weight of America's economy and the increasing importance of foreign trade in it, our internal decisions—monetary and budgetary—shape the world economy, not just our own. On the other hand, as a trading nation, as an advanced industrial economy, and as the leader of several alliances, we have an interest in an open world economy that allows us to export goods and to import indispensable raw materials and sources of energy. At home, this requires not only adjustment and compensation measures for industries and workers affected by foreign competition, but above all measures of industrial policy aimed at redirecting our industry *away* from sectors in which we are no longer competitive and *toward* areas in which we have a comparative advantage. Otherwise, protectionist pressures will keep rising.

V.

Clearly, the suggestions presented here are sufficiently different from current policies, and also both from the visions that guided earlier strategies in the 1950s and 1960s and from the more complex but still fundamentally bipolar (or geopolitical) conception of Henry Kissinger, to raise formidable questions about their acceptability by the American public, about the chances for bipartisan support, and about the many other problems of internal consensus. But this ought to be the subject of another essay—indeed, a more important one. After all, what use is there is presenting what may be sensible suggestions for coping with the outside world if there is no basis for support of these suggestions at home?

The internal preconditions relating to the process of foreign policy-making can only be sketched here. They are:

First, unity of direction, which in my opinion requires restoration of the secretary of state's preeminence as the person who shapes America's external relations, by delegation from the president (if the latter has little expertise or interest in foreign affairs), or as the person who carries out the president's foreign policy;

Second, a strong NSC staff, to provide the president not only with options but also with the information required to coordinate external, defense, and domestic policies (however, the head of the staff should not be a policy-maker, a negotiator, or a public defender of the policy);

Third, an effort at involving key Congressional figures in both the definition and the extension of policy, to avoid disastrous delays or disavowals from Congress;

Fourth, a constant educational effort by the president, aimed at helping the public understand both the realities and the policies—that is, an effort to rise above the oversimplifications and slogans that too many people seem to believe indispensable for achieving consensus; and

DEAD ENDS

Fifth, greater reliance on professionals and less on political appointees who tend to believe that everything that preceded their coming (or returning) to power was wrong, and who give to American diplomacy discontinuity, amateurishness, and a hucksterish tone that are both unique and detrimental to our interests.

The main task ahead of us is to convert the American people and the American political system to a strategy that faces the real world—not the world of the 1950s—and that defines our goals in a sober and realistic way.

NOTES

1. Karl Kaiser, et al., *Western Security: What has changed? What should be done?* (New York: Council on Foreign Relations, January 1981).

2. "Toward Peace in the Middle East: Report of a Study Group" (Washington, D.C.: The Brookings Institution, 1975).

INDEX

Abrams, General, 41
Acheson, Dean, 21, 26, 81, 164
Adenauer, Konrad, 230
Afghanistan, Soviet invasion of:
Carter policy and, 71-72,
187-188; and Soviet-American
relations, 145, 192, 194, 253;
Western European response to,
185-186
Africa, 113, 115, 249, 254, 260
Albertz, Heinrich, 237
Algeria, 183
Allen, Richard, 137
Allende, Salvador, 20-21, 30, 36,
37, 47, 54-55, 251
Allies, U.S.: machinery for co-
ordination of, 261-262; relations
with Soviet Union, 164-165,
172, 261, 279; and U.S. uni-
lateralism, 167-168, 172. *See
also* Japan; Western Europe and
the U.S.
American national psychology, 93-
95, 105-106, 123-124, 202, 255,
270-271. *See also* New orthodoxy
Amin, Idi, 250, 252
Andropov, Yuri, 86
Angola, 140, 159, 191, 266
Antinuclear movement: in Western
Europe, 148, 157, 175-176, 205,
219-239; in U.S., 173
Arab states, 141, 183-184, 266,
284. *See also* Middle East
Argentina, 4, 139, 162
Arms control: under Carter, 75, 189;

of conventional weapons, 110,
269; as objective in Soviet-
American relations, 110-112,
147-148, 268-269, 280; under
Reagan, 166, 172; of theatre
nuclear forces, 111, 160, 166,
172, 213-214, 229-230; Western
European view of, 76, 148,
204-205
Art, Robert, 255
Aron, Raymond, 121, 200
Assad, Hafez Al, 55, 101-102
ASEAN, 261, 286
Authoritarianism, 54-55, 162, 257

Bailer, Seweryn, 248
Balance of power, 5, 63; Kissinger
view of, 30-38, 62-63; main-
tenance of, 110, 276-277
Bangladesh crisis, 20, 22, 26, 34, 36
Barre, Siad, 116
Begin, Menachem, 71, 76-77, 187,
195, 284; and Reagan, 158, 164,
169-171
Belgium, 229
Boumedienne, 55
Bowie, Robert, 181
Brazil, 138, 171
Brandt, Willy, 24, 31, 36, 50, 221,
237
Brandt Report, 267
Brezhnev, Leonid, 24, 25, 43, 47,
50, 86; and détente 63; and
nuclear arms, 111, 145, 147; and
October 1973 war, 59-60

Brown, Harold, 69-70, 99, 102
Brzezinski, Zbigniew, 72-73, 74, 79, 109, 139, 155
Bundy, McGeorge, 23, 224, 232, 240, 268-269
Bureaucracy and foreign policy, 25-26, 48-49. *See also* Institutional control of policy-making

Cambodia, 3, 22, 53, 284; bombing of, 26, 34, 41-42, 54, 57-58; and Kissinger policy, 18, 37, 38, 41-43; and Soviet-American relations, 113
Camp David agreements. *See* Middle East, peace process in
Capitalism and developing nations, 157, 163, 284
Carrington, Lord, 184, 185-186
Carter, Jimmy, 12, 118, 154, 156, 157, 163, 209, 282-283; Presidential Directive, 59, 204, 225, 228; and SALT II, 36; and Western Europe, 179, 201, 229
Carter doctrine, 187-188
Carter foreign policy, 10, 15, 16, 67-83, 89, 91-92, 124; absence of coherence in, 1-2, 71-72, 97-98; and China, 70, 76; domestic politics and, 79-81, 105-106; global perspective of, 69, 73, 91; and human rights, 68-69, 73, 91, 117-118; institutional control of, 72-73, 104-105, 155, 189; and Middle East, 76-77; and Soviet-American relations, 1-2, 73-77, 79, 97-98, 122, 187-189, 191, 274
Castro, Fidel, 252
Central America, 254, 266; and Reagan foreign policy, 141, 159, 161-162, 171-172

CIA, 37
CENTO, 261
Chad, 3
Cheysson, Claude, 11
Chile, 20, 30, 36, 37, 138, 140, 189
China, 51, 54, 284-285; opening to, 20, 22, 44, 90-91, 208; and Reagan, 169; and the Soviet Union, 248; and Vietnam, 40-41, 114-115, 284-285
Chou En-lai, 36, 53-54; and Cambodia, 57-58; and Kissinger, 17, 22, 24-25, 26
Church, Frank, 105
Clark, William, 168
Client states: Soviet, 7, 35, 109, 149, 248, 249, 260; and Soviet-American relations, 165, 193, 252-253; superpower dependency on, 7, 159, 283; U.S., and internal instability, 139, 159, 285; U.S. pressure against Soviet, 159, 249, 259; Western European, 183-184
Committee on the Present Danger, 12, 154
Communism, U.S. fear of: and foreign policy, 11-12, 116, 131, 157-159; as ideological power, 129, 131-132. *See also* Radicalism; Revolutions; Totalitarianism
Complexity, 140-142; American denial of, 82-83, 86-87, 89-96, 124, 138, 208, 270-271; Carter's recognition of, 69; and selection of objectives, 142, 258-260. *See also* Exceptionalism; New orthodoxy
Congo, 248
Congress, role of, in policymaking, 104-105, 137-138, 287

Connally, John, 18, 21-22, 26, 189
Consensus, lack of, and policy-
    making, 128, 155
Conservative tradition, 126-127
Consistency in foreign policy, 117,
    135-136, 155
Containment, 29, 130-131, 189,
    256-257, 269-270, 277-278; Kiss-
    inger view of, 15-16, 33, 90
Conventional weaponry, 212-213,
    233, 277; arms control and, 110,
    269; and nuclear weaponry,
    101-102, 142-145, 156, 264-265
Cooper, Richard, 248
Cooperative relations, Soviet-
    American, 110-113, 193, 268-
    269. See also Arms control;
    Economic cooperation
Counterforce strategy, 99, 110-111,
    143, 225
Crisis stability and management,
    143-144, 249, 279
Credibility, 37-38, 40-41
Crocker, Chester, 160
Crozier, Michel, 82, 126; Le mal
    américain, 124
Cuba, 22, 77, 249; Soviet brigade
    in, 79, 98, 109; and U.S. in
    Central America, 159, 171-172
Cyprus, 3, 53, 163

Dallin, Alexander, 85
Dayan, Moshe, 50
Decolonization, 3, 8, 206, 249,
    254, 260
DeGaulle, Charles, 38, 71, 96,
    179, 220, 236, 261; and détente,
    205; memoirs of, 18; and
    Western Alliance, 176, 182
dePorte, A.W., 237
Détente, 11, 15-16, 82, 122, 145-
    146, 278; campaign against, 48,

91-92, 128, 207, 208; divisibility
    of, 185, 203-204. See also
    Western Europe and the U.S.,
    differences over Soviet policy.
    and Kissinger, 1, 32, 43, 56,
    61-64, 74, 92, 122, 206; and
    Western Europe-U.S. relations,
    183, 185, 199, 203-206. See also
    Soviet-American relations
Deterrence, 4, 5, 99-102, 204-205,
    224-225, 228, 231-233
Dewey, Thomas, 22
Developing nations, 163, 171, 267-
    268, 283-284. See also Capi-
    talism and developing nations;
    International economy; North-
    South relations
Diplomacy, 130, 167, 190; Kiss-
    inger style of, 27-28, 49-50. See
    also Preventive diplomacy;
    Shuttle diplomacy; Triangular
    diplomacy
Dobrynin, Anatoly, 26, 49
Domestic affairs, intervention in,
    37, 247-250, 257-258, 262-264
Domestic change and foreign
    policy, 12, 124-125
Domestic politics of foreign policy:
    and Carter, 79-81, 105-106; and
    complexity, 89-96, 137-138, 243-
    244, 287-288; and détente,
    62-63, 207; and Kissinger, 34-35,
    53-54, 89-91; and Reagan, 160,
    161, 173, 190; and Vietnam, 40,
    54. See also Antinuclear move-
    ment
Duarte, José Napoleón, 161-162
Dulles, John Foster, 29, 155, 169,
    189

East Asia and regional conflict, 253
    254, 284-285. See also Vietnam

East Germany, 205, 206, 207
Eastern Europe, 146, 165, 183, 208
Eban, Abba, 26
Economic cooperation: and linkage, 31, 278-279; Soviet-American, 112-113, 148, 166, 186, 214-215; Soviet-West European. *See* West European-Soviet relations
Economic power, U.S.: coercive use of, 4, 165-166, 185, 214-215, 251-252, 279; disadvantages of, 117; limitations of, 125-126, 133, 255. *See also* Developing nations; North-South relations
Economy, U.S., and foreign policy, 136-137, 156, 248, 251, 270, 286-287; under Carter, 77-79; under Johnson, 149; under Reagan, 81, 150, 156, 173, 202-203
Eden, Anthony, 231
Egypt, 34, 53, 59, 60, 159, 250; and the Soviet Union, 248; and the U.S., 164, 183
Ehrlichman, John, 51
Eisenhower, Dwight D., 155, 173, 182, 189
Ellsberg, Daniel, 34
El Salvador, 3, 142, 159, 161-162, 171-172
Energy policy, 78, 136-137. *See also* Oil and foreign policy
Eppler, Erhard, 237
Ethopia, 3, 138
European Defense Community, 229, 231
European defense organization, 213, 282
European Economic Community, 58, 59, 183, 208, 281

Exceptionalism, American, 13, 82-83, 95, 124, 209

Fallaci, Oriana, 19, 22
Falkland Islands, 2
Farer, Tom, 132
Force: as American archetype, 93-96, 209, 270-271; Kissinger view of, 29, 31-32
France: and Africa, 203, 265; domestic politics of, 207; foreign policy of, 180-181, 207, 216; military power of, 183, 201, 206, 211, 236; relations with U.S., 147, 180; and West European defense, 196, 213, 282
Frei, Eduardo, 37
Fundamentalist response, 123-124, 129, 150, 202, 222-223, 270-271. *See also* New orthodoxy

Gallois, General, 204
Gaddis, John Lewis, 15
Gandhi, Indira, 36
Gelb, Leslie, 110
Geopolitics, Kissinger's, 29-38, 41-44, 92
Geography and U.S.-West European differences, 204-205
Gierek, Edward, 146
Gilpin, Robert, 248
Giscard d'Estaing, Valéry, 181, 207
Goldborough, James, *Rebel Europe*, 177
Great Britain, 59, 180-181, 200, 201, 213, 216; and France, 240; and NATO, 229; and South Africa, 141
Greece, 3, 158-159, 163
Gromyko, Andrei, 20, 26, 63
Guatemala, 3

Habib, Philip, 163, 169
Haig, Alexander, 44n8, 51, 155, 157, 160, 168, 215
Haldeman, Robert, 51, 53
Hallstein, Walter, 181
Hansen, Roger, 267
Hassner, Pierre, 123, 173, 237
Heath, Edward, 24, 50
Helsinki agreements, 146, 206
Hirsch, Fred, 124
Historical differences between the U.S. and Western Europe, 205-207
Hoffmann, Stanley, *Primacy or World Order*, 1
Holland, 176
Horn of Africa, 35-36
Human rights policy, 117-118, 139, 282-283; under Carter, 68-69, 73, 91; under Reagan, 162-163, 171
Huntington, Samuel P., 124, 263

Idealism in foreign policy, 67-68, 124
Illusion of Peace (Szulc), 19
Imperialism and nationalism, 3
India, 20, 31, 34, 35, 158, 261
Institutional control of policy-making, 25-27, 48-49, 106, 118, 137-138, 287-288; in absence of consensus, 128, 155; under Carter, 72-73, 104-105, 155, 189; under Reagan, 155-156, 161, 168
International economy, 246-247, 248, 251, 286-287; and inequality, 247, 267-268, 283-284. *See also* North-South relations
Internal problems, 36, 53-54. *See also* Revolutions
International Monetary Fund, 171, 267

International security, 245-256
Internationalism and isolationism, 127
Iraq, 3, 37, 183, 253
Iran, 3, 253; hostage crisis, 70; internal problems of, 53-54; and U.S. policy, 44, 72, 76-77, 183-184
Ismail, Hafiz, 49
Israel, 33, 37, 49, 150; and Carter, 76-77; and Kissinger, 52, 54; and Middle East policy, 141, 284; and October 1973 war, 59-61; and Reagan, 158, 162, 163-164, 169-171; and Western Europe, 183
Italy, 213, 216, 229

Jackson, Henry, 48, 50, 53, 62-63, 92
Japan, 25, 51-52, 172, 261-262, 281
Jaruzelski, General, 165
Jaster, Robert, 265
Jay, Peter, 259
Jobert, Michel, 50, 58, 59, 207
Johnson, Lyndon, 149, 189, 229
Jordan, 22, 30, 169, 170, 171

Kahler, Miles, 254
Kahn, Herman, 164
Karmal, Babrak, 186, 188, 194
Kashmir, 3
Keohane, Robert, 78, 127
Kennan, George, 15-16, 29, 86, 105, 243; and nuclear weapons, 165, 240; and the Soviet Union, 167, 185, 186, 200
Khan, Yahya, 20, 31, 36
Khmer Rouge, 42, 43, 57-58
Khomeini, Ayatollah Ruhollah, 77
Khrushchev, Nikita, 240
King Hussein, 61

Kirkpatrick, Jean, 135, 168
Kissinger, Henry, 10, 70, 71, 81-82, 92, 95, 192, 257, 278, 287; and Cambodia, 41-43, 56-58; détente policy of, 1, 32, 43, 56, 61-64, 74, 92, 122, 206; and the Middle East, 18-19, 44, 59-61, 200; as negotiator, 23, 24-25, 27-28, 49-50; and nuclear arms, 204, 224, 225, 228; personal qualities of, 23-28, 52-53, 64-65; relationship of, with Richard Nixon, 21-23, 24, 51; theories of, 9, 28-38, 53-56, 69, 168; and Vietnam, 19, 38-43, 44, 56-58; and Western Europe, 182, 208, 224; *White House Years*, 17-45, 47, 51; *World Restored, A*, 20; *Years of Upheaval*, 47-65
Kissinger-Nixon foreign policy, 15-16, 104; in Cambodia, 41-43, 57-58; and domestic politics, 89-91; in the Middle East, 44, 49, 61; method of policy-making, 25-27, 48-49, 155; in Vietnam, 38-43, 44, 56-58
Korean nationalism, 3

Laird, Melvin, 18, 26
Laos, 20, 34, 41
Lapidus, Gail, 85
Laqueur, Walter, 183
Latin America, 115, 141, 159, 260, 266
Lebanon, 3, 169-171. See also Middle East
Le Duc Tho, 26, 28, 42, 44n4
Lefever, Ernest, 135, 162
Legvold, Robert, 98, 209
Le mal américain (Crozier), 124
Liberalism, 126
Libya, 159

Linkage, 31, 62, 257, 278; and arms control, 111-112, 280; and Carter policy, 74-75, 187; and cooperative relations, 110, 278-279; and human rights policy, 118
Linowitz, Sol, 163
Lon Nol, 31, 41-43, 53, 57-58

Mao Tse-tung, 20, 24-25, 47, 50, 58
Marcos, Ferdinand, 68
McCloy, John, 21, 181
McNamara, Robert, 240
Meese, Edward, 137
Meir, Golda, 19, 26
Mendès-France, Pierre, 231
Mengistu, General, 260
Mexico, 3, 141, 171
Middle East, 26, 30, 33-34, 37, 38, 49, 141, 260; Carter and, 76-77; European strategy for, 195-196, 215-216; Kissinger and, 18-19, 44, 59-61, 200; peace process in, 59, 163-164, 169-171, 284; Reagan and, 157, 158, 169-171; as regional conflict, 113, 115, 253, 254, 266; Soviet-American cooperation in, 148, 279-280; West European-U.S. relations and, 181-182. See also Arab states; Begin; Egypt; Israel; Jordan; Sadat; Saudi Arabia
Military power, 102; and Kissinger, 37; limitations of, 6, 86, 103-106, 129-135, 243, 255, 262-265, 277; and the new orthodoxy, 99-106, 129-135; and Reagan, 156, 161, 189-190, 202; and Western Europe, 183, 196
Mill, John Stuart, 135
Mitterand, François, 207

Mixed relationship, 10-11, 74-77,
90-91, 108-118, 122, 144-148,
193, 278-280
Moderation of conflict, 4-5, 108-
118. *See also* Crisis stability and
management
Modernization, economic, 3, 164,
251
Monnet, Jean, 181
Morality in foreign policy, 37.
See also Virtue as archetype
Morgenthau, Hans, 29
Morocco, 159
Moynihan, Daniel Patrick, 92,
126, 132
Mozambique, 140
Mujib, (Mujibur Rahman), 36
MIRVs, 19
Muskie, Edmund, 155, 187
Namibia, 2, 141, 160, 169, 266
Nationalism, 2-3, 35, 142, 259-260.
See also Revolutions
National Security Council and
Adviser, 48, 104-105, 137, 161,
287
Neto, Agostinho, 116
New orthodoxy, 122-135, 149-150;
adaptation of, to reality,
170-173; and military power,
99-106, 129-135. *See also*
Power. triumph of, in 1980, 2,
9-10, 222-223; and Western
Europe, 201-202. *See also*
American national psychology,
Complexity
Nicaragua, 3, 140, 159, 171-172,
266
Nixon, Richard, 2, 25, 31, 47-48,
65, 99, 118, 130, 257; and China
policy, 20; and control of
foreign policy, 26; and détente,
1, 92; *The Real War*, 89, 92;

relations of, with Kissinger,
21-23, 24, 51; and Vietnam
negotiations, 19, 39-40, 56; and
Watergate, 12, 54. *See also*
Kissinger-Nixon foreign policy
NATO, 206, 233-234; limitations
of, as policy-making body, 211,
262, 281-282; political base of,
148, 157; and Reagan, 157-158;
and theatre nuclear forces, 111,
144-145, 160, 166, 201, 204-205,
212-213, 231-233, 240. *See also*
Western Europe; Western
Europe and the U.S.
NATO 1979 agreements, 204-205,
226-227, 229; and antinuclear
movement, 219, 223; and arms
control, 213-214, 230; and deterrence, 224, 225; lessons of,
233-239
North-South relations, 157, 163,
171, 183, 267-268. *See also*
Capitalism and developing nations; Developing nations; International economy
Nuclear weaponry, 4-5, 8-9, 99-102,
106, 157-158, 165, 276-277. *See
also* Arms control; Conventional
weaponry; Theatre nuclear
forces; Vulnerability, missile

October 1973 war, 47, 53, 59-61,
101-102
Oganden, 261
Oil and foreign policy, 47-48, 53,
59-61, 78, 259, 264, 270. *See
also* Energy policy
OPEC, 36, 78, 103
Oman, 183
OAU, 261, 286
OAS, 286
Organizations, international, 286

Ostpolitik, 31, 36, 207, 237

Pacifism, European. *See* Anti-
nuclear movement
Pakistan: and Afghanistan, 145,
158, 188; and Bangladesh crisis,
36; and India, 31, 261; internal
problems of, 3, 53-54, 159; and
nuclear proliferation, 163
Palestine, 3, 169-171, 265-266, 284
PLO, 55, 61, 169-171, 266. *See
also* Middle East, peace process
in
Panama Canal treaties, 69, 141
Pentagon, 49, 53, 62, 163
Philippines, 3
Pinochet, General, 54
Poland, 4, 145, 146, 162-163,
165-166, 206, 221
Pol Pot, 43, 159
Pompidou, George, 21, 63, 65,
207, 237
Power, 5-8, 68, 250-251; as Ameri-
can archetype, 93-96; decline of
American, 102-103, 117, 128,
182, 255; ideological, 131-132;
international diffusion of, 252,
255; limitations of, 6, 86,
103-106, 127, 132-135, 255-256;
and the new orthodoxy, 99-106,
129-135, 190; U.S. economic.
See Economic power, U.S. *See
also* Military power
Pragmatism, 10, 173
Preventive diplomacy 69, 265-269
Primacy or World Order
(Hoffmann), 1
Proliferation, nuclear, 113, 266-
267, 282-283; Reagan policy on,
162, 163, 171; as threat to
Soviet-American relations, 4-5,
266-267

Qadaffi, Colonel, 159, 275
Quandt, William, 37

Rabin, Yitzhak, 18, 26, 36
Radicalism, U.S. policy and, 30,
35, 54-55, 60, 116, 140, 257-258.
See also Revolutions; Third
World; Totalitarianism
Rapid Deployment Force, 156,
187-188, 264
Reagan, Ronald, 2, 12, 232, 244
Reagan foreign policy: adaptations
in, 159-160, 169-173; and allies,
172, 190; and anticommunism,
157-159, 162-163, 169, 189-190,
257; in Central America, 142,
159, 161-162, 171-172; and complexity, 86-87, 92; decalogue of,
153-155, 172; and developing
countries, 157, 163, 171; and the
economy, 81, 150, 156, 173,
202-203; and exceptionalism, 83,
138; and human rights, 162-163,
171; incoherence of, 161-173; in
Middle East, 150, 157, 158,
169-171; and military power,
161, 189-190, 202-203; and process of policy-making, 155-156,
161, 168; as response to failure,
9-10, 202; and Soviet-American
relations, 85, 150, 164-167,
172-173, 189-190; and
unilateralism, 142, 190
Realism, 29
Real War, The (Nixon), 89, 92
Rebel Europe (Goldborough), 177
Reform, encouragement of, by
U.S., 140, 285
Regional conflict, 101-102, 248-
256; and Soviet-American relations, 113-117, 252-253; U.S.
approach to, 256-260, 284-285;

U.S. unilateralism in, 140-142
Revolutions: and alignments, 250;
causes of, 4, 274-275; Kissinger
and, 54-55; Soviet exploitation
of, 148, 248, 252; U.S. and,
94-95, 113, 116-117, 138-140,
266, 274-275, 285; and U.S. anticommunism, 11-12, 116-117,
131-132, 139. *See also* Central
America; Radicalism; Third
World
Rhodesia, 69
Rockefeller, Nelson, 17, 23
Rogers, William, 19, 26, 48
Rostow, Eugene, 166

Sadat, Anwar, 50-51, 164, 187;
expulsion of Soviet Union by,
34, 184; and Kissinger, 26, 36;
and the October 1973 war, 53,
59-60, 101-102; peace initiative
of, 141, 192, 284. *See also*
Egypt
Sandinistas, 159, 161, 171-172
Saudi Arabia, 51, 158, 162, 250,
264
Scalapino, Robert, 261
Schneider, 37
Schlesinger, James, 50, 62, 204
Schmidt, Helmut, 36, 76, 147, 176,
201
Schmitt, Karl, 29
Secrecy, 34-35, 49
Shah of Iran (Mohammad Reza
Pahlavi), 21, 31, 36, 37, 54, 72
Sharon, Ariel, 163-164, 169-171
Shawcross, William, 41, 42-43
Sideshow, 58
Shultz, George, 168, 173
Shuttle diplomacy, 47-48, 50
Sihanouk, 34, 41, 42, 43; and Lon
Nol, 53, 57-58
Smith, Gerard, 240

Smith, Ian, 252
Solidarity, 146, 162
Somalia, 248, 261
Somoza, Anastasio, 258
South Africa, 3, 4, 249, 253;
and Namibia, 141, 160; and
nuclear proliferation, 171;
Western pressure on, 4, 266
SEATO, 261
South Korea, 138
SWAPO, 160
Soviet-American relations, 60-61;
and Afghanistan crisis, 71-72,
145, 187-188, 192, 194, 253; and
arms control, 110-112, 147-148,
268-269, 280; asymmetries in,
3-5, 104, 191-193, 256, 273-274,
278; under Carter, 1-2, 73-77,
79, 97-98, 122, 187-189, 191,
274; and China, 114-115,
284-285; and domestic politics,
79, 80-81, 173; economic,
112-113, 148, 166, 214-215,
278-279; goals and strategy for,
8-9, 10-11, 106-113, 191-194,
268-269, 279-280; and Kissinger,
30-38, 61-64, 122; and the Middle East, 60-61, 148, 279-280;
under Reagan, 85, 150, 164-167,
172-173, 189-190; and regional
conflict, 113-117, 181-182, 252,
254, 262-265
Soviet foreign policy, 6-8, 98-99,
103, 107, 191-192, 200-201, 248,
249
Soviet influence: in Indochina, 36.
See also Vietnam. method of
limiting, 115-116, 158-159,
256-257, 278; in the Middle
East, 33, 34, 76; in revolutionary situations, 139, 148,
252. *See also* Revolutions; Third
World. in South Africa, 33; in

the Third World, 69, 115-116, 248, 252

Stability as goal of foreign policy, 209-210, 257, 275. *See also* Crisis stability and management; Soviet-American relations, goals and strategy for

START negotiations, 172

State Department, 48, 53, 104-105, 137, 160, 161, 287

SALT I, 19, 26, 31, 32, 62

SALT II, 36, 48, 49, 53, 79, 110, 269, 280; and Carter, 75, 98, 187; and Kissinger, 62, 64; linked to Afghanistan, 187, 194; and SALT III, 147, 194

Strauss, Franz-Josef, 163

Sudan, 159, 248

Syria, 30, 35, 52, 55, 59, 60

Szulc, Tad, *Illusion of Peace*, 19

Taiwan, 138, 158, 169

Thatcher, Margaret, 11, 147, 184

Theatre nuclear forces in Western Europe, 102, 144-145, 160, 204-205, 224-241; and arms control, 111, 160, 166, 172, 213-214, 229-230; popular opposition to, 219-239. *See also* NATO

Thieu, General, 19, 22, 26, 28, 31, 36, 39-40, 56

Third World: economic development of, 251, 267-268. *See also* North-South relations. regional conflict in, 248-256, 259-260; revolutions, Soviet exploitation of, 148, 201, 248, 252, 256-257, 260; revolutions, and U.S. policy, 11-12, 54, 250, 266. *See also* Radicalism. and Western Europe, 206. *See also* Soviet influence

Thompson, E.P., "Letter to America," 205

Thurow, Lester, 137

Tirpitz, Admiral von, 254

Totalitarianism, 37, 54, 162, 257

Triangular diplomacy, 27, 32-33, 44, 47, 56, 90-91, 114-115

Truman, Harry, 70, 209

Tucker, Robert W., 16, 82, 190, 129-135 *passim*

Turkey, 3, 53-54, 158-159

Uganda, 4, 138

Unilateralism, American: and allies, 167-168, 172, 211, 216; end of, 140-142, 167-168, 275-276

Vance, Cyrus, 35, 72, 92, 155, 187, 190, 191

Venezuela, 141, 159

Vietnam war, 25, 34, 37, 38, 53, 121, 188; Kissinger Nixon policy in, 19, 20, 30-31, 38-43, 44, 54, 56-58; treaty of 1972, 19, 22-23, 39-40, 44n4, 47, 49

Vietnam, 188; in East Asian conflict, 113-115, 249, 284-285; Soviet influence in, 35, 159. *See also* East Asia

Vulnerability, missile, 100-101, 110-111, 143, 172, 276. *See also* Nuclear weaponry

Virtue as archetype in America, 93-96, 270-271

Walzer, Michael, 124

War-fighting strategy, 99-100, 143, 204-205, 225, 249

Watergate, 12, 47-48, 51; and Kissinger foreign policy, 20, 23, 34-35, 40, 53, 54

Weinberger, Caspar, 157, 168

Western Europe-Soviet détente 76, 146-147, 164-166, 175, 186, 214-215, 281; vs. U.S.-Soviet détente, 183, 185, 205-206

Western Europe: antinuclear movement in, 148, 157, 175-176, 205, 219-239; arms control and, 76, 148, 204-205; attitude towards U.S. of, 25, 176-177, 178, 194, 196, 208; common strategy for, 194-197; fear of war in, 234-235; formation of defense organization in, 213, 238-239, 282; and invasion of Afghanistan, 185-186; and Middle Eastern oil, 180, 195. *See also* Oil and foreign policy. military balance in, 102, 199. *See also* NATO

Western Europe and the U.S.: difference in political systems, 181, 207-210; differences over military power, 203, 206-207, 209; differences over Soviet policy, 76, 172, 175-176, 183-190, 190-195, 199-210, 214-215, 221-223, 228-229, 235-236; economic relations of, 176, 180; EEC and, 58-59, 147, 183, 205; and extra-European crises, 181-182, 199, 203, 282; leadership among nations of, 55, 96, 182-183, 190, 194-197, 202, 211, 216, 236-239, 261-262; machinery for coordination of, 211-213, 215, 261-262, 281-282; and the Middle East, 183-184, 186, 195, 196, 215-216; and Reagan anti-Sovietism, 157-158,

190; reasons for divergences between, 204-210; theatre nuclear forces of, 204-205, 226. *See also* Theatre nuclear forces in Western Europe; NATO. *See also* Allies, U.S.

West Germany, 180-181, 200, 203, 213, 216; antinuclear movement in, 220, 221, 230-231; domestic politics of, 176, 207; and East Germany, 205, 207; and France, 237, 240-241; links with Soviet Union, 146, 166, 180, 205, 214-215. *See also* Western Europe-Soviet détente. and NATO, 229, 230-231; and nuclear weapons, 238, 239; and Year of Europe, 59

White House Years (Kissinger), 17-45, 47, 51
Whiting, Allen, 261
Whitman, Marina v. N., 68
Wiretapping of aides, 34, 48
Wohlstetter, Albert, 101
Wolfers, Arnold, 250
World Bank, 267
World Restored, A (Kissinger), 20

Xuan Thuy, 44n4

Year of Europe (1973), 47, 48, 52-53, 58-59, 182
Years of Upheaval (Kissinger), 47-65
Young, Andrew, 72

Zaire, 4, 138
Zero option, 160, 166, 172
Zimbabwe, 140, 258, 269

ABOUT THE AUTHOR

Stanley Hoffmann is Douglas Dillon Professor of the Civilization of France at Harvard University, where he has taught since 1955. He has been the Chairman of the Center for European Studies at Harvard since its creation in 1969.

Professor Hoffmann was born in Vienna in 1928. He lived and studied in France from 1929 to 1955 and has taught at the Institut d'Etudes Politiques of Paris.

At Harvard he teaches French intellectual and political history, American foreign policy, the sociology of war, international politics, ethics and world affairs, and modern political ideologies.

His books include *Contemporary Theory in International Relations* (1960), *The State of War* (1965), *Gulliver's Troubles* (1968), *Decline and Renewal: France since the 30's* (1974), *Primacy or World Order* (1978), and *Duties Beyond Borders* (1981). He is co-author of *In Search of France* (1963), *The Relevance of International Law* (1968), *The Fifth Republic at Twenty* (1981), and the forthcoming *Living with Nuclear Weapons*.